Environmental Decline
and
Public Policy

Pattern, Trend and Prospect

Timothy C. Weiskel
and
Richard A. Gray

THE PIERIAN PRESS
Ann Arbor, Michigan

1992

Cover by: Beverly Brann

Knowledge Windows Series, No. 1
ISBN 0-87650-289-3

Acknowledgements:

Figures 3 - 4: adapted from *Extinction and Survival in Human Populations*, by Charles D. Laughlin, Jr. and Ivan A. Brady, copyright 1978, © Columbia University Press, New York. Reprinted with the permission of the publisher.

Figures 7 - 10: adapted from John S. Steinhart and Carol E. Steinhart, *Energy: Sources, Use and Role in Human Affairs* (Duxbury, MA: Wadsworth/Duxbury Press, 1974); *The Fires of Culture* (Duxbury, MA: Wadsworth/Duxbury Press, 1974); and "Energy Use in U.S. Food Systems," *Science* 184 (19 April 1974): 307. Copyright 1974, © John S. Steinhart and Carol E. Steinhart. Reprinted with permission of the copyright holders.

Pierian Press
Box 1808
Ann Arbor, Michigan 48106
1 (800) 678-2435

Contents

Preface

In August and September of 1988 two subcommittees of the United States Senate *Committee on Environment and Public Works* held joint hearings on S. 2666, the "Global Environmental Protection Act of 1988." To inform their deliberations with a broad range of evidence, staff members for the Senate subcommittees sought testimony from both natural scientists and social scientists acquainted with problems of global change. When the subcommittee staff contacted me, I suggested that as an anthropologist and historian I would best be able to present an overview to the Senate of our contemporary environmental circumstance in light of the larger context of human evolution and the history of cultural adaptation to environmental change. They indicated that this is what they would like me to provide, so I prepared a formal written statement and testified before the Senate subcommittees on 14 September 1988.[1]

Having read the Senate proceedings, Mr. Edward Wall, President of the Pierian Press, in Ann Arbor, Michigan, felt that this testimony would be of general interest and that it should be published for broader circulation to expand the range of public discussion of the current environmental crisis. Mr. Richard Gray, Senior Editor of the Pierian Press, agreed to provide supplementary annotations to the works cited in the initial testimony. In the first instance, then, the testimony and annotated sources were published as a collaborative effort in the form of an extended three-part article entitled "The Anthropology of Environmental Decline," in three issues of the professional journal *Reference Services Review* during 1990.

Since that time, substantial new material has been collected both by Mr. Gray and myself to update and supplement the information and assessments first presented to the Senate. The resulting cumulative work is presented here in a single volume to provide college professors, librarians, high school teachers, students, and the general reading public with informative summaries of the key literature touching upon global environmental change and public policy in its widest setting. It can be used in its entirety or chapter by chapter as a useful introduction to much of the background literature relating to large-scale and long-term environmental change as it relates to human history and culture.

If public policy initiatives on environmental matters are going to be effective, a massive shift will be required in public awareness and thinking about global environmental trends. Experts and specialists have been issuing serious warnings for years, but so far the general public continues to believe that environmental matters are secondary or optional issues, to be dealt with only after concerns about jobs and a growing economy are addressed. This public belief needs to change quickly if industrial societies are to have any realistic hope of sustaining viable economies and creating stable jobs in the years and decades ahead.

Because of the urgency of these issues, specialized environmental research and expert Senate testimony can no longer be confined to the narrow leadership audiences to which it was initially addressed. An informed and involved citizenry is the only hope of generating forward-looking political leadership, and without this kind of leadership public policy will surely fail. The present work, then, should be of interest to anyone engaged in public education—in the broadest possible sense.

* * *

The gist of the evidence presented in the Senate hearing and elaborated with annotated references in the following pages can be summarized quite succinctly. First, environmental crises are not as unheard of in natural and human history as one might think at first. While some of the circumstances we currently face are clearly unprecedented, environmental catastrophes in the past were not rare. On the contrary, periods of environmental decline occurred repeatedly in the past with devastating impact on human populations over the full course of evolutionary history. While some of these environmental disasters have been attributed to "acts of God," it is now becoming clear that many more can be attributed over the long term to ill-conceived or misdirected public policy.

Secondly, as evidence from environmental archaeology is beginning to suggest, the history of environmental decline does not reflect a uniform or gradual process. Instead, the general continuum of the environmental history in most civilizations is punctuated with short intervals of intense environmental destruction, followed by long periods of subsequent recovery. Ecosystems are characterized by the complex interaction of bio-geo-chemical exchanges between life forms and material support systems. As the nature and pace of these exchanges are altered, ecosystems can experience relatively short-lived periods of marked instability, often characterized by the runaway growth of selected populations and the massive extinction of others.

These seemingly sudden syndromes or spasms of environmental instability are expressed in system terms as moments of heightened positive feedback interactions in systems that have become hypercoherent—that is, periods of an explosive chain reaction between two or more mutually aggravating circumstances. Stable ecosystems are characterized by the dominance of negative feedback mechanisms or self-corrective, countervailing processes. It is when these mechanisms are blocked, overwhelmed, or fail to function that positive feedback interactions take over, escalating system exchanges out of control in a vicious circle and pushing populations toward the classic pattern of "overshoot" and collapse.

Thirdly, while syndromes of environmental degradation constituted an important component in the fall of ancient civilizations, in the modern world the phenomenon of European overseas expansion and subsequent global patterns of natural resource and agricultural commodity trade have been the most powerful driving force behind the radical degradation of ecosystems throughout the world. It is in areas of the Third World formerly under European colonial control that one can witness in our day the most dramatic instances of these runaway syndromes of environmental decline. For this reason it is upon these areas that public policy makers should focus their efforts in trying to formulate policy for global environmental change. In particular, the syndrome of environmental decline in Africa since the end of World War II deserves special attention.

Finally, the evidence presented to the Senate subcommittees emphasized that, despite the new energy sources from nuclear and petroleum-based technologies, modern civilizations—no less than ancient ones—will prove in the long run to be viable only if they can manage to make the transition to a solar-sustainable agriculture designed to support a human population that succeeds in restraining itself to remain below the earth's carrying capacity.

In effect, global industrial civilization is currently bound up in an escalating syndrome of rapid population growth, uncontrolled urbanization, and the accelerated petro-intensification of agriculture. Deliberate public policy needs to be devised now to slow and eventually reverse this large-scale positive feedback syndrome. Failure to recognize this as the long-term goal of public policy, it was argued, will result in public confusion, conflict, and the tragic squandering of remaining natural assets as nation-states and smaller factions within them splinter apart and struggle with one another to control a declining resource base and an ever more precarious food supply.

Tragic cases of this syndrome are already dramatically apparent in the countries in the horn of Africa and elsewhere on that continent. It remains to be seen whether deliberate public policy will be devised by the international community to assure that these instances are exceptional or whether the failure of public policy, on the contrary, will assure that they become the general pattern in growing numbers of Third World countries. If this proves to be the case, the syndrome will not be confined to the Third World. Pressure will build for the massive migration of desperate and destitute souls from Third World cities to any available points of entry in the more prosperous industrial countries of the north, thereby aggravating social, ethnic, and political tensions and exacerbating patterns of environmental decline in these regions as well.

In order to achieve the self-imposed self restraint on the part of the public at large which will be required for secure survival, political leadership will have to devise persuasive means of informing the public about the gravity of our global environmental circumstance and novel ways of eliciting and inspiring cooperation to avoid open conflict. A new style of responsible political leadership based on an enlarged sense of community and citizenship will be required as the basis for effective environmental policy.

Public policy predicated primarily on returning advantage to a narrow electoral constituency or providing particular privileges to a traditional patronage structure is too narrowly conceived and will inevitably fail. Worse yet, such a strategy will most likely accentuate the syndrome of environmental decline as smaller and smaller groups compete more intensely for control over diminishing resources. In short, "politics as usual" is a recipe for ecological disaster. If this is to be avoided, policy makers will need to develop a sober understanding and clear presentation of our collective condition combined with a new willingness to lead the public toward an enlarged sense of responsibility for the broader ecological community we now inhabit.

Natural scientists describe ecosystemic processes as characterized by positive or negative feedback loops. Social scientists add that when human activity is involved it is necessary to include what might be called the "cognitive feedback loop," because human behavior is often altered by what we learn and what we have come to believe. Since as a species we have become an important agent in ecosystemic change, it is the cognitive feedback loop that may well determine the direction and pace of global ecological change.

The question remains, however, whether this cognitive feedback process will in the future improve or diminish the prospect for human survival. In the past, insufficient knowledge and inappropriate beliefs have repeatedly led to public policies that have exacerbated the positive feedback patterns involved in environmental overshoot and collapse. As for the future, it will take a deliberate effort beginning now on the part of a new kind of public leadership and a newly informed citizenry to assure that public policy will be devised instead to stabilize human interaction with the ecosystem and thereby sustain the human prospect for generations to come.

* * *

In developing the initial Senate testimony and subsequent supporting material I have incurred debts to numerous people and institutions which made this work possible. In the first place, I am grateful to Professor William Cronon of the University of Wisconsin, whose suggestion made the Senate testimony possible and who was a constant source of encouragement and helpful criticism over the years that we both taught at Yale University.

At the time of the Senate hearings I was conducting research on environmental values and belief systems as a Henry Luce Fellow at Harvard Divinity School. In this respect I owe special gratitude to the Henry Luce Foundation, Dean Constance Buchanan, and the entire Theology Department of the Divinity School. Professors Margaret Miles and Richard Niebuhr were especially helpful. Moreover, Dean Constance Buchanan, and Professors Ted Hiebert and Gordon Kaufman deserve particular thanks for their patient discussions with me concerning the values imbedded and implicit in Judeo-Christian tradition and the implications these values have for formulating public policy on environmental matters.

Finally, in this context, I owe special thanks to Professor Ronald Thiemann, Dean of the Harvard Divinity School, for his continuing encouragement and support for my work as Director of the Harvard Seminar on Environmental Values. He has been a strong advocate for exploring the interaction between values questions and public policy, and his commitment to examine environmental issues and religious beliefs has made him a national leader among religious educators on these questions.

During 1989-90, I was granted a year's leave from the Harvard Divinity School, to work as a Warren Weaver Fellow at the Rockefeller Foundation in New York. For this opportunity I am grateful to the officers of the Rockefeller Foundation, and in particular the Senior Vice-President, Dr. Kenneth Prewitt, as well as Dr. Joyce Moock and Mr. Joseph Bookmeyer.

During the year at the Foundation I was asked to develop a system to monitor global environmental change as part of the Foundation's effort to launch an environmental initiative. With the able assistance of Meredith Avril and the support of Frank Karel, I was able to develop a series of software programs known as *Eco-Link*, which made it possible to monitor news and academic research about environmental change from around the globe.[2] In developing these research tools, I was thankful for the criticism, advice, and encouragement of several other Warren Weaver Fellows, especially Dr. Hadi Dowlatabadi, Mr. Steven Bass, and Ms. Elizabeth Beaman. This software has been used to update much of the information in this book beyond the initial Senate hearings, and it now serves as the basis for a computer research facility in support of the Harvard Seminar on Environmental Values.

Since 1991 I have worked on a joint appointment at Harvard University, on the one hand, as a Research Associate in Environmental Ethics at the Divinity School, and on the other, as Research Fellow in the Pacific Basin Research Center—a program within the John F. Kennedy School of Government's Center for Science and International Affairs. In this context I am grateful to a number of people at the Kennedy School including Dr. Ashton Carter, Director of the Center for Science and International Affairs, Susan Fox, Program Director at the Center, and particularly Professor William Clark, its Associate Director. Professor Clark has encouraged my work on agricultural policy and environmental issues as part of the broader research I am undertaking on international trade and environment issues. I owe him particular thanks for the support of the Center for Science and International Affairs, and I continue to learn from his wisdom and insight on problems of formulating and implementing effective public policy.

Above all I owe thanks at the Kennedy School to Professor John Montgomery, Director of the Pacific Basin Research Center, and to the Soka University of America for their fellowship support at that Center. In 1990 Professor Montgomery launched a series of investigations on the necessary components of what he called "mega-policies"—major innovative public policy initiatives that can be seen in retrospect to have changed the course of history. In this context he has focused upon the importance of developing policies that transcend the traditional sectoral realms of specialization of defense, cultural development, economic development, and the environment.

Upon examining past patterns and current trends in environmental change for the Pacific basin and elsewhere, Professor Montgomery has suggested that mega-policies on the scale of the historically important Marshall plan will be required to achieve stable and equitable development in the Pacific region. As an aspect of his interest in evolving mega-policies, Professor Montgomery has encouraged, guided, and supported my research on the impact of international trade agreements upon environmental conditions in the Pacific basin and throughout the Third World. Moreover, on a personal level, he has been a source of spirited wit and energetic inspiration for all those around him, goading us to achieve more than we thought possible. For this and many other unsung virtues I owe Professor Montgomery abundant thanks.

Students at Williams College, Yale, and Harvard have always been helpful over the years that I have taught both history and anthropology. In this context Elliott Gimble, Paul Trawick, Dan Smith, Jock Conyngham, Katina Lillios, Jim McKinley, and Joe Simonetta as well as many others have all asked penetrating questions, and they have proved remarkably patient with the tentative thoughts I have offered in response. They all deserve explicit thanks.

Finally, I wish to express special gratitude to Dr. Peter Weiskel of the U.S. Geological Survey for his continuous instruction and guidance on matters of ecosystem science and to Portia Weiskel of Hillhouse Farm in Leverett, Massachusetts, for her insight and inspiration on agricultural, food and farming matters. Beyond all words, I am indebted to Catherine Lacny Weiskel for the constant commitment and support she has provided in all my endeavors.

Timothy C. Weiskel
September 1992

* * *

Notes

1. For the original testimony see: Timothy C. Weiskel, "The Anthropology of Environmental Decline," testimony presented at the *Joint Hearings before the Subcommittee on Hazardous Wastes and Toxic Substances and the Subcommittee on Environmental Protection of the Committee on Environment and Public Works,* United States Senate, *on S. 2666, A Bill Entitled the "Global Environmental Protection Act of 1988,"* (14 September 1988) [Committee Print], pp. 35-37, 114-157.

2. For a description of this program see: Timothy C. Weiskel, "Environmental Information Resources and Electronic Research Systems (ERSs): *Eco-Link* as an Example of Future Tools," *Library Hi Tech* 9:2 consecutive issue 34 (1991), pp. 7-19.

Chapter I

Devising Public Policy in an

Ecological Community

I believe we are on the road to tragedy.
MAURICE STRONG
Secretary General of UNCED, 14 June 1992

It is hard to read the newspapers on environmental matters without being left with an uneasy sense that we face an enormous mismatch problem. The institutions, the leadership, the public understanding, and the collective vision that we currently possess simply do not match the immense ecological crises we now face. Moreover, the available tools for formulating public policy seem woefully inadequate for the range of global problems before us.

The tragedy is not simply the lack of tools. Indeed, tools of all shapes and sizes abound. Everyone seems to have a favorite formula or a technological marvel to arrest or reverse environmental decline. But tools in themselves are only part of the solution. The larger problem is one of matching the tools to the tasks. There is nothing intrinsically wrong with a dentist's pick; nor is there anything wrong with a jack-hammer. There is, however, something fundamentally misguided in trying to repair a public highway with a dentist's pick or in attempting to undertake the work of dentistry with a jack-hammer. In the first instance the effort is clearly silly; in the second, it would turn out to be excruciatingly painful and destructive.

In addressing the social and economic aspects of environmental change we face the same problem: the tools available and tasks at hand are sadly mismatched. Using mechanisms like market pricing, taxation, government regulation, and negotiated treaties to fine-tune human behavior in a complex and fragile ecosystem can prove to be either patently silly or painfully destructive. In short, we have a long way to go and not much time left to match the appropriate tools to the needed tasks.

Difficult as they may seem, our problems would be relatively simple if all we had to do was mix and match existing tools with well-known tasks. But this is not the case. Scientists persistently point out that in an ecosystem nothing remains static. All the components are perpetually in motion. Thus, as agents in the ecosystem, the tasks required of us are always changing as well. In response, new tools of public policy, new institutions, new leadership qualities, and a new common vision and commitment need to be forged. Here lies the true challenge before us as a human community within the global ecosystem.

Are we up to the task? Does our leadership see what is at stake? Are the world's citizens prepared to change their habitual behavior and make the necessary sacrifices for our collective survival?

Unfortunately there is mounting evidence that our collective capacity to forge new policy tools, create new institutions, and develop new leadership qualities may be declining just when it is most urgently required. At the very least, it seems that our ability to formulate effective public policy is not evolving quickly enough to match the accelerating pace of global environmental decline.

The year 1992 may well be remembered by future generations as a tragic milestone in this regard. The year is barely half over as this manuscript goes to press, yet several events have already occurred that will no doubt serve to single out this year as particularly significant in the history of humanity's relation to its earth environment.

Most notable on a global level, 1992 was the year of the Earth summit. For the first time in the history of humankind, heads of state from around the world convened specifically to consider the condition of the earth's ecological systems, the growing needs of humankind, and numerous concrete proposals to move the world's economies toward sustainable development. The United Nations Conference on Environment and Development (UNCED) convened in Rio, Brazil for twelve days in early June of 1992 after more than two years of advanced preparation. As the Secretary General of the UNCED conference, Maurice Strong, concluded at the end of the historic meeting: "After the summit, the world will never be the same."[1] In the presence of over one hundred heads of state who attended the meetings, Maurice Strong emphasized the importance of the events: "This indeed is a historic moment for humanity....It has indeed been a profound human experience from which none of us can emerge unchanged."[2]

Compared with the fitful and fragmentary efforts in the past, the accomplishments of the Rio Conference were in fact impressive. Five major documents emerged from the meetings: the Rio Declaration, setting forth general principles of environmental protection and sustainable development; a convention on global warming; a convention on biodiversity; a protocol on global forests; and a massive document known as "Agenda 21," designed as a blueprint for explicit actions by nation-states as the world approaches the twenty-first century.

But by the end of the summit, an air of disappointment hung over the proceedings. Because of the United States government's refusal to sign the biodiversity convention and its successful efforts to lobby against language to set any timetables or targets for reducing carbon emissions, many participants felt that the summit fell short of its promise. Moreover, Third World participants from the nations of the "South" were bitterly disappointed at the unwillingness of "Northern" countries to provide the substantial new funding necessary to execute the ambitious plans outlined in the Agenda 21.

Throughout the conference the debate was starkly drawn between the contrasting perspectives of the North and the South. The tension was poignantly expressed in the words of India's Prime Minister, Narasimha Rao, when he observed in his address to the summit that "We have only one planet, but many worlds."[3]

As if to underscore the sad truth of this observation the American government insisted upon distancing itself from efforts to reach global agreement on key environmental issues. In Washington on Thursday, 11 June, before leaving for the summit, President George Bush announced that "If the United States has to be the only country to challenge the biodiversity treaty, so be it."[4] As he stepped on to Air Force One to begin his trip to Rio, Bush reasserted in a defiant tone that he refused to sign the biodiversity agreement because he felt it had the potential of costing Americans both jobs and money. "I am determined to protect the environment, and I am determined to protect U.S. taxpayers. The day of the open checkbook is over."[5]

Upon arriving in Rio, President Bush seemed to sense the disapproval and disappointment of other world leaders, but he responded with chauvinism and defiance. In his speech before the world gathering on Friday, 12 June, Bush declared:

> Let's face it, there has been some criticism of the United States. But I must tell you, we come to Rio proud of what we have accomplished and committed to extending the record on American leadership on the environment. In the United States, we have the world's tightest air quality standards on cars and factories, the most advanced laws for protecting lands and waters, and the most open processes for public participation.
>
> And now for a simple truth: America's record on environmental protection is second to none. So I did not come here to apologize.[6]

In a flourish of rhetorical bravado apparently designed to counteract criticism for not signing the biodiversity treaty, President Bush went on to affirm:

> We come to Rio prepared to continue America's unparal-
> leled efforts to preserve species and habitat. And let me be
> clear, our efforts to protect biodiversity itself will exceed,
> *will exceed* the requirements of the treaty....
>
> [I]t is never easy, *it is never easy* to stand alone on
> principle, but sometimes leadership requires that you do.
> And now is such a time.[7]

Even as he was making this emphatic declaration of principle,
however, President Bush's words were contradicted by events in the
United States. On the morning of 12 June it was announced in Washington that the Supreme Court had ruled in favor of a long-standing Bush
administration legal suit to *reduce* the rights of U.S. citizens to take legal
action on behalf of endangered species in the United States and around
the world. James H. Rubin of the *Associated Press* filed a report on the
Court's decision only hours before the President's speech in Rio,
commenting in his story on the coincidence of the two events:

> The Supreme Court today limited the right of envi-
> ronmentalists to sue over federal support of projects
> overseas that allegedly threaten endangered species.
>
> The 7-2 ruling, a victory for the Bush administration
> coincidentally handed down the day the president attends
> the Earth Summit in Brazil, overturned a victory for
> wildlife groups that seek to preserve endangered species
> outside U.S. borders.
>
> The dissenters condemned the decision as "a slash and
> burn expedition" that could cost the environment dearly.[8]

Neither President Bush nor any of the American delegation commented
on the apparent discrepancy between the President's solemn declarations
to world leaders and the administration's final victory in the legal battle
that Bush had waged *against* the environmental groups that work to
protect endangered species. Reporters covering the Rio summit were
apparently unaware of the Supreme Court's announcement, and no one
in Rio questioned the President about this glaring contradiction.

Some observers speculated in the days surrounding the summit that
President Bush's behavior at Rio had little to do with the summit in any
case. The Rio statements, they suggested, were part of a calculated effort
to appeal to particular business interests and conservative political
constituents in an election year.[9] While President Bush denied this in a
news conference in Rio on Saturday, 13 June, his choice of words
indicated that what he called "business rights" were an important part of
his decision not to sign the biodiversity treaty.

I'm not pressured by domestic politics as to what our sound environmental practices are. We've got sound environmental practices. We are not going to sign up to things that we can't do. We're not going to sign up to things we don't believe in. I happen to believe that in biodiversity, it is important to protect our rights, our business rights.[10]

The international reaction to the Bush position was nearly universal. Even before Bush's speech José Goldemberg, Brazil's Minister of Education and Minister of the Environment, summed it up plainly: "There is a generalized feeling of resentment against President Bush....Most delegates, who will obviously receive the American president in a respectful manner, are disappointed in him because of his refusal to sign the biological diversity treaty."[11] In addition leaders of various non-governmental organizations expressed their disappointment with the American President. Magda Renner, president of Friends of the Earth International, made the distinction between the American government and its people: "We can't blame Americans, but we blame the government....For years, we tried not to be personal.... Now it's time to point the finger and say, 'You are responsible. You are accountable.' And Bush is," Renner said.[12]

Whether Bush was defending narrow business interests, or appealing to the political right wing, or—for that matter—whether he genuinely felt himself to be acting "to protect U.S. taxpayers," it became clear to the world at large from Bush's performance at Rio that the United States had abdicated its role as an international leader on matters relating to the environment.

By the end of the meetings the official summit organizers were clearly disappointed as well. On Sunday, 14 June, in a news conference Maurice Strong issued a final impassioned appeal to the world leaders to respond to the gravity of the deteriorating environmental situation, particularly the circumstances in the Third World. He insisted that the summit had not been a failure, but as he put it: "We have got agreements without sufficient commitments." He added, "I would have liked to have seen a more solid and a more forthcoming commitment by major donors."[13]

In what many took to be a direct reference to the disappointing positions taken by the United States government, Strong underscored that political leadership in North America seemed to remain blind to the realities at hand, preferring instead to pursue traditional strategies of economic growth that protect the status quo:

"The current [North America] lifestyles are not sustainable. But that message has still not got through to some political leaders," he said. "I don't agree that the status quo is the answer because the status quo will not survive. The evidence is very clear."[14]

Then, as he reflected over the last twenty years of his own efforts since the 1972 Stockholm United Nations Conference on the Environment, Maurice Strong seemed momentarily overwhelmed by a certain sense of frustration that more had not been achieved in Rio to convince the world's political leadership of the need to act now in consort. Reporters from the *Washington Post* described the scene, capturing the drama of his candid remarks:

"When we thought we did it in Stockholm, we didn't," said Canadian Strong, choking back tears as he recalled the 1972 conference on the environment in Sweden. "And, we don't have another 20 years now. I believe we are on the road to tragedy."[15]

* * *

We will not know for years or even decades whether Maurice Strong's bleak assessment at the close of the Rio summit will turn out to be true. Nevertheless, it seems clear that if collective ecological decline is to be arrested and reversed, a new kind of vision will need to inform political leaders and public policy makers around the globe. Moreover this vision and a sense of common commitment will have to be generated and shared by ordinary citizens throughout the world. If the Rio summit proved anything, it is that current political leaders are by and large far too short-sighted to respond effectively to the global environmental challenges before the human community.

The reasons for this are understandable if not pardonable. In autocratic or authoritarian regimes the environment has often been ignored, or—worse yet—simply pillaged and ravaged in pursuit of state production goals or personal enrichment of a few. Democratic regimes have not fared much better. Here the reason is that in most of the world's representative democracies the means and methods of ascending to political leadership have traditionally had little or nothing to do with developing an awareness of the environment or demonstrating an understanding of global systemic process.

On the contrary, political elites in democracies are typically quite skilled in focusing upon immediate crises and localized constituencies. In these circumstances the calculus of visible, short-term mutual benefit is preeminent. This leaves out most of the world, most of the time. Public policy decisions made in the United States frequently have grave and enduring implications for the welfare of citizens in foreign countries, but their interests are rarely considered paramount in determining policy for one simple reason: foreigners cannot vote in United States elections so politicians can afford to be indifferent to their plight. The same is true for future generations. As one Senator put it in defending his lack of resolute action on environmental matters, "What have future generations done for me lately?"

In most democracies there is no sizable, well organized group that will vote on behalf of these structurally disenfranchised populations so it is hardly surprising that in elective democracies global environmental concerns are of secondary importance to traditional political elites. Indeed, in these days of television and media pollsters, the so-called political leadership has transformed itself into a species of political followership, capable of shifting a carefully crafted message instantaneously to target just the right combination of constituencies needed to win fifty percent of the vote plus one in order to declare victory.

After the twenty years of reflection and environmental action since the 1972 U.N. conference on the environment in Stockholm, citizens around the globe may well have hoped to see heads of state meet in Rio at the world's first Earth summit to make important and timely decisions for the future benefit of humankind, but what we all witnessed instead was a gathering of politicians, most of whom were preoccupied with the narrow calculus of partisan debate and constituent patronage. Few of these political figures demonstrated that they were capable of seeing let alone responding to the global ecological crisis facing humankind as a whole.

Even if eventually a well functioning democratic process manages some day to take the interests of future generations, of the socially disenfranchised, and of citizens outside its borders into account in making public policy, our problems would not be solved. The reason for this is simple: humans are only one species in a vast and complex web of life-forms on the planet. In responding to *human* needs and *human* desires, elective democracies may eventually improve their capacity to respond to short-term human need. But what about the myriad other species upon whom we depend in ways we are just beginning to discover or do not yet recognize? What of the welfare of the planet as a whole?

No known ecosystem has ever functioned for long when the needs of only one of its constituent species are met to the exclusion of others. The needs of all constituent species must be met for the system to function as a complete system. The earth's entire ecosystem will be no exception to this universal law of ecology. Similarly, no organism can outlive its life support system for very long, so it would make sense for all humans to preserve and protect the multiple life forms upon whom our life depends.

It is tempting to declare that human needs must come first, yet ironically, pursuing this as the singular logic of public policy would lead to accelerated ecological collapse. Humans cannot always come first. Some principle of restraint must come into play for each species in an ecosystem—for humans as well as for all others. Without a governing principle of self-limitation populations rapidly escalate out of control driving the ecosystem toward chronic instability. While it is true that humans select or elect those who formulate public policy, developing that policy solely on the basis of immediate human needs would be a formula for ecological suicide. The preservation and health of plant and animal biodiversity must be an urgent task for anyone who seeks to formulate public policy for a sustainable world.

How then are we to devise effective public policy for the environment in the broader ecological community we inhabit? Even the most refined political institutions that we possess are still designed primarily to meet human needs, but as we have just seen, responding to human needs alone will not be enough to enable us to preserve and survive in a functioning ecosystem. What then are we to do? How can we make wise public policy for the ecological community as a whole?

The answer to this conundrum lies in fashioning a radically new sense of citizenship and an entirely new political process to reflect that citizenship. Public policy needs to be formulated on the basis of a fundamentally new and more inclusive sense of community. Snails and whales do not vote—indeed they cannot vote. Yet if their interests—and the interests of all the other seen and unseen species—cannot be represented in our political process, public policy is bound to fail even its human constituency. We need, in short, to work hard in the months, years, and decades ahead to forge a new and compelling sensibility in the public at large that we all are citizens of a global ecological community and a new kind of political leadership is required to reflect that fact.

In spite of the structural impediments of the political process and despite Maurice Strong's momentary personal sense of discouragement, it is worth noting that there are at least some encouraging signs that this process is already underway. A series of committees in the United States House of Representatives and the Senate have for a number of years been listening to the testimony of citizens, consumer groups, environmental activists, and scientists who have all emphasized the urgency of impending environmental changes and the need to develop a new style of political leadership to address them.

Years of organizing among a sizable coalition of scientists, environmentalists, and national religious leaders culminated in joint hearings between the House and Senate in May 1992, just prior to the Rio summit. Calling themselves the "Joint Appeal by Religion and Science for the Environment," the group held two days of hearings, seminars, and briefing sessions for members of Congress. In addition, they presented a statement to the Senate leadership signed by over one hundred eminent scientists, national religious leaders, and sympathetic House and Senate members, outlining the dimensions of their global environmental concern and asserting, "We believe that the dimensions of this crisis are still not sufficiently taken to heart by our leaders, institutions and industries." The Joint Appeal's declaration went on to state: "We call upon our government to change national policy so that the United States will begin to ease, not continue to increase, the burdens on our biosphere and their effect upon the planet's people."[16]

In part as a result of this crescendo of public concern, some of the Congressional leadership have begun to articulate the need for a more inclusive political process and a longer-term vision to match the scope of global environmental change. On 13 May, Senate majority leader George Mitchell read the full text of the Joint Appeal declaration into the Congressional Record, applauding the efforts of the group to bring these issues to the top of the public policy agenda.[17]

Individual senators had already taken leadership roles on selected environmental issues. Senator Timothy Wirth of Colorado had long been an advocate of environmental legislation. Environmentalists were disappointed when he decided not to run for reelection to his Senate seat, but other senators have become more vocal on environmental issues. Senator Albert Gore, Jr., of Tennessee, for example, developed a national reputation for leadership on global environmental issues. Building upon the scientific evidence presented to him in numerous Senate hearings, expressing a personal sense of obligation for future generations, and drawing upon a deep spiritual commitment to honor the sacredness of creation, Senator Gore published a remarkable book in February 1992 entitled *Earth in the Balance*, in which he summarized the global environmental challenge before us.[18]

The book provides an excellent summary of the evidence on population growth, environmental deterioration, global warming, and stratospheric ozone depletion. In addition, however, Senator Gore discusses both the values questions inherent in formulating environmental policy and the political changes that will need to occur to address global environmental issues. In a chapter entitled "A New Common Purpose," Senator Gore puts the issue quite clearly:

> I have come to believe that we must take bold and unequiv-
> ocal action: we must make the rescue of the environment
> the central organizing principle for civilization. Whether
> we realize it or not, we are now engaged in an epic battle

to right the balance of our earth, and the tide of this battle
will turn only when the majority of people in the world
become sufficiently aroused by a shared sense of urgent
danger to join an all-out effort.[19]

As the American public learned in early July, it was in part because
of his demonstrated knowledge of and commitment to environmental
matters that Governor Bill Clinton selected Al Gore to be his Vice
Presidential running mate.[20] Senator Gore made no secret of his
commitments in these matters. After years of holding hearings, writing
articles, and giving speeches on environmental matters, he led the United
States Congressional delegation to the Earth summit in June. There he
witnessed President Bush's disappointing performance.

Referring to the conduct of President Bush and his advisors at Rio
during his acceptance speech at the Democratic National Convention
Senator Gore was blunt: "They embarrassed our nation when the whole
world was asking for American leadership in confronting the environmental crisis. It is time for them to go."[21] Within hours of Senator
Gore's speech, the highly popular but still undeclared candidate for
President, Ross Perot, decided that the Democratic party had indeed been
"revitalized" and he announced he was withdrawing from the presidential
race.[22]

Rarely has there been such a swift and dramatic political response to
the failure of environmental leadership. Within one month of President
Bush's provocative pronouncements in Brazil, the largest political party
in the United States embraced a forceful and effective spokesperson for
environmental causes and began to campaign to reverse the Bush
administration's record on environmental matters. Having been despon-
dent in mid-June after Rio, many environmentalists were elated by mid-
July.[23] They began to feel that for the first time in a national election
they had the possibility of campaigning for and voting for a proven pro-
environment candidate. At least in some instances, then, there seems to
have been a shift of perspective on environmental issues in national
political circles. It remains to be seen whether this kind of leadership
will prevail in a national election, but the issues are squarely joined and
a clear choice will be presented to the electorate in November 1992.

If political leadership has begun to reorient itself toward recognizing
the urgency of the environmental crisis, it is not yet clear that beyond the
environmentalist community the general public is equally informed or
motivated to act on these issues. Electoral appeals for fundamental
change on environmental matters may be novel and even moving, but
such appeals will only succeed if ordinary citizens recognize and respond
to a radically new concept of community and accept the responsibilities
of ecological citizenship that this new sense of community requires.

To begin with it is helpful to reexamine the historical patterns of environmental decline that have characterized past cultures and then turn to a sober assessment of the trends currently underway in the contemporary world.

Notes

1. Ken Silverstein, "Earth Summit," *AP Newswire*, 14 June 1992, 15:02.

2. "Earth Summit Ends 12-Day Meeting to Save Planet," *Reuter Newswire*, 14 June 1992, 17:24.

3. "Earth Summit: Speakers Mix Accusations and Promises," *IPS Newswire*, 12 June 1992.

4. "Earth Summit: Leaving for Rio, Bush Says No More Blank Checks," *IPS Newswire*, 14 June 1992.

5. "Earth Summit: Leaving for Rio, Bush Says No More Blank Checks."

6. "Bush-Summit-Text," *AP Newswire*, 12 June 1992, 15:14.

7. "Bush-Summit Text."

8. James H. Rubin, "Scotus-Endangered Species," *AP Newswire*, 12 June 1992, 10:22 aed. The case was known as 90-1424 Manuel Lujan Jr., Secretary of the Interior vs. Defenders of Wildlife, et al. See also: Greg Henderson, "Court Says Environmental Groups Can't Sue U.S. for ...," *UPI Newswire*, 12 June 1992, 13:23; and Ruth Marcus, "Justices Make It Harder to Press Environmental Enforcement Cases," *Washington Post*, 13 June 1992.

9. Senator Tim Wirth of Colorado, a member of the U.S. Congressional delegation, indicated that he felt the President's entire strategy surrounding the summit was motivated by domestic political concerns. "The U.S. has allowed itself to be isolated here because of its rigid adherence to the...right wing." See: Michael Weisskopf, "Behind the Curve in Rio; Unhappy Allies Await Bush in Rio," *Washington Post*, 11 June 1992.

10. "Bush-Excerpts," *AP Newswire*, 13 June 1992, 12:02.

11. Ruth Sinai, "Bush-Summit," *AP Newswire*, 12 June 1992, 00:36.

12. Ruth Sinai.

13. "Earth Summit: UNCED—'A High Point, but not the End Point'," *IPS Newswire*, 14 June 1992.

14. "Earth Summit: UNCED—'A High Point, but not the End Point'."

15. Julia Preston and Michael Weisskopf, "Rio Organizer Says Summit Fell Short," *Washington Post*, 15 June 1992.

16. "ENVIRONMENT: U.S. Scientists, Clergy Pledge Joint Efforts," *IPS Newswire*, 15 May 1992, 12:11 aed.

17. *The Congressional Record*, 102d Congress, Second Session, vol. 138, no. 66, 13 May 1992.

18. Al Gore, *Earth in the Balance: Ecology and the Human Spirit* (Boston: Houghton Mifflin, 1992).

19. Al Gore, p. 269.

20. In announcing his choice of Senator Gore, Governor Clinton said: "Today, he [Senator Gore] is perhaps better known than anything else for his willingness and readiness, his commitment and his ability to do something that George Bush is not willing to do, to be a leader in protecting the world's environment. Al Gore has spent the last decade working on the global environmental challenges; we desperately need to address: global warming, ozone depletion, energy conservation. He has written a magnificent book on his thoughts and recommendations. He has asked me to join in his commitment to preserve not only the environment of America, but to preserve the environment of our globe for future generations. And together, we will finally give the United States a real environmental presidency." "CVN--Clinton-Gore Excerpts," *AP Newswire*, 9 July 1992, 19:14 ped.

21. "CVN--Gore-Text," *AP Newswire*, 17 July 1992, 03:40 aed.

22. The UPI news service reported on the Perot news conference quoting Perot: "'I decided that it was definitely going into the House of Representatives,' he said, adding that the Democratic Party had done 'a brilliant job' of revitalizing the party." *UPI Newswire*, 16 July 1992, 0:32 aed.

23. The Associated Press reported that: "Sierra Club political director Reid Wilson issued a statement calling Gore 'an outstanding choice'."

"There is a world of difference between Sen. Gore and his counterpart, Vice President Quayle," Wilson said. "Sen. Gore is extremely knowledgeable about environmental problems and has worked hard to keep the environment at the top of the nation's agenda. He's a leader on the issue."

"Al Gore will ignite the environmental community at the grassroot levels," said Jim Maddy, executive director of the League of Conservation Voters. And the group's president, Bruce Babbitt, another 1988 candidate, said Gore was recognized as "someone who is committed to environmental issues."

Sen. Tim Wirth, D-Colo., said the ticket represented "a new generation of leadership to guide the United States from the Cold War into the 21st century." *AP Newswire*, 10 July 1992, 01:45 aed; "Gore-Environment," *AP Newswire*, 10 July 1992, 16:42 ped.

Chapter II

Historical Aspects of
Environmental Decline

Is Our Predicament New?

Current news on environmental problems frequently emphasizes the totally unprecedented nature of the ecological crises that beset us in this nation and the Western world as a whole. We are told, for example, that the summer of 1988 constituted "the hottest summer on record" in North America. Similarly we hear that Boston Harbor has never in its history been so polluted, and in European waters seal populations died of an epidemic in 1988 on a scale never before witnessed by man. By stressing this "never before" aspect of events, it is sometimes argued that the experience of the past is largely irrelevant for policy planners. Since our circumstances are new, so the argument runs, past experience leaves us with little or no instruction for the formulation of a practical public policy for the environment.

The Current Crisis Has Precedents

This is not altogether true. While particular types of industrial pollution may be new and the scale of ecological devastation may be greater now than previously, recent research demonstrates that the Western world is not confronting completely unprecedented circumstances. We need only cast our gaze over a somewhat enlarged horizon to realize that numerous civilizations before our own have confronted environmental degradation. Moreover, many regions of the non-Western world are currently facing and some are coping with environmental deterioration in our own time. Historians and archaeologists have studied examples of ecological collapse in past civilizations while anthropologists are examining contemporary examples of ecological degradation in non-Western cultures.

In our urgent concern to formulate effective environmental policy in the United States, we would be wise to keep the insights of this historical and cross-cultural research clearly in mind, lest public leaders commit our society to repeating and amplifying the tragic blunders of other cultures and past civilizations. If we continue to tie our society's infrastructure and agricultural production to a declining resource base, as ancient civilizations did with such depressing regularity, we too will suffer the fate of unavoidable collapse.

The Ecological Decline of Ancient Civilizations

Anthropogenic ecological degradation is, unfortunately, very ancient indeed. Since at least the advent of sedentary agriculture, humankind has acted as a powerful biological and geological agent in complex ecosystems, almost invariably without a corresponding awareness of its own impact upon the environment. For this reason, conscious statements by witnesses from the past or from other cultures in our own day have not adequately reflected the full scope of human involvement in ecological decline. Thus, written records or oral traditions are not in themselves sufficient for investigating the question of human agency in ecosystems.

Archaeologists have debated the relative importance of human agency or environmental change as the primary factor in explaining accelerated patterns of soil erosion in the circum-Mediterranean over historic time. While climate theories were favored at an early date, theories stressing anthropogenic activity are gaining ascendancy. As Kevin Greene says in *The Archaeology of the Roman Economy*:

> Recent work around the Mediterranean has tended to favour human rather than climatic factors as the cause of the dramatic accumulations of sediment which took place in so many areas.

Thus many catastrophes which have long been understood as "acts of God" or "natural disasters" were in fact largely generated or substantially aggravated by collective and cumulative human behavior.[1] The recurrent pattern of the rise and fall of ancient civilizations in the circum-Mediterranean region, Mesopotamia, Phoenecia, Palestine, Egypt, Greece, and Rome[2] is clearly revealed in the emergence and collapse of their agricultural complexes.

These urban-based civilizations had to solve the basic problem of producing food surpluses and collecting raw materials from rural areas to sustain the non-agricultural activities of populations engaged in commerce, ritual, government, and the arts. Over time the strategies that each society pursued to produce food and procure resources left their characteristic mark on the environment. Many of these strategies proved not to be sustainable in the long run. Local populations overtaxed the natural resource base of the region through depletion of water, soil, or forest reserves, and their continuous agricultural demands on the land exceeded its long-term carrying capacity. The general pattern was one of gradual emergence, brief efflorescence, and rapid collapse of civilizations, often taking the form in the final stages of devastating military struggles for the control of arable land or a declining resource base.

Techniques of agricultural intensification—terracing, crop selection, animal husbandry, irrigation, and the like—were devised to meet repeated crises of production. Despite short-term improvements in output, however, the long-term consequences of these technologies were not foreseeable by early agricultural innovators. In subsequent decades or centuries problems of overgrazing, watershed deforestation, soil erosion, siltation, water-logging, soil salinization, and crop blight often emerged as the long-term consequences of earlier innovations, sometimes leaving whole regions permanently destroyed for agricultural use.

Written documentation of these phenomena frequently presents explanations in terms of military, political, or religious rivalry and conflict, perhaps most obviously because the elites who wrote such literature were part of military, political, or religious institutions in the societies concerned. Nevertheless, no matter how persuasive this literature may seem to be, explanations of this kind inevitably oversimplify and distort a more fundamental understanding of the dynamic of agricultural civilizations.

Current archaeological research based upon scientific analysis of soil profiles, vegetation, and landscape evolution indicates that in the rise and fall of ancient civilizations there was at the base of nearly all sustained conflict an irreducible ecological component. Patterns of rivalry in the circum-Mediterranean could express either a momentary ecological crisis or a long-standing decline of some fundamental element of ecological capital of the agricultural systems concerned. The ecological dislocations were frequently most visible in the "peripheral" areas of the great Mediterranean empires, for it was here that the imperial powers established systems of commercial agriculture and proceeded to exact levels of agricultural production that exceeded the ecological capacity of the land.[3]

The Ecology of European Expansion

The sobering ecological lessons of the ancient world may well have remained clear in our collective consciousness were it not for the experience of the Western world over the last five hundred years. In no other period of history does there appear to have been as much exploration, outward migration, trade, and conquest in such a comparatively short interval of time.

This recent experience has overshadowed—indeed all but eclipsed—the lessons that we should have learned from the recurrent decline and collapse of ancient agricultural civilizations. It can be argued that recent history has been responsible for a potentially fatal, cultural blind spot concerning the vulnerability of our current industrial system of agriculture. Because of its experiences between roughly 1450 and 1950—a period marked by seemingly unlimited expansion—the Western industrial world now finds itself conceptually ill-equipped to understand and politically impotent to cope with the problems of ecological adjustment that currently face all societies in our modern, finite world.

The Europeans' "Biological Allies"

Ironically, it is precisely the remarkable "ecological success" of European cultures that has led to their current ecological myopia. Recent research on the historical ecology of European expansion makes this abundantly clear. Briefly put, Europeans were able to expand with such rapid success throughout great portions of the world between 1450 and 1950 largely because their microbes, viruses, weeds, pests, and plant and animal domesticates proved to be heartier than indigenous species in competition for survival in distant lands around the world. It was the success of their "biological allies" that paved the way for Europeans to dominate much of the modern world.[4]

The comparative success of the Europeans' biological allies ultimately stemmed from the evolutionary history of microbes, plants, and animals. Essentially, the antiquity of agricultural practice and urban civilization in the Old World meant that diseases, weeds, cultigens, and herbivorous domestic animals had developed highly effective mechanisms for feeding or breeding simply to remain alive in the context of close competition with other species. Hence, many of these organisms were equipped with more effective defenses, better dispersal mechanisms, or more aggressive behavior than the species occupying similar eco-niches in the newly discovered colonial territories. With the help of their "biological allies" European agriculturalists quickly exploited the natural capital of vegetation and fertile soils in regions where indigenous populations were either sparsely settled agriculturalists or foraging nomads. The ensuing biological intrusion was frequently devastating for populations of indigenous flora and fauna and often led to substantial modifications of local biotic communities, alterations of the regional hydrology, and the devastation of age-old topsoils.[5]

Loss of Ancient Agricultural Wisdom

European agricultural techniques were substantially transformed in the New World colonies, even as the New World itself was being physically transformed. In this process, some age-old agricultural wisdom appears to have been lost. Conservation of resources simply seemed no longer necessary in the circumstances of comparative abundance. Whereas intensive techniques of resource husbandry had come to characterize the confined land-base of medieval European agriculture, the New World afforded rich new possibilities for agricultural expansion. In effect, since the discovery of the New World, predatory expansive agriculture and parasitic resource use came to characterize European civilization, leading some emergent cultures, including our own, to believe in a mythology of expanding "frontiers." Because historically this was a plausible mythic image, the mythology of "frontier cultures" could be sustained for centuries and verified by numerous cases of parochial experience.

It is important to realize, however, that the overall expansion of the land surface under cultivation, and not improvements in basic technology, accounted for increases in agricultural output over most of the period. While total production rose dramatically, productivity per acre and productivity per unit of energy input often declined. Nevertheless, profits from total agricultural surpluses helped to finance the emergence of urban-based industrial systems. The dynamic of industrial growth served, in turn, to sustain the mythology of "unlimited frontiers" and further transformed these formative frontier myths into a belief in perpetual economic growth. Having expanded upon the things of nature, the West came to believe that expansion was in the nature of things. Perpetual growth was considered both good and natural.

The European experience of overseas expansion and ensuing industrialization has engendered deep-seated habits of thought and images of cultural self-perception.[6] In our day, these images and metaphors leave the industrial world unable to construct a viable system of stable production in our finite circumstance. In effect, we are trying to sustain a "frontier culture" in a post-frontier world. Little wonder that our environmental policy is so embarrassingly immature.

NOTES

1. J. Donald Hughes, *Ecology in Ancient Civilizations* (Albuquerque: U. of New Mexico Press, 1975). Kevin Greene, *The Archaeology of the Roman Economy* (Berkeley: U. of California Press, 1986), p. 85. See also: S. Judson, "Alluviation and Erosion," in E. Fentess, et al., *Excavations at Fosso della Crescenza 1962* (Rome: 1982) [Papers of the British School of Rome, No. 51], pp. 58-101; and Claudio Vita-Finzi, *Archaeological Sites in Their Setting* (London: 1978), especially, pp. 8 and 11-13.

2. H. W. Lawton and P.J. Wilke, "Ancient Agricultural Systems in Dry Regions," in A. E. Hall, G. H. Cannell, and H. W. Lawton, eds., *Agriculture in Semi-Arid Environments* (New York: Springer-Verlag, 1979), pp. 1-44. Popular, if somewhat dated, accounts include: Edward Hyams, *Soil and Civilization* (New York: Harper and Row, [1952] 1976); and Vernon Gill Carter and Tom Dale, *Topsoil and Civilization* (Norman: University of Oklahoma Press, 1976).

3. W. Groenman-van Waateringe, "The Disastrous Effect of the Roman Occupation," in: R. Brandt and J. Slofstra, eds., *Roman and Native in the Low Countries: Spheres of Interaction* (Oxford: British Archaeological Reports, s184, 1983), pp. 147-157; and Claudio Vita-Finzi, "Roman Dams in Tripolitania," *Antiquity* 35 (1961), pp. 14-20; and Z. Naveh and J. Dan, "The Human Degradation of Mediterranean Landscapes," in: F. Di Castri and H. A. Mooney, eds., *Mediterranean Type Ecosystems* (New York: Springer-Verlag, 1973), pp. 373-390.

4. Alfred W. Crosby, Jr. *The Columbian Exchange: Biological and Cultural Consequences of 1492* (Westport, CT: Greenwood Press, 1972); also his *Ecological Imperialism: The Biological Expansion of Europe, 900-1900* (New York: Cambridge University Press, 1986). For a detailed account of the ecological impact of early colonial presence of Europeans see: William Cronon, *Changes in the Land: Indians Colonists, and the Ecology of New England* (New York: Hill and Wang, 1983).

5. For an overview of the patterns of ecological interaction that characterize colonial circumstances see: Timothy C. Weiskel, "Agents of Empire: Steps Toward and Ecology of Imperialism," *Environmental Review* 11:4 (1987), pp. 275-288.

6. For a discussion of the impact of the frontier experience upon ecological consciousness in America see: Timothy C. Weiskel, "Rubbish and Racism: Problems of Boundary in an Ecosystem," *Yale Review* (Winter 1983), pp. 225-244.

ANNOTATED BIBLIOGRAPHY FOR CHAPTER II

ECOLOGICAL DECLINE OF ANCIENT CIVILIZATIONS

* 2.1 *

Dale, Tom, and Vernon Gill Carter. *Topsoil and Civilization*. rev. ed. Norman: University of Oklahoma Press, 1974. LC 74-175105. ISBN 0-8061-0332-9. (The 1st edition, published in 1955, was used to prepare these notes.)

In these pages, Dale and Carter seek to validate an ecological basis for the rise and decline of civilizations. In its initial stages civilization rests on a flourishing agriculture which, in turn, presupposes availability of productive topsoil. After a civilization has established itself, it can survive or even expand for a time, despite the loss or depletion of its topsoil. It can do this by military conquest, by colonization, or by economic diversification, through manufacture and trade. Ultimately, however, such strategies will fail. Civilizations that suffer a fatal loss of topsoil inevitably decline.

Some historians have tended to deny the central importance of the presence or absence of topsoil as a causative or contributing factor in the rise and decline of civilizations. Toynbee, for example, asserts that the very poverty of the soils of Attica played a critical role in the emergence of Athens as a high civilization, in accordance with his "challenge and response" theory. Thus Toynbee and many other historians, including Thucydides, have claimed that Greek soil was never fruitful, bountiful. Thucydides ascribed Attica's "freedom from faction" to the supposed poverty of Greek soil from the earliest days. Plato, who lived from 427 to 347 B.C., disagreed with all such theorists, however.

In one of his dialogues, Plato, speaking through Critias, described changes that had occurred in the land of Attica over time: ."... what now remains of the once rich land is like a skeleton of a sick man, all the fat and soft earth having wasted away, only the bare framework is left. Formerly, many of the present mountains were arable hills, the present marshes were plains full of rich soil; hills were once covered with forests, and produced boundless pasturage that now produce only food for bees. Moreover, the land was enriched by yearly rains, which were not lost, as now, by flowing from the bare land into the sea; the soil was deep, it received the water, storing it up in the retentive loamy soil; the water that soaked into the hills provided abundant springs and flowing streams in all districts. Some of the now abandoned shrines, at spots where former fountains existed, testify that our description of the land is true."

Evidence gathered from modern soil surveys definitely supports Plato. According to the authors, "in their virgin state, most of these rolling plains [of Attica] had a black or red clay-loam soil of fair depth that was highly productive. Beneath this soil was a layer of soft limestone that weathered fairly fast and helped build up or enrich the soil above.... Today there is a layer of soil only a few inches deep over most of the Attica plains and hills, and limestone outcroppings protrude from the surface every few feet."

The Roman philosopher and poet Lucretius, writing circa 60 B.C. before the Empire was established, bemoaned the fact that the earth itself seemed to be dying. The once bountiful land, he observed, was nearing exhaustion as rivers and rain eroded it and carried its topsoil into the sea. Other thinkers and observers were able to note shrinking food supplies and diminishing populations of regions where the land was seriously eroded. Roman observers and imperial administrators could and did recognize the threatening effects of soil erosion but they did not understand soil science. They devised various carrot and stick legislative devices to compel farmers to renew cultivation of barren, eroded, and even abandoned farms. All such devices, unaccompanied by programs of soil conservation and reclamation, proved to be fatal as the impoverished lands were subjected to increasingly intense cultivation. In completing the destruction of the land, the emperors and their administrators hastened the disintegration of the empire.

Edward Gibbon attributed the fall of Rome to "barbarism and religion." In the view of Dale and Carter, far more to the point in accounting for that fall was the fact that Roman agricultural regions were being progressively depopulated because their impoverished agricultural base could no longer sustain the previous levels of population density.

* 2.2 *

Greene, Kevin. *The Archaeology of the Roman Economy.* Berkeley: University of California Press, 1986. LC 86-7024. ISBN 0-520-059158.

In his book, Greene summarizes the findings of archaeology as it—archaeology—has been applied to the Roman economy. Because agriculture was by universal agreement the most important element in that economy, it may legitimately be made our sole focus of interest.

Modern archaeological excavation of the villas and farmsteads in what was the Roman empire, when undertaken in conjunction with geomorphology, soil science, climatology, paleobotany, and pollen analysis, has made it possible to study the manner, intensity, and consequences of Roman exploitation of the land. An analysis of the layered soils shown by an excavation can contribute to an understanding of the changes that have occurred over thousands of years, either through climatic change or through the intensification of land use—which is agriculture.

A revealing example of a soil science analysis of an excavated layer of soil is the "dark earth" found in many urban excavations in Britain in the late Roman and early medieval phases. "Dark earth" has been found to be "an accretion of rubbish, frequently disturbed by human and animal activity which could also be characteristic of a market garden soil."

Multidisciplinary studies have shown unmistakably that a dramatic decline did occur over time in both the productivity of the soil and in population levels, a decline that was caused in the first instance by erosion and sedimentation. Some theorists have argued that changes in climate were responsible for the observed decline in soil conditions. An example of climatological causation is an increase in rainfall which leads to flooding, and hence to soil erosion and sedimentation, siltation, and other problems.

Greene, however, observes: "Recent work around the Mediterranean has tended to favour human rather than climatic factors as the cause of the dramatic accumulations of sediment which took place in so many areas. By 1978, Vita-Finzi had virtually dismissed climate from the study of geomorphology." Critics of climate change as a major causative factor point out that the natural processes involved in erosion and sedimentation are extremely complex. A change toward wetter conditions could decrease erosion by increasing vegetation. Agricultural exploitation of the land can be shown to increase the rate of deposition up to 100 times.

Furthermore, many Roman documents mention floods in Rome and relate them to patterns of forest exploitation and to the number of settlement sites in central Italy. A recession in agriculture would reduce the number of sites, the amount of forest clearing that could be done, and the number and severity of floods. Thus historical evidence confirms the evidence of archaeology. Finally there is evidence that farmers in the Adige Valley of northern Italy, by adopting adequate methods of terracing, forestalled serious erosion until 600 AD.

* 2.3 *

Groenman-van Waateringe, W. "The Disastrous Effect of the Roman Occupation." In: *Roman and Native in the Low Countries: Spheres of Interaction*, edited by Roel Brandt and Jan Slofstra. B A R International Series 184. Oxford: British Archaeological Reports, 1983. ISBN 0-86054-237-8.

Interaction between the Roman occupation and the low countries occurred primarily in the sphere of a local economy that was made subservient to an imperial design. "In a pre-industrial society, wealth is highly dependent on the productivity of land." A serious agrarian crisis, therefore, followed from the Roman-directed over-exploitation of the land.

That there was over-exploitation is manifest: 1) There was a move away from small-scale mixed agriculture to large-scale monoculture; 2) The overseas market was given preference to the native market; 3) Existing market and exchange patterns were dismantled in order to augment Roman control; 4) The trading network was transformed into a taxation network.

Initially Roman administration, with its centralized economic control and its greater ability to rectify local food shortages, resulted in large increases in population. Thereafter, "a vicious cycle develops." Improved markets for local producers providing food for expanding populations led to increased food production. Not only did food producers have to feed the local populace but also the Roman military and civilian occupation force as well as the people of the towns that came into being in the wake of the Roman occupation. With farming methods, for all we know, remaining unchanged, increased production "must have exacted a heavy toll from the entire ecosystem." On the poorer soils of the low countries, that is, those that are not "on the fertile ridges of sandy loam of the northwest European littoral and in the terp-region of Friesland, Groningen and Ostfriesland," there was overgrazing, soil erosion, and acidification, in consequence of which came epidemic disease and sharp declines in both food production and population.

Groenman-van Waateringe argues that this vicious cycle was ultimately caused by the fragility of the complex Roman economic/ecological system. Complex systems have finely tuned regulating mechanisms. When these malfunction, the entire system is jeopardized. The native low country system, on the other hand, was simple, poorly developed, and consequently robust.

* 2.4 *

Hughes, J. Donald. *Ecology in Ancient Civilizations.* Albuquerque: University of New Mexico Press, 1975. LC 74-27446. ISBN 0-8263-0367-6.

"A human community determines its relationship to the natural environment in many ways. Among the most important are its members' attitudes toward nature, the knowledge of nature and the understanding of its balance and structure which they attain, the technology they are able to use, and the social control the community can exert over its members to direct their actions which affect the environment. The ancient world shows us the roots of our present problems in each of these areas." (p. 147)

Primitive attitudes of humans toward nature can be characterized as animism according to which nature and humankind are made of the same essential stuff, thus eliminating the human-nature dichotomy. Animism is an ecologically more discerning natural philosophy than the dominance or indifference views that succeeded it. All the great ancient civilizations—Egyptian, Mesopatomian, Israeli, Greek, and Roman—accepted the view that nature existed to serve the needs and whims of humans. The Jewish and the Christian world views added to the notion of dominance the further view that the visible world was unimportant in comparison with the unseen, spiritual world of god. The Romans were most blatant in their assertion of dominance over nature. They treated all of nature under their sway as though it were one of their conquered provinces.

In the sphere of knowledge, in Greece, as we might expect, there was evidence that a few of their more empirically-inclined thinkers were beginning to approach an ecological science. The Romans, by contrast, had no ecological science at all. In technology and in technologically-driven devastation of the environment, however, the Romans surpassed everyone. The technologically superb network of Roman aqueducts was linked, in many direct and indirect ways, to the degradation of the environment and to the deaths of innumerable Romans. The highly efficient aqueducts brought into Rome debilitating industrial poisons in large quantities. Finally, all the ancient civilizations were aware, in varying degrees, of the dire consequences of such forms of anthropogenic devastation as deforestation and soil erosion. Each civilization enacted some prohibitive environmental laws to constrain the most flagrant offenders.

Hughes ably documents his central thesis that the roots of our environmental difficulties lie in our cultural past. Furthermore he demonstrates that what can be called the ecological consciousness of our own day is made up of the components he specifies: a philosophy of nature, ecological science, technology, and prohibitive environmental legislation.

* 2.5 *

Hyams, Edward Solomon. *Soil and Civilization.* London and New York: Thames and Hudson, 1952. Re-print. New York: Harper and Row, 1976. LC 75-43490. The Harper and Row edition contains a new preface by Hyams; otherwise, the 1952 text remains unaltered.

Hyams assigns precise meanings to a few frequently repeated concepts as follows:

"Farming—scientific, industrial, ecological":
> Speech commonly perverts the word "scientific" when it uses such phrases as "scientific farming." In fact, as that phrase is conventionally used, it means only "profitable"

farming—profitable, that is, for a brief time, either for the farmer or his banker. Such farming is better called "industrial farming" for it entails the application of chemistry and mechanics to the soil in order to maximize production, and consequently profits, in the shortest possible time and in the belief that agriculture is capable of indefinite expansion. Truly scientific farming is that farming which is controlled by an ecological understanding. Ecological farming has come into existence only since circa 1930.

"Artificial soil community":
An agricultural region, large or small, but in either case integral, in which the natural balance of a wild countryside, which sustains and enhances soil fertility, has been successfully replaced, as a rule over a long period of time, by an artificial balance of cultivated instead of wild plant, domestic instead of wild animals. Such a community must, of course, include men as members, men living not off the soil as capital, but off the increment of fertility which they themselves are engaged in producing. The community is self-sustained and self-supporting in essentials.

These and other concepts are necessary to the development of Hyams' thesis that topsoil and subsoil have played a central role in the rise, continuation, and decline of civilizations. As Hyams concedes in his preface, he does run the risk of distortion in stressing, to the exclusion of all others, the influence "of men on soil and soil on men." Nonetheless, many of his specific documentations of the effects of soil degradation are persuasive.

1) Deforestation and the soils of Rome
"Other things being equal, the aridity of a soil climate is proportional to the numbers of trees present. As the early Italians cut trees to clear soil, they were unwittingly engaged in changing the climate of their country in an unfavorable sense." Hyams quotes Varro (116-28 B.C.) to the effect that in Latium wheat was harvested in July. Today Italians must harvest wheat in June to save it from the withering drought. Hyams speculates that, probably several hundred years before Varro, it may have been harvested in August, just as it now is in southeastern England. The soil of Campagna, the region of about 800 square miles surrounding Rome, was thin and fertile at the beginning of intensive agriculture, circa 500 B.C. Hyams enumerates the sequential steps in the downward spiral of degradation.

The water-cycle was disturbed. Torrential run-off of the decreasing rainfall carried away the hillside soils, silting up streams and rivers, causing flooding and creating malaria-infested marshes; the most mortal symptom of soil disease, gully-erosion, appeared on the hillsides.

2) The exploitation of subsoil in Attica
When a people finds itself upon a thin and stony soil, the product of natural erosion, or of the tactless mauling of the natural soil community by the people's predecessors, it may, in certain climatic and economic conditions, save itself by the ingenious exploitation of its subsoil. Such a people may, even in the absence of a fertile top-soil, create a balanced soil community, but one which will be of a peculiarly artificial and precarious kind. For one of its "members" must be a foreign market.

Fig trees, olive trees, and the vine will grow in subsoil after the topsoil has been eroded. Although Athens was able to cultivate these plants on the austere soils it inherited from its improvident predecessors, it had to export its wines and olives abroad in ceramic containers. This necessity became the stimulus to the Athenian ceramics industry.

3) Industrial farming
Industrial farming that seeks to maximize production and profits using all available sciences is as old as human efforts to go beyond subsistence agriculture. The industrial approach is evident in the parasitism on alluvium in the Tigris-Euphrates valley; in the growth of the deserts around Carthage; throughout the Roman Empire; and in a starkly dramatic form in Oklahoma.

4) Artificial soil communities
In only two parts of the world does Hyams find evidence of what he calls artificial soil communities in which human beings as members of that community have intelligently augmented soil fertility. These soil communities are those of the former Inca Empire in the Western Andes and existing Atlantic Europe.

* 2.6 *
Jacobsen, Thorkild, and Robert M. Adams. "Salt and Silt in Ancient Mesopotamian Agriculture." *Science* 128 (21 November 1958): 1,251-1,258.
    "The semiarid climate and generally low permeability of the soils of central and southern Iraq expose the soils to dangerous accumulations of

salt and exchangeable sodium, which are harmful to crops and soil texture and which can eventually force the farmer from the land." An examination of ancient records establishes that destructive levels of salinity have occurred at least three times. The earliest period, occurring between 2400 and 1700 B.C., is important historically in as much as it coincided with the northward movement of political power from southern to central Iraq. Several parallel lines of historical and archaeological evidence allow the increasing salinization to be followed quantitatively: 1) The presence of patches of saline ground is noted in the reports of surveyors in the reign of Entemenak; 2) Crops to be planted were chosen in part on the basis of which were most salt-tolerant. Wheat has low salt tolerance, whereas barley has more. Counts of grain impressions in excavated pottery show that, from 3500 to 1700 B.C., the proportion of wheat to barley steadily diminished. By 1700 wheat had been abandoned as a crop; 3) Records also show that fertility, measured in liters per hectare, also declined markedly.

> As the rate of sedimentation is affected by the extent of irrigation, so also were the processes of sedimentation—and their importance as agricultural problems—closely related to the prevailing patterns of settlement, land-use, and even sociopolitical control. The character of this ecological interaction can be shown most clearly at present from archaeological surveys in the lower Diyala basin....

Two successive phases of settlement and irrigation, "each operating in a different ecological background and each facing problems of sedimentation of a different character and magnitude," can be distinguished. The earlier phase, lasting from about 4000 B.C. and ending in the final centuries of the pre-Christian era, was one in which there was a fluctuating pattern of settlement and abandonment. Water seems not to have been drawn great distances from the main watercourses. "Under these circumstances, silt accumulation would not have been the serious problem to the agriculturalist that it later became. The short branch canals upon which irrigation depended could have been cleaned easily or even replaced without the intervention of a powerful, centralized authority."

The second phase of settlement was characterized by a much greater exploitation of available land and water resources. The population expanded; the area of cultivated land was enlarged, as was the irrigation system. It became necessary "to crisscross formerly unused desert and depression areas with a complex—and entirely artificial—brachiating system of branch canals." The length and complexity of the irrigation canals led to their filling up with silt more rapidly than before under conditions of a simpler design. With increasing siltation came the need to expend more time and energy on maintenance. "With the converging effects of mounting maintenance requirements on the one hand, and declining capacity for more than rudimentary maintenance tasks on the other, the virtual desertion of the lower Diyala that followed assumes in retrospect a kind of historical inevitability."

* 2.7 *

Judson, Sheldon. "Alluviation and Erosion." In: *Excavations at Fosso della Crescenza, 1962*, edited by E. Fentess et al. Papers of the British School at Rome, no. 51. London: R. Clay and Sons, 1983. OCLC 1537364.

"Alluviation begins when a stream is no longer able to remove all of the sediments brought to it from its drainage basins. Possible causes are several, but we need here to consider only three: climate, land use and normal stream dynamics." Judson provisionally rejects the evidence from climatic change. Stream dynamics have not been found to offer a sufficient basis for observed alluviation and erosion in Italian streams. The author concludes: "It seems reasonable to us that the cause of increased alluviation along sediment-clogged streamways has been due to land use on the slopes."

* 2.8 *

Judson, Sheldon. "Erosion Rates Near Rome, Italy." *Science* 160 (28 June 1968): 1,444-1,446.

"Near the beginning of the Christian era, small stream valleys in the Mediterranean region began to silt up, and various works of man were buried." Judson reports on the rates of the production of sedimentation in west-central Italian streams, past and present.

For the early period before human beings intensively used the land, lake cores provide estimates of the rates of erosion. "The basin of Boccano, astride Via Cassia about thirty km north of Rome, is a volcanic crater; the lake originally filling it was drained by the Romans in about the second century before Christ. Bonatti, in a pollen analysis of cores from the old lake deposits, reports a single carbon-14 age of 8429 + or - 180 years. This date enables one to estimate the rate of sedimentation, which can be converted to rate of erosion of watershed. The resultant estimate is about 3 cm/1,000 years between 6600 B.C. and drainage of the lake. This rate of erosion compares closely with the low rate of erosion around Lago di Monterosi before the days of agriculture."

To determine the rates of production of sedimentation for the period since the second century before Christ, Judson averaged the modern rates of erosion over entire drainage basins, as shown by stream records. "In addition archeological sites provide rates over periods ranging up to 2500 years." The erosion rates for the drainage basins ranged from 9 to 73 cm/1,000 years. The rates of erosion of the archeological sites were comparable, though higher. They commonly ranged between 20 and 40 cm/1,000 years.

"With intensive occupation by man the rates have increased by an order of magnitude."

* 2.9 *

Lawton, H. W., and P.J. Wilke. "Ancient Agricultural Systems in Dry Regions." In: *Agriculture in Semi-Arid Environments*, edited by A.E. Hall, G. H. Cannell, and H. W. Lawton. New York: Springer-Verlag, 1979. LC 79-13995. ISBN 0-387-09414-8.

"There can be little question that agriculture did and does increase the food supply. Nevertheless, agriculture has also had many deleterious effects, including environmental degradation, astronomical increases in human population, nucleation of population into large permanent settlements, greater susceptibility to social and medical adversities, dietary deficiencies, and widespread famine. Thus agriculture has resulted in an over-all loss of man's ecological flexibility."

Ancient irrigation systems, widely used in the dry regions of the Near East, curtailed ecological flexibility still further. In Mesopotamia, the ancient land lying between the Tigris and Euphrates Rivers, irrigation systems as they evolved over time tended to fall into three configurations of increasing complexity. The third and last configuration was a large-scale system, planned and controlled by the central government. "The Sassanian period saw massive irrigation projects, such as the construction of the gigantic Nahrwan canal, which took water from the Tigris River." The authors claim that the canals "probably" had inadequate slopes "which led to greater and more rapid silt accumulation." These systems required continual maintenance in order to remain operational, and in times of military crisis, an adequate maintenance force was not available. "Such large-scale systems could not survive the pressures placed upon them."

In one instance, a Near Eastern irrigation project "appears" to have been ecologically sound. The Nabatean systems of water harvesting used in the Negev desert of Israel is one example of an "early farming technology that made use of their environments with a minimum of disruption." Lawton and Wilke continue: "Study of the ancient farms on the Negev, including data gathered from reconstruction of two farms, showed that they had two essential features: (1) several cultivated terraced fields located in the deep valley soils, and (2) a cleared upland watershed area averaging about 10-50 ha [hectare] on the surrounding slopes." After describing the subdivisions of watershed areas, the authors add: "The division of the overall catchment into smaller subcatchments, each with diversion channels leading to specific parts of a farm, prevented destructive peak flows and made it easier for the farmer to exercise control over the flood."

Siltation of irrigation canals, salinization, and depletion of soil fertility were problems that plagued the farmers of the ancient Near East. They still exist to plague the farmers of today.

* 2.10 *

Naveh, Z., and J. Dan. "The Human Degradation of Mediterranean Landscapes in Israel." In: *Mediterranean Type Ecosystems—Origins and Structure,* edited by Francesco di Castri and Harold A. Money. New York, Heidelberg, Berlin: Springer-Verlag, 1973. LC 72-95688. ISBN 0-387-06106-1 (New York).

Relying on pedological and geomorphological evidence, Naveh and Dan analyze anthropogenic landscape degradation in Israel as a function of the soil-vegetation system. While granting that quantification of the interactions between mode, duration, and intensity of human interference, among other factors, is still extremely difficult, the authors believe that several generalizations are warranted.

"The harsher and more fragile the environment, the more far-reaching and irreversible will be the man-induced changes in state variables and the slower and more difficult will be the process of recovery." The destruction of the vegetable canopy in Israel's semi-arid zone at an early date exposed the soil to the direct influence of the harsh climate and to unimpeded rainfall. In this way there arose conditions similar to those of more arid regions with a sparse plant cover, flashfloods, and extremes of climate.

On the upland arable slopes, several cycles of degradation and regeneration have occurred. Early clearance of forest and woodlands caused the first erosion cycle. Later there was an aggradation cycle of terracing. Still later neglect of the terraces generated catastrophic erosion.

> As illustrated in examples from Judean hills and Western Galilee, this has been followed by a regeneration cycle, leading to maquis, garrigue, batha and derived grasslands. But recently [with] increasing human and livestock pressure the erosive degradation cycle has been renewed....
>
> The soil recovery process has been slowest on shallow soils covering hard rocks, and faster on soft rock....The dynamics of recovery are apparently determined by the recent "bio-function" and especially by soil depth, by slope exposure and by the "initial floristic composition" of the abandoned site.

During the long phase of agricultural decay and population decline in the mountainous region of Israel, a new equilibrium was established on the uncultivated upland ecosystems. This new equilibrium is now endangered by population explosion, by increasing traditional land use with its accompanying erosion, by urban sprawl, and by neo-technological despoliation.

* 2.11 *

Vita-Finzi, Claudio. "Roman Dams in Tripolitania." *Antiquity* 35 (1961): 14-20.

The Roman wadi dams of Tripolitania were effective in both conserving and creating cultivable soil in the difficult area of northern Libya. *Wadi* is an Arabic word for a gully, valley, or river bed that remains dry for much of the year but flows during rare winter floods. The Roman soil and water retention dams, while they continued in good repair, caused the flow of silt-laden water through the wadis to be fairly well distributed. When the dams and their concomitant works fell into disrepair, trees on the slopes of wadis decreased and erosion became severe. Vita-Finzi concludes his report:

> The wadi floods of today are both more violent and more short-lived than they were two thousand years ago.

ECOLOGY OF EUROPEAN EXPANSION

* 2.12 *

Cronon, William. *Changes in the Land: Indians, Colonists, and the Ecology of New England.* New York: Hill and Wang, 1983. LC 83-7899. ISBN 0-8090-3405-0.

Cronon concludes his argument with two summarizing passages: "By integrating New England ecosystems into an ultimately global capitalist economy, colonists and Indians together began an unstable process of ecological change which had in no way ended in 1800. We live with their legacy today." After quoting Carl Sauer to the effect that Americans had "not yet learned the difference between yield and loot," Cronon says "Ecological abundance and economic prodigality went hand in hand: the people of plenty were a people of waste." The English colonists of New England believed in the Biblical injunction to "subdue" and to "improve" the land and to use it for the augmentation of wealth. Because of the apparent abundance of land, they came to believe that the supply of the commodity was limitless. They assumed that ecological abundance would be convertible into economic abundance indefinitely.

The colonists believed that improvements of the land were the true mark of ownership. The English conception of land ownership entailed boundaries, enclosures, fencing, restricted access to others, laws of trespass, permanent occupancy, a fixed abode, and intensive agricultural practices such as plowing with an animal team. Indians had a quite different conception of ownership. Strictly speaking, what they possessed was not ownership but usufruct, the right to use land so long as the property was not damaged or altered. Because Indian customs enshrined the idea of usufruct as distinguished from the legal concept of ownership, the colonists declined to recognize that the Indians owned any land at all, not agricultural fields, ponds, lakes, river banks or forests, however the Indians may have used these resources in accordance with their seasonally modulated migratory way of life. Ultimately the land came under almost complete English ownership. Cronon states the consequences of the colonial land grab:

> Strictly speaking in terms of precolonial New England, Indian conceptions of property were central to Indian uses of the land, and Indians could not live as Indians had lived unless the land was owned as Indians had owned it. Conversely, the land could not long remain unchanged if it were owned in a different way. The sweeping alterations of the colonial landscape which Dwight himself so shrewdly described were testimony that a people who loved property little had been overwhelmed by a people who loved it much.

One particular example of the sweeping alterations will be mentioned here. Because Indian occupancy of agricultural fields was shifting and temporary, abandoned sections of land would revert to forest and become "edge habitats" which were especially good for many species of wildlife. When lands ceased to be owned in the Indian fashion, these edge habitats also ceased and with them many species became endangered.

The devastating epidemics that struck the Indians of southern New England during the years from 1616 through the 1630s were reliably reported to have caused unbelievable levels of mortality. Death rates of 90 to 95 percent were common. In some instances, entire villages were wiped out. This was the most brutal manifestation of ecological imperialism. The Indian population of New England in 1600 is estimated to have been 73,000. By 1700, that population had dwindled to about 12,000. Radical depopulation of this order disrupted the normal patterns of Indian economic life. Because they had to find a substitute for their former reliance on hunting and subsistence agriculture, they became the partners of the colonists in the fur trade. They exchanged animal pelts for brass and iron ware and woven fabrics of European and colonial manufacture; they also received a form of monetary payment, wampum. Far more efficient as trappers of fur-bearing animals than the English, they soon hunted the animals to the point of exhaustion of supply. Prior to this period, the Indians had not taken animals beyond the level of their immediate need. As a consequence of the widespread extinction of species, the Indians were driven back into the poverty of what later came to be called reservations.

Most of the ecological and legal conflict between the colonists and the Indians turned on what constitutes a "resource." As Cronon points out, a "resource" exists only to the extent that a culture at a certain point in its evolution defines it as such. "By drawing the boundaries within which their exchange and production occur, human communities label certain subsets of their surrounding ecosystems as resources, and so locate the meeting places between economics and ecology."

* 2.13 *

Crosby, Alfred W., Jr. *Ecological Imperialism: The Biological Expansion of Europe, 900-1900*. New York: Cambridge University Press, 1986. LC 86-6106. ISBN 0-521-32009-7.

In *The Voyage of the Beagle*, Charles Darwin declared: "Wherever the European had trod, death seems to pursue the aboriginal. We may look to the wide extent of the Americas, Polynesia, the Cape of Good Hope, and Australia, and we find the same result." In their ecological conquests of the "New Europes," Europeans received vigorous support from their "biological allies," the plants, animals, and pathogens of Europe. What Crosby calls the "New Europes" are those lands which resemble Europe climatically and yet are separated from it by vast stretches of ocean, lands that lie across the "seams of Pangaea," to use Crosby's geological metaphor. They are the precise lands that Darwin specifies. The significance of lying across Pangaea's seams is that, because of their long-term trans-oceanic isolation, the New Europes possessed no natural competitors or predators with which to oppose Europe's plants and animals, and the aborigines of the New Europes were sustained by no immunities with which to resist Europe's pathogens. The result was that Europe's plants and animals flourished in the Americas and in Australia and New Zealand beyond anyone's wildest expectations. English plants did far better in Australia than they had ever done in England. European sheep prospered in New Zealand just as European cattle did in Texas. The case of the European rabbit in Australia is an extreme one that proves the point. The rabbit multiplied menacingly in Australia because in the entire continental island it had not one natural predator to hold its fecundity in check.

The plants that flourished most vigorously in the New Europes were weeds, a term Crosby defines as opportunistic or aggressive plants that spread rapidly and out-compete other plants on disturbed soil. When Europe's weeds, the best forage grasses, were introduced into New Europe, they quickly and invariably ousted the native grasses wherever the soil was disturbed. European grazing quadrupeds—horses, cattle, sheep—are notorious for disturbing the soil. Hence a symbiotic relationship between the imported weeds and animals soon developed, to the incalculable economic advantage of the New Europeans.

Because their agriculture flourished in New Europe, the immigrant Europeans themselves thrived and multiplied. Their numbers increased in an unprecedented geometric progression. As their numbers increased, the numbers of aborigines declined sharply. Diseases among aborigines caused by Europe's pathogens engendered virtual genocide in many instances. William Bradford of Plymouth Plantation said of an epidemic of smallpox among the Algonkins of Massachusetts in the early 1630s: "Whole towns of them were swept away, in some not so much as one soul escaping Destruction." Crosby continues his account by alleging: "Smallpox whipsawed back and forth across New York and surrounding areas in the 1630s and 1640s, reducing the Huron and Iroquois federations by an estimated fifty percent."

In his account of the expansion of European civilization, Crosby has skillfully gathered and integrated the various skeins of ecological evidence. Although much of his story is not new—the consequences of the lack of immunity to European diseases among aboriginal peoples have been known for some time—Crosby has contributed a clarifying frame of reference that interrelates European history and the ecology of exotic plants and animals with Wegener's theory of continental drift. That body of theory is central to his account as he makes clear by his repeated allusions to Wegener in the phrase "the seams of Pangaea." Pangaea is Wegener's hypothesized unitary landmass which over millions of years broke up to form the continents as we know them today.

* 2.14 *

Crosby, Alfred W., Jr. *The Columbian Exchange: Biological And Cultural Consequences of 1492*. Westport, CT: Greenwood Press, 1972. LC 73-140916. ISBN 0-8371-5821-4.

To a degree, Crosby's 1972 book can be regarded as a preliminary and less well developed version of his 1986 book. As he was to demonstrate conclusively in his later book, Old World plants, animals, and pathogens devastated the ecological balance of the New World. A point he makes uniquely in the present book, however, furnishes the significance of his title. The destructive biotic traffic that Columbus let loose was a two-way traffic. There was an exchange. Some of the New World's plants and pathogens retorted on Europe to benefit and to plague it.

Although Crosby acknowledges that there is still substantial disagreement on the American origin of syphilis, he is provisionally committed to the view that the disease was inflicted on Europe in the first instance by one of Columbus' returning sailors in 1493. The evidence for the Columbian exchange is substantial. First of all, there are no unambiguous pre-Columbian references to syphilis in European literature. More importantly, archaeology provides no pre-Columbian bones showing characteristically syphilitic disfigurement. Euphemisms bestowed on the disease by European nations exhibited European xenophobia at its most intense. The English called it the "French" disease. The French either returned the courtesy or called it the "Spanish" disease. Under whatever name, its effects were always disfiguring; its course was frequently fatal; and physicians' purported "cures" were quackery at its most ludicrous.

Many European pathogens, but particularly smallpox, ravaged the Indians of Mexico, a fact that illuminates the otherwise inexplicable Spanish conquest of the Aztecs. Having no immunities to smallpox, they died in incalculable numbers. Crosby's text is filled with quotations relating to Indian mortality rates. Toribio Motolinia said they died "in heaps, like bedbugs." After having been driven out of the Aztec capital on their *noche triste* of 30 June 1520, the small Spanish force under Cortés returned to the city which they then besieged. Crosby explains the circumstances of the final defeat of the Aztecs:

> The triumphant Aztecs had not expected the Spaniards to return after their expulsion from Tenochtitlán. The sixty days during which the epidemic lasted in the city, however, gave Cortés and his troops a desperately needed respite to re-organize and prepare a counter-attack. When the epidemic subsided, the siege of the Aztec capital began. Had there been no epidemic, the Aztecs, their war-making potential unimpaired and their warriors fired with victory, could have pursued the Spaniards, and Cortés might have ended his life spread-eagled beneath the obsidian blade of a priest of Huitzilopochtli. Clearly the epidemic sapped the endurance of Tenochtitlán. As it was the siege went on for seventy-five days, until the deaths within the city from combat, starvation, and disease—probably not smallpox now—numbered many thousands. When the city fell "the streets, squares, houses, and courts were filled with bodies, so that it was almost impossible to pass. Even Cortés was sick from the stench in his nostrils."

To call smallpox the Spaniards' "biological ally" is more than a clever metaphor. To the extent that accounts of the Spanish conquest of

Hispanic America have neglected the devastating effects of exotic diseases on peoples lacking protective antibodies, those accounts are manifestly inadequate.

In his first chapter, Crosby reviews the evidence relating to the predominant "O" blood type of the American Indian, which contrasts sharply with the diverse blood types found in the indigenous peoples of Europe, Asia, and Africa. He does not develop the implications of blood type for differential susceptibility to disease. See Diamond on blood type A and susceptibility to smallpox.

* 2.15 *

Diamond, Jared. "A Pox upon Our Genes: Smallpox Vanished Twelve Years Ago, but Its Legacy May Still Linger within Us." *Natural History* (February 1990): 26-30.

Diamond reviews the evidence for a causal relationship between blood type and susceptibility to smallpox, relying on a comparative study of survivors and victims of an epidemic in India in the 1960s. "They (investigators Vogel and Chakravartti) found a total of 415 unvaccinated smallpox patients. For all but eight of these patients, they were able to find a healthy brother or sister to consider as a 'control subject'—that is, someone as similar as possible genetically to the patient and living in the same house, but differing in not having contracted smallpox despite close exposure." 261 of the patients carried blood group A; 154 lacked it. "Among the 407 healthy subjects, only eighty carried group A." These data strongly suggest that the As were susceptible and the non-As resistant to infection. "The ratio of A to non-A among the patients (261:154), divided by the ratio of A to non-A among the controls (80:327), was 7—meaning that a person with group A had a seven times greater risk of contracting smallpox than someone without group A."

Diamond also considers statistical studies that compare the frequencies of blood group A in different sections of India and Africa with reported epidemics of smallpox in those same sections." Areas with high frequencies of smallpox proved to have low frequencies of group A, suggesting that smallpox had killed off people with group A." These correlations for India and Africa are close to those for the Americas. See Crosby's 1972 book for statistical data on the very low incidence of blood group A among the indigenous peoples of the Western hemisphere.

* 2.16 *

Mourant, A. E. "Associations Between Hereditary Blood Factors and Diseases." *World Health Organization. Bulletin* 49:1 (1973): 93-101.

Mourant carefully considers all the evidence relating to the relationship between blood groups and susceptibility to disease in the course of which he identifies the work of the scientists on whom Diamond relies.

That study has the following citation: Vogel, F. and M. R. Chakravartti. *Humangenetik* 3 (1966): 166+. Mourant also refers to the same body of work that Diamond discusses on the possibility that modern distributions of blood groups are consistent with people having group A being particularly susceptible to smallpox.

Mourant had to acknowledge that some investigators have failed to confirm the correlations that Vogel and Chakravartti found in their studies of smallpox epidemics in India. Mourant therefore considers that the question is still unresolved.

* 2.17 *

Ponting, Clive. *A Green History of the World.* London: Sinclair-Stevenson, Ltd., 1991. ISBN 1-85619-050-1. GB 91-3508. Publisher's address: 7/8 Kendrick Mews; London SW7 3HG, England. Price (pounds sterling) 17.95.

Environmental issues are not only those that pertain strictly to the state of the natural world. They ramify out into all domains of culture and society, most importantly in the use of resources and energy, the distribution of wealth—and consequently of poverty, the way people treat people, and the way people think about the world they inhabit. Ponting's book is a "green" history of the world in the sense that it places in the foreground the force of the environment in shaping and limiting the events of human history. Ponting grants that his book is not based on original research. He has assimilated the research of others and presented it in a succinct narrative.

Ponting begins with a reconstruction of the prehistory of Easter Island where a technologically advanced Polynesian culture had once flourished. The evidence for a high culture having once existed there consisted of the presence of about 600 huge stone statues of gods or tribal chiefs that lay scattered about the island in varying states of completion and repair. The people who occupied the island in 1722 lived in a condition of barbarism and squalor, their only interest being incessant internecine warfare. When Europeans first saw the island in 1722, it was devoid of trees, but pollen analyses show that, at the time of its settlement by Polynesians, it was heavily forested. Moreover trees, or rather logs, were essential to the transport of the huge statues, each averaging about twenty feet in height, from the quarry to their final disposition. Deforestation undermined the possibility that Easter Island's specialized culture might continue.

Human attitudes and presuppositions about the natural world are of the utmost importance in determining how we interact with the environment. Unfortunately for ecological understanding, the Greek philosophers gave no support to the idea that nature is to be respected. The Jewish scriptures were emphatic that God enjoined man to exercise dominion over the earth and all living things that dwell thereon. Christianity perpetuated the ecologically destructive attitudes of both Greek philosophy and Hebraic religion. To the weight of these three traditions was soon added the secular religions of the doctrine of progress and the "cancer cell" view of economic growth as endless and perpetual. Although ecological science and the modern concern for preservation have significantly modified the Greek and Hebraic inheritances, the secular religions continue with a virtually unabated strength.

Endowed with a divine mandate to subdue the earth, Western man proceeded to ravage the world's animals. Dominion over fish and fowl was interpreted as a license to extinguish species without restraint, either prudential or ethical.

> As late as 1420 and 1438 wolf packs were seen in the streets of Paris in daylight. In 1520 enough still survived for Francis I to organize official hunts and about a hundred years later in 1640 there are accounts of wolves coming down from the hills of the Jura to terrorize the inhabitants of Besancon. The last recorded sighting of a wolf came in 1486 in England, 1576 in Wales, in Scotland in 1743 and in Ireland during the early nineteenth century.

The disappearance of the passenger pigeon from the skies of the United States ranks as the consummate effort to attain dominion over a fowl, when dominion is construed as annihilation. From a population of more than two billion circa 1850, the number dwindled down to a single female bird by 1914. That bird, whose name was Martha, died in the Cincinnati Zoo on 1 September 1914. Ponting vividly describes the American killing fields. When a dense passenger pigeon overflight occurred, assembled farmers, waiting below with their hogs in tow, would fire every available piece of light artillery at the birds while their hogs feasted on the falling carnage. When Indians, who had exercised their usual restraint in hunting passenger pigeons, observed this annihilatory carnage, they would say: "The white man is insane." In a state park in Wisconsin there is a monument to the passenger pigeon. The inscription reads: "This species became extinct through the avarice and thoughtlessness of man."

About 10,000 years ago, the first great transition to intensive cultivation of the soil began. The agricultural revolution vastly increased the efficiency of human labor in relation to the land, with the result that the population was able to increase rapidly. About the time that agriculture was adopted the world's population was approximately four million. That number then began to double every thousand years to reach 50 million by 1,000 B.C. That number then doubled every 500 years, reaching 100 million by 500 B.C. Thereafter human history can be characterized as an alternation between cycles of expanding population and a contraction of population through famine. Societies and governments were wont to overtax the agricultural system, demanding ever more of it to feed huge military establishments. All too often the result was ecological breakdown. Only fairly recent improvements in agricultural technique in Europe enabled Europeans to break the cycle of expansion and contraction of human numbers.

Agroculture-based destruction of the environment has had a long and sadly recurrent history. The author recounts numerous instances of great civilizations that have collapsed because they exceeded their ecological base. Sometimes economic decline occurred because of the causal chain marked by deforestation, erosion and loss of fertility of the soil, declines in agricultural productivity, and famine. In the Tigris and Euphrates Valley, ecological decline proceeded through extreme salinization of the soil due, in the last analysis, to technically inadequate irrigation systems. Ponting adds an updated account of the breakdown of the Maya civilization. On the basis of recent investigations, it is now clear that ecological breakdown occurred in Mexico and Central America just as it has in the homelands of other great civilizations around the world.

Over-cultivation and over-grazing of fragile lands are responsible for further ecological degradation. The creation of the American "dust bowl" aptly illustrates the conjunction of these practices. After the extermination of the American bison on the Great Plains, the land was plowed using a heavy plow that turned up the cover of vegetation which alone held the dry soil together. Once this was gone, the land, thus stripped of its vegetation cover, was subjected to either excessive continuing cultivation or to the compacting and desiccating effects of great herds of grazing animals. The creation of the dust bowl was entirely anthropogenic. It was occasioned by the wanton misuse of land in defiance of sound ecological practice.

In the wake of industrialization, ecological deterioration has intensified to the point that it now threatens the survival of human society on this planet. Among the gravest threats are acid rain; toxic wastes; nuclear pollution; chemical pollution of rivers, lakes, air, and oceans; depletion of the ozone layer; and the ultimate threat, global warming. Ponting summarizes his position in these words:

> The problem for all human societies has been to find a means of extracting from the environment their food, clothing, shelter, and other goods in a way that does not render it incapable of supporting them. Some damage is clearly inevitable. Some depradation is tolerable. The challenge has been to anticipate or recognize at what point

the environment is being badly degraded by the demands placed upon it and to find the political, economic and social means to respond accordingly.

* 2.18 *
Weiskel, Timothy C. "Agents of Empire: Steps toward an Ecology of Imperialism." *Environmental Review* 11:4 (1987): 275-288.

Weiskel likens the course of ecological imperialism to a five-act tragedy, a drama that has been enacted on the world's stage many times. The first enactments occurred when the Phoenicians began colonizing the Mediterranean. They were followed by other expansionist peoples, but most notably by the Greeks and the Romans who performed their own versions of the ecological tragedy. The version that most immediately concerns us is the one that European man initiated, circa 1500. The series of Acts in the often-repeated tragedy as Weiskel describes them can be summarized in schematic form.

Act I—the period of biotic interchange.

Act II—the population explosion of intrusive, opportunistic, exogenous species that are able to exploit under-occupied eco-niches in the "new world."

Act III—"the explosive expansion of some populations generates an entirely new eco-niche space for other resident populations, differentially intruding upon their prospects for successful feeding or breeding." This is the correlative collapse phase of Act II's explosion phase.

Act IV—The explosion/collapse syndrome works itself out in the form of a radical destruction of both endogenous species and human inhabitants. Because of this massive death, the "white settler" in the "new world" typically has the sense that he is in the process of occupying "virgin" or "empty" land. This sense of virgin land is, in Weiskel's phrase, "largely ideological bravado, deliberate obfuscation, or simply self-delusion."

Act V—"involves the development of mature pest and predator populations that emerge within the colonial ecosystem to establish new kinds of enduring symbiotic relations with the intrusive species or populations, keeping their explosive behavior in check and deriving sustenance from them."

The tragedy of Weiskel's eco-drama is consummated in Act IV, for the effect of the massive death of endogenous species is a simplification of indigenous ecosystems and an active propagation of "a *narrow* range of genetically selected, opportunistic species." Nowhere are the dangers of genetic impoverishment more acutely manifest than in the "development" plans of agencies like the World Bank. Plans for monocropping a narrow range of cultivars merely accentuate a dangerous depletion of genetic variability. With his full approval and endorsement, Weiskel quotes Paul Ehrlich on this point:

> One of the most serious side-effects of the Green Revolution is the accelerating loss of reserves of genetic variability in crop plants, variability that is badly needed for continuing development of new strains. A multitude of traditional crop varieties...are rapidly being replaced by a relatively few high-yielding varieties throughout large areas. *Aside from nuclear war, there is probably no more serious environmental threat than the continued decay of the genetic variability of crops.* [Emphasis in Ehrlich, et. al., *Ecoscience: Population, Resources, Environment* (San Francisco, 1977)].

Weiskel admonishes us that there is "no such thing as a *predictive ecology.*" Although we can intrude on and alter specific organisms, we lack the sophistication needed to conceive the intricate connectedness of organisms in their total environment. "In the global circumstance that now confronts us, our long-term survival depends upon learning how to function *within* plant and animal kingdoms, not in setting ourselves up against them or in cultivating the sadly characteristic imperial illusion of control." The consequences of that imperial illusion are deforestation, plant genetic impoverishment, and degradation and erosion of the soil. At the end of his article, Weiskel expresses a guarded optimism for the future. It is possible, he suggests, that, in understanding ourselves and our history as agents of ecological imperialism, we may be able to avert the final ecological catastrophe.

* 2.19 *

Weiskel, Timothy C. "Rubbish and Racism: Problems of Boundary in an Ecosystem." *Yale Review* 72:2 (Winter 1983): 225-244.

Weiskel directs our attention to the core of a paradox when he says: "While nature draws no boundaries between elements in an ecosystem, a human society, which occupies a particular 'niche' within the total system, has no meaning without them. Just where one draws a line between one part of the system and another may not be particularly important for an analyst of nature, but it is of vital importance to men in society." Indeed, belief systems may be said to exist to delineate, clarify, and reinforce boundaries.

At the physiological level, human cultures "bound" perceptions of color and sound. People without defective color vision in Western cultures normally perceive six primary colors whereas the people of the Bassa culture perceive only two; people of the Shona language group in Zimbabwe perceive four. In the realm of phonetics, the situation is essentially the same. The Japanese perceive the "l" and the "r" as a single unit of sound whereas speakers of the Indo-European languages readily distinguish them.

At the conceptual level, bounding is a universal and fundamental operation of culture. Beliefs and rituals represent society's endeavor to define itself and to distinguish itself from other societies and from the non-human. Among the belief systems Weiskel considers are those of pollution and taboo and of the outsider. These two ideas are his two key concepts: rubbish and racism. Racism for Weiskel is a feature "only of societies which bound themselves off from nature." He is not confident that racism will ever disappear from American society, despite recent and continuing amelioration of its most virulent manifestations.

Weiskel delineates two contrasting systems of subsistence, each with its own boundary definitions of nature, culture, and rubbish. The first is typified by the Mbuti pygmies of Zaire. They are a foraging people who frequently move to new locations in the forest as previous locations are exhausted. They regard the forest as their benevolent friend and protector. For them there is no people/nature antagonism. In sharp contrast, the Bantu agriculturalists are a people bounded off from nature. They practice swidden agriculture, according to which they cut down a section of forest growth, burn it off, and cultivate the field thus prepared. When the section is exhausted, they abandon it and move to another part of the forest and begin the process anew.

Because the Bantu are always battling a forest whose power they fear, they see nature itself as hostile. Their approach to the natural world is one of "conquest, subjugation, exploitation, and abandonment." Because of the way in which they separate themselves from nature, bound themselves from it, they create for themselves a linear view of the physical environment which ranges from that which is still to be mastered to that which has already been mastered and now remains only to be spat out and excreted. For the Bantu, this statement is literally true. Their villages are ringed with garbage, household debris, and fecal matter, with only the most superficial attention being given to the science of garbage disposal. When the encircling garbage dumps become intolerably noxious, the Bantus simply abandon their existing villages and move on to another part of the forest.

Although Western peoples do not practice swidden agriculture, their attitudes toward the physical environment have much in common with the Bantu agriculturalists with their relentless slash and burn policies.

Nowhere is that commonality more in evidence than in the continued generation of intolerable quantities of toxic chemical and nuclear wastes. Weiskel warns: .".. we are rapidly approaching circumstances globally where there are no new lands to 'slash and burn' and no more room to retreat from the waste of our own making."

These "swidden" agriculturalist attitudes toward nature, its conquest and cultural transformation, and its consequent rubbish were very prominent on the American frontier. As Weiskel construes it, the frontier affected American attitudes primarily by its very abundance, its seeming inexhaustibility. These perceptions reinforced the already-existing tendency to regard nature as something to be conquered, exploited, and then abandoned in a rubbish heap when its richness is significantly diminished.

WOOD AND ITS USES

* 2.20 *

Meiggs, Russel. *Trees and Timber in the Ancient Mediterranean World*. Oxford: Oxford University Press, 1982. LC 81-22471. ISBN 0-19-814840-2.

In assessing Plato's well-known description and chronology of deforestation in Attica, it is necessary to bear in mind that Plato in *Critias* was joining factual observation and inference to a mythical idealization of Athens' glorious past. A literal interpretation of the passage suggests that all of the mountains of Attica had been stripped of timber by the fifth century B.C. However Plato refers to the roof-timbers of his own day (427-347) as being still sound; considering the susceptibility of wood to deterioration, it is not possible for such roofing timbers to have been put in place more than two hundred years prior to the date of writing.

Accepting as veridical Plato's classic description of the deforestation of Attica and the consequent degradation of the region's once fertile soils, we are obliged to adjust his chronology. An expansion of the city in the seventh and sixth centuries probably denuded the mountains closest to its center. Timber reserves close to Athens then became insufficient to meet the city's requirements for waging the naval wars of the fifth century. At the beginning of the fifth century, Athens had only 100 ships, most of which were pentekonters. When the Persians invaded Greece in 480, the Athenians contributed a fleet of 200 triremes warships with three tiers of oars on each side to the common defense at the Battle of Salamis. Construction of these warships required an enormous expenditure of timber which could only have come from the hinterland of Attica or further North, from colonies like Amphipolis. When, more than fifty years later, the Spartans captured the colony and deprived the Athenians of their timber reserves, Athenian recuperative powers were dangerously undermined.

Athens' wealth and power increased markedly in the fifth century after her triumph over Persia in 489 or 479, and so did the magnificence of her public buildings. Although the Parthenon, on which work began in 447/6, is a marble structure, massive wooden cross-beams of thirty-five feet and ridge-beams of seventy feet were used to support the roof. The monumental door of 10 by 4.92 meters was also made of wood. Not only did the Parthenon itself consume vast amounts of timber, so also did Phidias' chryselephantine statue of Athena.

> Athena was here the warrior goddess, with spear, shield, and helmet, holding Victory in her outstretched hand. The gleam of gold from the dress, the white ivory of the flesh, and the blue-grey eyes must have been very impressive as one passed from the bright light of the sun into the dim cella, lit only from the great doorway. One could not have seen the strong timber that was the chief supporting member of the armature of the statue. A cutting in the pedestal shows that it was 0.75 meters wide and 0.45 meters thick and was sunk to a depth of 1.83 meters implying a total height of roughly 12 meters.

The building program carried out in fifth-century Athens created a demand for timber that was unprecedented in quantity and quality. Even moving the timbers to be used in building required additional timbers with which to fashion the animal-drawn wagons.

Rome waged three imperialistic wars against Carthage, the first beginning in 264 B.C. The third Punic War ended in 146 with, literally, the extirpation of Carthage, a city-state on the northern coast of Africa and Rome's only rival for the domination of the western Mediterranean. After the victory, Roman society underwent a subtle change that in part mimicked the behavior of fifth-century Athenians. Affluent Romans, in disdaining the crudities of their triumphant warrior state, began to imitate Hellenic architectural models. Roman architects proceeded to naturalize the Greek peristyle and stoa and in the process their consumption of building timbers increased markedly.

> The basilica, the "royal building" was the Roman answer to the Greek stoa, though its form owed more to the Greek peristyle. Its function was to provide a sheltered setting for legal hearings, commercial transactions, and social meetings,

and its natural place was in or near the Forum, Rome's civic centre.

The Romans made a few engineering and architectural improvements on their Greek models. Typically they used ridge-beams and tie-beam trusses in roofing basilicas and temples. Timbers exceeding eighty feet were required for the cross-beams. Such timbers could only rarely be cut from oaks and other hardwoods. They had to come from fir trees growing at high altitudes in the Apennine forests.

Meiggs' work is the comprehensive treatise on trees and timber in the Mediterranean. He covers such additional topics as woods for farms, parks, gardens, furniture, and sculpture; the timber trade; and the qualities and attributes of woods from various species of trees.

* 2.21 *

Perlin, John. *A Forest Journey: The Role of Wood in the Development of Civilization.* Foreword by Lester R. Brown. New York and London: W. W. Norton & Co., 1989. LC 88-25291. ISBN 0-393-02667-1.

Wood, the most versatile of all natural products, is the crucial enabling agency that sustains human civilization. Perhaps because the importance of wood is so transparently obvious, philosophers and historians have tended to neglect it as a major determinant of history. From trees comes the fuel that sustains the fires that have permitted our naked species, first, to survive in inclement weather and, second, to reshape the earth. Wood-fueled fires have transformed inedible grains into primary sources of food, converted clay into pottery, extracted metal from stone, and molded innumerable objects made of iron and other metals extracted from stone. An indispensable adjunct to all industrial arts and crafts, wood is itself either a primary building material or, once again, an indispensable adjunct to the building arts. When the Parthenon was under construction, its builders used huge wooden winches to lift the massive blocks of marble into place.

Until the early nineteenth century, all ships, military and non-military alike, were made of wood. In no other domain of human activity did the existence of accessible timber reserves have such fateful consequences as it had in the fortunes of naval war. In the course of the Peloponnesian Wars, 431-404 B.C., the destruction of the forests on which the Athenians depended for their navy ultimately led to the defeat of Athens by Sparta. Pericles naively boasted to his Athenians of the naval supremacy afforded by their three hundred ships, but he ignored the strategic implications of undefended timber reserves. The Spartans displayed greater strategic insight. When they invaded Attica, they systematically cut down all of its trees and turned it into a barren wasteland. In the winter that followed the Spartan ravages, torrential rains severely eroded the deforested land; lower-lying areas became marshy, and mosquito-borne diseases, malaria and typhus in all probability, reached epidemic proportions. From this early defeat in the war, the Athenians never fully recovered.

Although intermitted by periods of precarious peace, the Peloponnesian Wars lasted for twenty-eight years. In 415 B.C., Alcibiades revived Athenian belligerency by sending a fleet to a remote ally, Segesta located on the island of Sicily. The Athenian purpose was to control Sicily's immense forests and to use them to build an armada with which to destroy Sparta. Alcibiades' plan backfired when the Athenian fleet was defeated.

The disposition of England's once bountiful forests was at the center of the country's sharp conflict of opinion on the primacy of industrial development versus the need to maintain naval preparedness. Until England entered the coal age, iron, copper, and glass manufacturers were totally dependent on indigenous supplies of timber to fuel their furnaces. Vast forests were consumed by these rapacious industries. One powerful interest, however, opposed the wholesale conversion of the forests, the Royal Navy. Its supporters, who included many of the most powerful in the land, pointed out that the navy could not continue as the dominant naval force on the high seas without access to abundant woods, particularly hard woods such as oak. The Navy's argument was unimpeachable and irresistible, in deference to which there arose an ecological consciousness in England that gave rise to efforts by Parliament to legislate conservation measures. Not only was Parliament involved in the effort to preserve timber for the use of the navy. The Tudor and Stuart kings intermittently acted for and against the conservation of forests. For the most part the monarchs agreed that it was necessary to preserve timber for the navy, but the sale of the remaining forests—and most of the forests in England were royal forests—afforded a convenient, and legal, way to raise revenue without the embarrassment of having to ask Parliament to appropriate it. Charles I in particular used this tactic and thereby exacerbated the tension that already existed between the Crown and the Parliament.

After the Restoration, Charles II and his brother James, the Duke of York, were devoted to the interests of the navy. Their approach to a solution relied less on conservation—conservation was probably a lost cause in England by the latter part of the seventeenth century—than on a monopoly control of North American timber. The British need for Maine timber, ideally suitable for the masts of its ships of the line, was a contributing cause of the growing hostility between Great Britain and its colonies. The British government, through its colonial administrators, tried to enforce the principle that trees of mast girth and height were to be reserved for the exclusive use of the Royal Navy. Colonial foresters chose to defy such regulations because greater profits were to be gained when all timbers could be cut up in sawmills and none reserved for special allocation.

With the exhaustion of England's home forests and the failure of the government's North American imperial strategies, British metalworking industries were forced to adopt a substitute fuel, coal. By the mid-1740s, the Darbys, father and son, had proved the effectiveness of coal-fired furnaces. "The coal revolution allowed England to leave the era of wood and put both feet in the Iron Age. Iron rails replaced their wooden predecessors, as did bridges, beams, machinery, and ships built with iron." However, it was wood that made the revolution possible. "Timber props held up mine shafts so coal could be extracted. Then the coal was initially shipped to ironworks in wooden carts on timber rails or in wooden boats through canals whose locks were also made of wood...."

Perlin investigates the question of wood in relation to many other civilizations beyond the two reported on at length here. We have chosen to emphasize his treatment of Athens and England because they, better perhaps than all others, illustrate the complex interrelationships that obtain between forests, deforestation, war policies, imperial strategies, and economic and industrial policies.

* 2.22 *

Thirgood, J. V. *Man and the Mediterranean Forest: A History of Resource Depletion*. London and New York: Academic Press, 1981. LC 81-66368. ISBN 0-12-687250-3.

Sea power in the Mediterranean Basin, as elsewhere before the early nineteenth century, always depended on a state's supply of timber. Minoan civilization (3000-1100 B.C.) may have perished because the extreme deforestation of the island of Crete made it impossible to maintain a strong naval defense. In 480 B.C., when Athens was in grave peril from the Persians under Xerxes, the Athenians consulted the oracle at Delphi. They were told that a "wooden wall" would shelter them against ruin. The "wooden wall" they interpreted as a line of wooden ships, which did prove to be decisive at the Battle of Salamis in 479 B.C.

Deforestation in the Hellenic homelands began about 600 years prior to the life of Plato. Between 500 and 400 B.C. the deforestation of Attica was virtually complete. Athens became dependent on the timber that was still available in parts of Greece further north. To safeguard timber reserves against disastrous depletion, governments began to institute controls. Athens banned the export and re-export of all ship materials, and access to timber reserves became a focus of both military alliances and military strategy. The Spartan seizure of Amphipolis, an Athenian colony and timber reserve along the Adriatic coast, was a devastating defeat for Athens. Alcibiades in 415 B.C. proposed an imperialist occupation of Sicily solely because the island was abundantly forested.

Thirgood devotes a long section of his book to a consideration of Cyprus as a case study in forest rehabilitation. Because originally the island was densely forested, Cyprus became a center of shipbuilding and the timber trade. Its strategic importance was enormous. As the first steppingstone east and west, it engrossed the attention of the dominant powers in the eastern Mediterranean, all of whom coveted its timber for naval purposes. In chronological order, those dominant powers have been: the Egyptians, Phoenicians, Greeks, Assyrians, Egyptians again, Persians, Egyptians, Macedonians, Egyptians, and Romans, among others during the pre-Islamic period. In 1571, Cyprus fell under the power of the Ottoman Empire. When in 1878 Turkey ceded the Island to Great Britain, the British found a devastated forest resource.

> Nicosia, the capital, stood a walled and isolated city, in the middle of an empty plain. Three large oriental plane trees outside the Paphos Gate were subject for universal comment. Within the towns, there was only an occasional date palm. The greater part of the cleared land remained uncultivated. In the words of an early writer: "Not cultivation, but sterility, a desert in fact has replaced the ancient forest vegetation of Cyprus."

The British authorities remarked that the only similarity between Greeks and Turks was their common hatred of trees. When the British took control, the assault on mountain forests was starting in earnest for the lowlands had become almost desert-like. Slopes, even the steepest of them, were being cleared for the cultivation of grapes and other crops. These cleared areas were quickly exhausted by erosion. Further, eroded lands became dangerously compacted by goats. "Flocks of goats, numbered in their hundreds, roamed in the charge of lawless shepherds who dominated the life of forest and countryside." Free-grazing goats were the greatest single threat to a revival of Cypriot forests. Goats became the target of a series of goat laws and finally the "Goat Exclusion Law of 1913." This law authorized villages to vote, by secret ballot, for an exclusion of goats from village lands. The secret ballot neutralized the fear villagers had of lawless shepherds and eventually led to a *cordon sanitaire* of goat-free villages around the periphery of forests.

British forest policy on Cyprus involved the replanting of deforested lowland areas with imported species of trees from Australia, the prohibition of felling in all official state forests, and a ban on exports of forest products. Gradually the attitudes of the Cypriots changed when they saw that trees could be grown on the arid plains. This widespread planting made an enormous contribution to the transition from the desert-like landscape of Turkish times, to the verdant towns of the present day. Progress to this satisfactory result was by no means uniform in its pace. There were periods of sabotage and outright defiance of the forest laws by Cypriot peasants who did not understand the importance of forests to the health of their environment.

Thirgood concludes with these words:

> The outstanding lesson to be gained from the Cyprus story is that, in a peasant society, progress can only come when close and personal contacts and mutual trust are established at village level, and the people are truly led to recognize the value of forest as a corporate resource.

DISEASE AND CIVILIZATION

* 2.23 *

Cohen, Mark Nathan. *Health and the Rise of Civilization*. New Haven and London: Yale University Press, 1989. LC 89-5405. ISBN 0-300-04006-7 (alk. pbk.)

Images of the primitive and the civilized in popular belief and in professional reconstructions of history are clearly contradictory. On the one hand, there is in Western society great admiration for the presumed simplicity of the primitive; on the other hand, there is disdain for the primitive and an idealization of a scientific civilization. If health and physical well-being are taken as measures of their truth, then both images are quite inaccurate. Ethnography, history, and archaeology do not confirm that there has been any reliably continuous advance either in diet or in freedom from diseases, "except in the last century, during which antibiotics have begun to offer serious protection against infection."

Except for the last century, archaeological evidence is ambiguous. Probably dietary deficiencies have increased and dietary quality has been sacrificed for quantity as hunters and foragers abandoned a diet of game in preference to grain cultivation. The generalization of declining dietary adequacy must be qualified in one important respect. In Western society, those who have been privileged economically have escaped the dietary stringency that has always been the lot of the poor.

The following representative observations and inferences are relevant to the relationship between skeletal analysis and a reconstruction of prehistoric diets:

1) The incidence of dental caries almost invariably increases with the soft, sticky foods of agricultural diets.

2) Bones and teeth can be analyzed to show trace amounts of strontium, zinc, magnesium, and so on.

3) Nutritional deficiency diseases are associated with bone composition and structure (i.e., iron deficiency anemia gives a spongy appearance to the thin bones of the skull vault).

4) The overall size of an adult skeleton indicates stature at the time of death.

5) Some infectious diseases can be detected through an analysis of bones.

Using these and many additional observational data, Cohen documents changes in the skeleton "from early (paleolithic) to later (mesolithic) hunter-gatherer economies." These skeletal changes, in turn, parallel what Cohen calls the "broad spectrum revolution." This occurred when large game animals disappeared and hunters turned to a broad spectrum of small animals, seeds, and aquatic foods. The new food orientation caused the health and nutrition of hunter-gatherers to decline. "In most locations studied so far, stature was declining or other measures of the skeleton were becoming smaller, rates of enamel hypoplasia were increasing, and rates of porotic hyperostosis and sign of infection were increasing."

The new food orientation led to increases in the size and permanence of human settlements for the obvious reason that the "broad spectrum" approach favored sedentarism. When human populations became more dense, the rate of infection increased. Further, there is no evidence to suggest that some infections declined or disappeared as people became more civilized.

Cohen concludes that "the organization and style of a civilization are at least as much the cause of biological stress as they are the cure." From the point of view of the individual, civilization has only one clear blessing, and that is the potential for investment in solutions to human problems.

* 2.24 *

Matossian, Mary Kilbourne. *Poisons of the Past: Molds, Epidemics, and History*. New Haven and London: Yale University Press, 1989. LC 89-5345. ISBN 0-300-03949-2 (alk. pbk.)

Ergot, a fungus of the genus *Claviceps*, infects cereal plants, such as wheat or rye, but rye has been the principal host of the fungus. When infected grains are eaten in sufficient quantities, they produce an often fatal disease known as ergotism. Matossian arranges the symptoms of ergotism under seven rubrics: cardiovascular, gastrointestinal, motor control, central nervous system, senses, skin, and reproductive system. Under central nervous system, she specifies the following: headache, dizziness, depression, confusion, drowsiness, unconsciousness, panic, hallucinations, delusions, and psychosis. Under motor control, she lists, inter alia, tremors, spasms, and writhing. Under reproductive system, she specifies fertility suppression, abortion (stillbirth), agalactia, and poisoning of mother's milk. These three sets of symptoms have special importance for the author's thesis, which is that ergotism underlies and explains such social and cultural phenomena as the persecution of witches, such as the Salem affair; sudden panics like the Great Fear in France in 1789; the Great Awakening and other manifestations of religious ecstacy; and the rise and decline of human fertility levels.

In witchcraft, there is an alleged victimizer, the witch or wizard, and alleged victims, the bewitched. Contrary to the view of some modern skeptics, the bewitched were not feigning. Their symptoms were oppressively real and, moreover, they were identical with those known to be associated with ergotism. In a trial for witchcraft in Europe or Massachusetts, the bewitched would experience tremors, spasms, writhings, and convulsions; there was occasional muscular paralysis and loss of speech. More importantly the victims, confused and panic-ridden, hallucinated and expressed persecutory delusions. Visions of heaven or hell and out-of-the-body experiences were commonplace as were voices purporting to come from the realm of the supernatural. In many cases of alleged bewitchment, the victim (female) complained that the witch was responsible for aborting a fetus or for poisoning a nursing mother's milk, or more generally for unwonted infertility.

Matossian conjectures that those accused of witchcraft were probably herbalists who had achieved some measure of success as healers of nervous disorders. Supposed witches were known to have possessed wortcunning (knowledge of herbs). Practicing the healing arts has always been a hazardous line of endeavor, but particularly was it so when the prevailing culture allowed the sudden onset of frightening, if not demoralizing, symptoms to be interpreted in accordance with presuppositions of supernatural intervention in mundane human affairs. Matossian speculates that an accusation of witchcraft may have been the sixteenth and seventeenth century equivalent of a modern action at law for medical malpractice.

To support her thesis that ergotism was the effective cause of accusations of witchcraft in early modern England, 1560-1660, Matossian examines the records of court trials for witchcraft in Essex County. She chose Essex County because that county has the oldest and least intermitted sequence of trial transcripts in England and because rye was grown and rye bread was eaten as a staple food in some precisely known parts of the county. Matossian does succeed in correlating trials for witchcraft with those sections of the county where rye was grown for an expanding market, particularly the Vale of London and the Essex coast. These two areas were lowland areas with wet, sandy soils, "where ergot was more likely to form on rye and where rye was cultivated intensely."

In order to attribute the 1691-92 eruption of witchcraft accusations and executions of condemned witches in Salem, Massachusetts, to an epidemic of ergotism, it is necessary that the author prove that ergot-infected rye was harvested and eaten over a ten-month period. She circumscribes the sequence of events.

> The first symptoms of bewitchment appeared in Salem Village in December 1691. Beginning about April 18, 1692, the pace of accusation increased. It slowed in June and then reached a peak between July and September. Exactly when the symptoms terminated is unknown. After October 12, 1692, there were no more trials for witchcraft by order of the governor of Massachusetts. During the winter of 1692-93, however, there were religious revivals in the area around Boston and Salem, during which people saw visions.

The timing is given precisely because it is critical to the proof. Normal New England practice was to delay threshing rye until December if other food was abundant, and so the infected rye crop of 1691 could have caused the first symptoms to appear in December. The Spring of 1692 saw violent rain and wind storms and grave damage to preferred crops like wheat. For this reason, the people of Salem Village were presumptively obliged to eat the infected rye crop of 1692 in July and August, the two months in which accusations peaked. There is one other causative factor that must be noted. The optimum temperature for ergot alkaloid production in New England is reached (17.4-18.9 degrees Centigrade) only during an unusually cold growing season. On the basis of tree ring evidence, it can be affirmed that the years 1690, 1691, and 1692 did have unusually cold growing seasons.

The last component in Matossian's probabilistic argument is the spatial distribution of symptoms in Salem Village. There were twenty-two households in which symptoms were reported, all twenty-two of which were located "on or at the edge of soils ideally suited to rye cultivation: moist, acid, sandy loams." She concludes her chapter on Salem thus.

> Although the limitations of surviving records make certainty impossible, the balance of the available evidence suggests that witchcraft accusations in 1692 in New England were prompted by an epidemic of ergotism.

Malthusian categories are usually invoked to explain such dramatic demographic changes as the explosion of the population of Europe in the years 1750 to 1850. The population of England and Wales, for example, increased 300 percent over the one-hundred year period. The statistical basis of Malthusianism is weak, however. In contrast to its unconvincing performance, a medical and climatic analysis may have more to offer. The presence or absence of ergotism must be considered as a major determinant of the rise and fall of population levels in as much as the disease directly affects both fertility and mortality rates. Moreover, it affects mortality in a differentiated manner. Ergotism proportionately kills more children than adults. A population tending toward expansion has a higher percentage of children than does a stable or declining population. For this reason, an otherwise expansive population will be most held in check by ergotism. Matossian cites evidence to show that the climate of Europe in 1750 to 1850 warmed to the point that temperatures were above those that favored production of ergot alkaloids. Therefore ergotism diminished if not disappeared, and the population of Europe could and did increase geometrically.

Chapter III

"Development" and Environmental

Decline in the

Contemporary Third World

The ecological decline of ancient Near Eastern civilizations and the violent and explosive characteristics of post-Columbian colonial ecologies might well remain comfortably remote from us in our twentieth century world were it not for the disturbing parallels that such case histories seem to evoke as we consider our contemporary global circumstance. Just as in ancient times and in the age of colonial expansion, it is in the "remote environments," usually quite distant from the centers of power, that the crucial indicators of environmental catastrophe first become apparent within the system as a whole. These regions are frequently characterized by weak economies and highly vulnerable ecosystems in our time, just as they were in the past. Accordingly, the environmental circumstances in these regions constitute for the modern world a kind of monitoring device that can provide early warnings of ecological instabilities in the global ecosystem.

If we begin to monitor this early warning system, we will come to realize that the signs are not encouraging. In country after country of the Third World we are beginning to recognize a repetitive syndrome—a seemingly irreversible spiral of ecological decline. One observer has summed up the overall situation quite succinctly:

> [T]he last thirty years have been the most disastrous in the history of most, if not all, Third World countries. There has been massive deforestation, soil erosion and desertification. The incidence of floods and droughts has increased dramatically as has their destructiveness, population growth has surged, as has urbanization, in particular the development of vast shanty-towns, in which human life has attained a degree of squalor probably unprecedented outside Hitler's concentration camps.
>
> With such developments have come increased malnutrition and hunger; so much so, that today we are witnessing

for the first time in human history, famine on a continental
scale, with two-thirds of African countries to some degree
affected.[1]

The Global Commissions

While it is most convincing to witness these trends in the field, their
reality is apparent to anyone capable of a sensitive reading of available
figures and reports that deal with aggregate populations or macro-level
change. Several environmental and economic trends of particular importance in this connection have been documented by various investigatory
bodies. A number of global "commissions" have been constituted to
investigate the widening gap between the "developed" and the "underde-
veloped" world. The gap has become wider since oil price hikes
triggered a global economic recession in the mid-1970s. Most notable of
these were the two commissions chaired by Willie Brandt, the former
West German head of state. The first commission report was finished in
1978 and the second in 1983. In addition, the United States Department
of State and the Council on Environmental Quality issued in 1980 a
document called *Global 2000: A Report to the President*, which detailed
environmental and resource supply trends throughout the world and
provided suggestions for future policy. More recently, the United
Nations commissioned Gro Harlem Brundtland, the Prime Minister of
Norway, to head a study group on global ecological and economic
issues. All of these reports deserve wide public consideration and
debate.[2]

Ironically, the Brundtland Report—the most deliberate and comprehensive of them all—was unveiled in the United States on 19 October
1987—the day of the largest stock market crash in American history. As
a result, the dramatic effect it might well have had, had it been issued a
week earlier or later, was largely eclipsed. Furthermore, it is probably
true that, since the Brundtland report was from a UN commission,
Americans may well have ignored its message. In recent years, top
public officials in the United States have held the UN and its service
organizations like UNESCO and FAO in open contempt, largely because
of the continuous criticism from Third World members leveled at
American policies in the global arena. American leadership seems to
have proceeded on the operative assumption: "If you don't like the news,
ignore it." It is not clear this is a wise strategy in the context of
worsening global ecological problems that require cooperation for their
solution.

Disturbing environmental and economic trends include problems of
deforestation, the expansion of petro-chemical agriculture, the shift in
weather patterns and perhaps climate in the semi-arid areas, continued

population growth, and the penetration of local food markets with Western food surpluses through dumping or foreign aid.

Tropical Deforestation

One of the most familiar among the measured environmental trends in the Third World is the phenomenon of tropical deforestation. While anthropologists have observed this on a micro-ecological basis for several decades, it is now becoming measurable from satellite monitors in space. The scope of the transformation is massive. President Carter's *Global 2000 Report* drew attention to the problem, and the data have been accumulating on the problem ever since. In March 1984, the Office of Technology Assessment (OTA) reported to the United States Congress that deforestation in tropical areas was proceeding at an alarming rate: "Each year approximately 11.3 million hectares (4.57 million acres) of the Earth's remaining tropical forests—an area roughly the size of Pennsylvania—are cleared and converted to other uses." If current trends persist, the report makes clear that much of the earth's tropical rain forest will be gone by the turn of the century. It estimates that at current rates, "Nine tropical countries would eliminate practically all of their closed forests within the next thirty years and another thirteen countries would exhaust theirs within fifty-five years."[3] A "closed forest" is one in which trees shade so much of the ground that a continuous layer of grass cannot grow. Attempts to re-forest denuded areas have been made, but estimates are that areas affected by re-forestation efforts account for only about one-tenth the acreage of deforested lands at the current time.

Those areas affected are in all of the tropical regions of the world. Nations experiencing the worst deforestation include the Ivory Coast in West Africa, where 6.5 percent of closed forests are lost each year; Nigeria in West Africa, 5 percent; Paraguay in South America, 4.7 percent; Nepal in Asia, 4.3 percent; Costa Rica in Central America, 4 percent; and Haiti in the Caribbean, 3.8 percent.[4] The OTA study joins a chorus of others that have been published recently, for efforts to publicize the fate of tropical forests have been made by scholars and researchers for several years.

Notable contributions have come from Norman Myers, whose study for the National Research Council and more popular works have done much to draw broad public attention to the problem, and from Earthscan, which has issued an action-oriented summary of what can be done. The World Resources Institute in coordination with the World Bank and the United Nations Development Programme has drawn up what it calls a "call for action" to help stop the loss of tropical rain forests. As one might expect, however, this proposal has come in for considerable criticism by those who argue that the World Bank's proposed solutions favor the very kind of development efforts that have devastated rain forests in the first place.[5]

As scientists are informing us, the tragedies involved in the loss of tropical forests are far greater than the hardships these losses impose on local peasantries or isolated ecologies. Indeed, the impact of tropical deforestation is global in scale for three main reasons. First, the tropical rain forests are perhaps the greatest remaining store of biological diversity left on the planet. Second, these ecosystems play a major role in the bio-geo-chemical cycling of carbon and the earth's atmospheric gases. Third, and partly as a result of their role in the bio-geo-chemical cycles, the tropical rain forests appear to play an as yet unclear but nonetheless important role in the regulation of the earth's climate.

Despite the volume of the scientific material already published over the last ten years and the large number of research programs currently underway that warn against the dangers, the pattern of deforestation has not been noticeably reversed by acts of policy in recent years. Third World countries involved in the process of forest loss are by now genuinely concerned about this form of ecological degradation, but they are frequently impotent to do anything more than monitor what has occurred. In 1987, for example, an environmental group known as The Mexican Ecological Movement indicated that: "The unplanned cutting of timberland in the past 30 years has caused Mexico to lose 45 percent of its forest reserves ... in 1957 Mexico had three million acres of forest, compared with some 1.8 million acres of current wooded lands."[6] Much of this forest loss is not of the same kind that has occurred by explicit timbering of tropical forest reserves, but the resource loss to peasants is nevertheless real and dramatic.

In some cases, localized patterns of deforestation can cause national and potentially international complications. Deforestation in the Himalayan highlands has been seen to be linked over time to the pattern of flooding down river in Bangladesh. More than twenty-five million people were made homeless and subjected to disease and food shortages in 1988 because of watershed deforestation in the Himalayan ranges. In addition, the process of deforestation currently proceeding in Panama seems to be affecting not only peasant welfare and local agriculture but potentially the integrity of the canal passageway itself. A report issued to the government of Panama indicated that the canal's most pressing problem is that of deforestation. In 1952, 80 percent of the Panama Canal basin was covered with forest, while today only 20 percent remains forested. "The jungle is being deforested at the rate of 5,000 acres per year," the report indicated.

The loss of forest cover on hills and mountainsides allows soil to be washed down into the lakes and connecting waterways causing siltation. The Panamanian governmental report estimated that this kind of erosion was expected to reduce the Panama Canal's capacity by 10 percent in the year 2000. The report, coordinated by Stanley Heckadon Moreno, an environmentalist at the Planning Ministry in Panama, stressed the urgency of acting immediately to reverse current forest-loss trends. "We believe," the authors said, "that unless corrective measures are taken immediately, the basin will be totally deforested and the useful life of the Canal will be reduced to less than 25 years."[7]

As the Panama circumstance indicates, many of the causes leading to deforestation are to be found in the desperation of landless peasant families seeking new territories for farming. UPI Reporter Elizabeth Love summarized the situation in these terms:

> A steady stream of landless peasants has been invading the land around the Canal. They earn a meager existence by raising cattle and raising crops by using slash and burn agriculture, both activities that destroy trees and native plant life that protect the soil. Some 40 underequipped forest rangers patrol the 1,280 square miles that make up the Canal watershed, but stemming the tide of migrants and persuading the farmers to move on is difficult.
>
> "(If) the government simply tells them by means of the armed forces or forest rangers, 'You can't cut the forest,' the peasants perceive that as you saying 'You can't eat,'" said Heckadon Moreno.
>
> He said some 50,000 peasants already live in the Canal basin area and the figure is expected to grow 7 percent annually.
>
> If peasants are not offered an alternative in the way of jobs or land, "political restlessness" could further hinder Canal programs, Heckadon Moreno said.
>
> "Just the other day, 50 or 60 families created a situation in which weapons had to be drawn (to evict them). What are we going to do in five years time when we have mass amounts of people there, demanding land?" he said.[8]

While deforestation in Panama and in many African countries may be the collective result of individual actions undertaken by small household peasants, elsewhere it seems to result from explicit policy decisions for development projects proposed by corporations or national governments and supported by the international financial community. Environmental groups like the Rainforest Action Network and the Tropical Forest Action Group have directly linked the loss of forest resources to the type of development strategies pursued by nation states and financed by the World Bank.[9] Randall Hayes, director of the Rainforest Action Network, indicated at a conference in Boulder, Colorado, in February 1987 that he intended to wage a campaign to arouse public opinion against the international financing of development projects that had the direct or indirect effect of destroying tropical rain forests. Pointing out that international financial backing is required to launch many of the cattle ranch and agriculture development projects that have a direct impact upon the tropical rain forest, Hayes argued that, if the flow of supporting capital could be stopped, the rate of deforestation could be slowed. "It's a battle that can be won...," he said. "It takes money to finance this destruction. If we can stop the money, we can stop the destruction."[10]

Other protests against World Bank development policies have taken more direct action. In September 1986 members of the Tropical Forest Action Group were arrested as they demonstrated against World Bank policies by unfurling a 40-foot by 20-foot banner from an eleven-story building near the World Bank headquarters. The banner read simply: "World Bank Destroys Tropical Forests." It was meant to be seen by finance ministers and world economic policy officials as they met in Washington to discuss future lending policies of the World Bank. More recently, adverse publicity for the Bank's policies has focused upon the ecological devastation that Bank lending helped engender by helping to finance extensive highway construction in the Amazon basin.[11] If changing the consciousness of international finance organizations is sufficient, there may be some room for optimism here.

At the highest official levels, at least, there seems to be an emerging consensus that something must be done. Perhaps in response to increasing accusations that it has been bankrolling environmental destruction or in response to its own internal policy review, the World Bank announced intentions in May 1987 to give environmental concerns top priority in future lending decisions. World Bank President Barber Conable indicated, in a speech to the World Resources Institute in Washington, that explicit efforts would be made in the future to halt the spread of deserts in Africa:

> "The World Bank is a force for development and will remain so," he said. "Our role in such projects, however, will include greater sensitivity to their long-term environmental effects. And we will put new emphasis both on correcting economic policy incentives that promote environmental abuse, and on stimulating the small-scale activities that can combat human and environmental deprivation."[12]

Despite all this official expression of good intentions, the most recent reports indicate that the rate of tropical deforestation over the last few years has, in fact, proceeded *faster* than initially predicted in the early

1980s. Whereas earlier estimates made by the United Nations Food and Agricultural Organization were in the range of 28 million acres lost per year, the latest report, based in part upon satellite photos, estimates the annual rate of destruction somewhere between 40 to 50 million acres—an area the size of the state of Washington.[13]

Against this background of the evident failure of economic development strategies to slow the rate of deforestation, it is perhaps significant that a long-standing critic of growth economics has recently been named to work on World Bank policy issues. Herman Daly, author of *Steady-State Economics*, and long-time critic of conventional economic growth theory, is currently working at the World Bank. Analysts of Bank policy regard Daly's appointment as a remarkable reversal, for Daly is raising embarrassing questions about the long-term ecological sustainability of proposed development strategies. Economists generally do not like to think of long-range time projections, and they are fond of quoting John Maynard Keynes who once dismissed concerns for the distant future by jesting that "in the long run we're all dead." Daly and others are pointing out to economists that such jokes are not funny anymore, and there is growing evidence that economists are finally sobering up to the realization that perpetual growth economies are just not sustainable in the ecological "real world."

In 1988 the Society for Ecological Economics was founded in a meeting in Barcelona, and it has proceeded to publish a journal called *Ecological Economics* under the editorship of Robert Costanza. Nevertheless, it remains to be seen whether market-oriented economists can ever fully commit themselves to explore and design steady-state economic systems based on homeostatic ecological models, and it is certainly not clear to what extent Daly's perspective can prevail in a bureaucracy as accustomed to growth-oriented criteria of success as the World Bank has proved to be in the past.[14]

The remaining questions are simply these:

- Is the effort to accommodate "ecological economics" simply a meaningless gesture? perhaps a case of too little, too late? or maybe worse, an obfuscatory smokescreen for old-fashioned resource extraction with a "kinder, gentler" face?

- Moreover, even with the best of intentions, can large international organizations like the World Bank effectively reverse a pattern of Third World decline that has been underway for over thirty years?

- Isn't there a fundamental contradiction between environmental conservation and "development" as it has traditionally been conceived?

Environmentalists are beginning to phrase the question in just these terms: "Is development the solution or is it the problem?"[15]

The issue of tropical deforestation may prove to be a weathervane case, indicating whether institutions can adapt quickly enough to changing circumstance in the Third World. The World Bank intends to raise its funding from $138 million to $350 by 1990 for studies to preserve tropical forests. Moreover, it recognizes the need to fund projects that promote conservation, but it may well be that projects of this kind would require flat opposition to "development" programs that have been launched and are likely to continue in the Third World. In any direct confrontation between the newly informed consciousness on the part of World Bank donors and the entrenched special interests advocating conventional forms of trade, aid, and development in the Third World, it is not clear that the newly discovered environmental sensitivities of World Bank officials will prevail. Indeed, there are mounting signs that the policies of development that have caused the most rapid and irreversible forms of environmental degradation are likely to endure. In fact, these policies are likely to be applied in an accelerated manner in the coming years, despite the best intentions of World Bank officials.

Warfare and the Underdevelopment Spiral

Although not always present in every Third World circumstance, warfare tends to accelerate the pace of the downward spiral. These compounding factors come into play when peasantries seek to arrest the underdevelopment spiral and take matters into their own hands. Typically peasant resistance involves attempts to:

1) resist direct government exactions in one form or another (taxes, fees, expropriations);

2) seek better trade terms for items they produce; or

3) seek control over arable land in order to pursue autonomous farming.

If these peasant movements are countered by the state or by other classes acting on their own, there will, in all likelihood, be noticeable ecological consequences:

1) escalating conflict in rural areas will divert efforts from agricultural production;

2) the growth in international arms trade will cause further drains on foreign exchange and thereby accentuate resource-extractive trade; and/or

3) crops, villages, and ground cover will sustain outright destruction through ground combat, bombing, chemical defoliation, or purposeful torching of biota to destroy an opponent's means of securing shelter, food, or a livelihood.

The potential ecological impact of nuclear war has attracted much attention recently, but all kinds of warfare are clearly costly to the environment. Perhaps the recent shift in public attention from the cold war to the "resource wars" in the Third World will heighten public concern on this issue. Attacks upon oil reserves became an avowed strategy of both parties during the recent Iran-Iraq war and provided a blatant example to the world of how the intentional destruction of ecological capital can emerge as a conscious goal of warfare in the modern world. Similar strategies may still be deployed by those who seek to keep Middle Eastern oil "safe" for consumption by Western industrial nations. It was, after all, American soldiers in Vietnam who became famous for the logic: "We had to destroy the village in order to save it."

As resource wars increase in frequency and intensity in the coming years, examples of this tragically short-sighted logic are likely to multiply. Rather than let valuable natural resources pass into the hands of perceived enemies, antagonists may choose to sell them quickly, deplete them at an accelerated rate, or simply destroy them to prevent all others from using them. Whatever sense this logic makes in political terms, it makes no sense whatsoever in ecological terms. Once they are destroyed, non-renewables—like oil, top soil, and tropical forests—are gone forever, no matter who claims a temporary political victory in the process.

Assessing the ecological impact of warfare must go beyond simply drawing up an inventory of the non-renewable resources destroyed. An examination of the ecological effects of "limited" wars, particularly those against peasantries in the Third World, should begin with the Stockholm International Peace Research Institute's study of warfare's impact on the environment and Arthur H. Westing's study of the long-term ecological consequences of the use of herbicides in warfare.[16] These internationally commissioned reports have been largely ignored in the United States, perhaps, once again, because current American political leadership finds it difficult to accept responsibility for the chemical warfare techniques used in recent wars in Indochina and advocated by some for use in ending conflicts in Central America. Indeed, given its opposition to compensation for alleged "agent orange" disabilities among its own veterans, the reluctance of the current and recent administrations to examine these issues publicly is perhaps understandable if not excusable.

Scholars have tended to neglect the ecological impact of open conflict that is predictably unleashed when particular development policies are pursued. This is a curious omission, and it marks a peculiar kind of blind spot in assessing development strategies. Not all businesses are similarly myopic. Some enterprises involved in Third World agriculture projects regularly include considerations of "security" as part of the operating costs they incur to protect their investments. If peasant resistance or sabotage to these projects becomes too expensive, the enterprise nearly always calls upon the state military apparatus to undertake the effort and expense of suppressing peasant opposition. The costs of repressing peasant revolts are readily calculable in terms of munitions and manpower, but the costs to the peasants' environment or the world's ecosystem of doing so are usually overlooked as an "externality" in the whole process.

If we are to develop a reasonable means of assessing the environmental costs of development strategies, we should try to include this "externality" in our calculations. The policy implications of undertaking these economic calculations would be significant, for, whatever the economic virtues of pursuing market-driven development strategies in regions like Central America, the ecological destruction involved in crushing peasant rebellions, supporting "contra" insurgencies, or launching "freedom fighter" rebellions is massive and needs to be counted as a substantial cost in a cost-benefit analysis of any proposed development strategy. Several government officials in El Salvador have now come to this realization. In forming a new organization called the Salvadorean Ecological Unity Movement, they have made urgent appeals to end the country's internal civil war in order to limit further ecological devastation. As Ricardo Navarro, leader of the new movement, has indicated, "if we carry on like this, El Salvador has only two decades to live...Ecological deterioration is killing us...."[17]

Elements of the Downward Spiral That Apply
to the Third World Generally

The development policies that have caused the most rapid and irreversible forms of environmental degradation are likely to continue to be applied in an accelerated manner in the coming years. The fundamental reason for this acceleration of decline can be located in what may be called most generally "the underdevelopment spiral"—a syndrome of closely related social, economic, and ecological phenomena, which when taken together work to engender a self-perpetuating cycle of environmental decline. As these phenomena interact they work to reinforce one another in a synergetic manner, accelerating a spiral of decline and making it increasingly difficult for any one party to intervene and arrest the process. To clarify, then, the reason that shifts in World Bank policy are not likely on their own to be sufficient to change conditions in the Third World, it is perhaps useful to outline the elements and interactions involved in the underdevelopment spiral. The basic elements of the spiral are these:

1) Cash-crop agriculture in the Third World has expanded enormously leading to commodity "gluts" on world markets.

2) Real prices of Third World commodities have declined in world trade over the last four decades.

3) Cash exchange has expanded and markets for petty manufactured goods have become international, eclipsing local artisan production and marketing.

4) Exogenous, hybrid, and/or petro-intensive cultivars have been introduced in rural areas throughout the world, often displacing indigenous food crops.

5) Small-hold agriculture has declined and the numbers of "landless peasants" have increased, as economies of scale with mechanized agriculture have favored larger landowners with greater capital assets.

6) Larger and larger portions of Third World populations have moved from rural to urban areas at the same time that the overall population numbers have increased at historically unprecedented levels.

7) Local weather and micro-climate patterns have changed in agricultural regions in unpredictable ways causing crop failures and shortfalls.

8) Overgrazing, loss of topsoil, salinization, flooding, and waterlogging have caused the destruction of many agricultural and pastoral lands and threatened the ecological viability of many others.

9) Local and regional food shortages have resulted in the growth of international food trade and aid to supply famine victims.

10) The industrialization of agriculture in developed nations has resulted in an overproduction of basic foodstuffs; these agricultural surpluses

are often exported to feed the exploding urban populations or famine victims in the Third World.

11) There have been fitful but secular increases (an overall upward trend) in the price of petroleum and petroleum products, over the last several decades, leading to unpredictable increases in agricultural inputs and transportation costs, and, thus, fluctuations in the price of imported food supplies.

12) In the long term, there has been an increase in relative prices of manufactured goods compared to agricultural commodities—reflecting, in part, the energy costs of producing and marketing the manufactured goods.

13) Third World indebtedness has increased as it has become necessary to pay both for expanded food imports and for increasingly expensive manufactured goods, while at the same time the price of their export commodities has declined in real terms.

14) Government bureaucracies have expanded, in part, to employ a burgeoning population of school graduates and thus avoid the problem of creating large numbers of urban, unemployed, articulate critics.

15) With foreign exchange being scarce, infrastructure, public services, and normal financial transactions have been difficult to maintain; sometimes they have collapsed all together, and corruption has grown, as private solutions to collective problems are sought by business owners, foreigners, and ordinary citizens.

The syndrome of environmental decline sets in as each of these elements reinforces the others. Thus, for example, pressure to repay international debts, combined with internal government corruption and inefficiency, a scarcity of profitable exchange commodities, and a growing level of rural desperation, has encouraged both governments and individuals in Third World countries to become "predators" upon the remaining natural capital in their immediate environment. Extractive industries and destructive agricultural processes are frequently established—often in the name of "development"—with the net effect of devastating the natural resource base in one country after another in the Third World.

Interaction of the Elements

Armed conflict or sustained warfare usually breaks out only where these basic elements have reinforced one another for years, decades, or generations. For general purposes, therefore, it is possible to set these obvious cases of environmental destruction aside for the moment to concentrate on the basic elements and examine how they interact to produce the steady and seemingly irreversible cycle of environmental decline in the Third World.

The principal aspect to note about the interactions between the elements is that, although they are presented above in a specific order, no particular order is needed. Each element reinforces aspects of other elements in cyclical and perpetual interaction, approaching what systems ecologists might call a "positive feedback" mechanism. This means that analysis can begin with any element and proceed through all the others. The links between them all strengthen themselves as the elements become more pronounced. The search for a "first cause" is, then, simply beside the point. Causation of these kinds of syndromes is best understood as a cyclical and cumulative process.

Different "experts" and academic professions will, no doubt, choose different points from which to start analyzing the links between the elements. Thus, economists may wish to begin by talking about the declining price of agricultural commodities, whereas demographers might begin with the population explosion, while sociologists may start with Third World urbanization patterns. Soil scientists will probably talk of wide-scale erosion, while ecologists might well begin with the massive transformation of the agricultural landscape, and journalists might choose to focus on massive corruption or bureaucratic incompetence. Since all of these processes are going on simultaneously in a self-reinforcing manner, just where one begins the analysis of connectedness is not crucial to understanding the underlying dynamic of the whole process so long as the interaction of all elements is kept clearly in mind. Much of the debate between social scientists analyzing environmental crises in the Third World is over the question of where to ground the fundamental starting point for analysis.

From the perspective of systems thinking adopted here, this kind of debate is as pointless as it is fruitless. Such debates often deteriorate into "Which is the better social science? economics? demography? sociology?" The point is simply that no particular perspective deserves priority, but all analysts must focus from now on upon the connectedness, the fundamental interrelatedness of these phenomena, if any effective means of addressing our environmental crises are to be developed. It is no longer sufficient to argue that our narrow expertise excuses us from the responsibility of addressing these larger issues or that the integrated approaches can be postponed until further technical breakthroughs can be achieved in one sector or another. There will be no miracle technical fixes, and collective deliberations must begin at once.

NOTES

1. Edward Goldsmith, "Is Development the Solution or the Problem?" *The Ecologist* 15:5/6 (1985): 210.

2. See: Independent Commission on International Development Issues (Brandt Commission), *North-South: A Program for Survival* (Cambridge, MA: MIT Press, 1980); and the Independent Commission, *Common Crisis: North-South: Cooperation for World Recovery* (Cambridge, MA: MIT Press, 1983). For a critique of the Independent (Brandt) Commission approach, see: Teresa Hayter, *The Creation of World Poverty: An Alternative View to the Brandt Report* (London: Pluto, 1981). Under President Carter, the United States Department of State and the Council on Environmental Quality issued in 1980 a document called *Global 2000: A Report to the President*. The most comprehensive multi-government global study is World Commission on Environment and Development (Brundtland Commission), *Our Common Future* (New York: Oxford University Press, 1987).

In addition to these global commissions, two reputable institutes issue regular reports on evolving global environmental circumstances. The World Watch Institute in Washington publishes an annual volume entitled *State of the World 1984* (with each successive year indicated in the title). Similarly, the World Resources Institute in Washington publishes a bi-annual volume entitled *World Resources, 1988-89* (etc.). The latest in the series is *World Resources, 1990-91*, which appeared in June of 1990. Both of these important series attempt to give accurate and timely information of crises situations and longer-term environmental trends in the Third World.

3. Robert Sangeorge, "Tropical Forests Face Destruction," *UPI News Wire Dispatch*, 23 March 1984, 1:49 pm.

4. Sangeorge, 1:49 pm.

5. Norman Myers, *Conversion of Tropical Moist Forests* (Washington, DC: National Academy of Sciences, 1980); and his *The Primary Source: Tropical Forests and Our Future* (New York: Norton, 1984). Earthscan has issued an action-oriented summary of what can be done. See: Judith Gradwohl and Russell Greenberg, *Saving the Tropical Forests* (Washington, DC: Earthscan, 1988). Also see: *Tropical Forests: A Call for Action, Pt. I, The Plan; Pt. II, Case Studies; and Pt. III, Country Investment Profiles* (Washington, DC: World Resources Institute, 1985). See: Magda Renner, "A Critical Review of Tropical Forests: A Call for Action," *The Ecologist* 17:4-5 (1987): 150; and Vandana Shiva, "Forestry Myths and the World Bank: A Critical Review of Tropical Forests: A Call for Action," *The Ecologist* 17:4-5 (1987): 142-149.

Ever since the world financial institutions have become involved with rain forest issues, books and lengthy articles have proliferated on the subject at a truly impressive rate. Many of them have been inspired by new scientific research on biodiversity or on the functions of rain forests in global bio-geo-chemical processes. See for example: Robert E. Dickinson, ed., *The Geophysiology of Amazonia: Vegetation and Climate Interactions* (New York: Wiley for the United Nations University, 1987); Les Kaufman and Ken Mallory, *The Last Extinction* (Cambridge,

MA: Published in cooperation with the New England Aquarium [by] the MIT Press, 1986); and E. O. Wilson, ed., *Biodiversity* (Washington, DC: National Academy Press, 1988).

Other works have been motivated by the desire to get available information into the hands and onto the agenda of major policymaking figures. Consider for example: J. C. Westoby, *The Purpose of Forests: Follies of Development* (Oxford: Basil Blackwell, 1987); Robert C. Repetto, *The Forest for the Trees?: Government Policies and the Misuse of Forest Resources* (Washington, DC: World Resources Institute, 1988); Robert C. Repetto and Malcolm Gillis, *Public Policies and the Misuse of Forest Resources* (Cambridge [Cambridgeshire] and New York: Cambridge University Press, 1988); and from the World Bank itself, Dennis J. Mahar, *Government Policies and Deforestation in Brazil's Amazon Region* (Washington, DC: World Bank, 1989).

Still other publications have looked at the role of indigenous peoples and focused on the struggle for their rights of access to and control over forest resources: Robert S. Anderson and Walter Huber, *The Hour of the Fox: Tropical Forests, the World Bank, and Indigenous People in Central India* (Seattle: University of Washington Press, 1988); Harry W. Blair and Porus Olpadwala, *Forestry in Development Planning: Lessons from the Rural Experience* (Boulder: Westview Press, 1988); Jason W. Clay, *Indigenous Peoples and Tropical Forests: Models of Land Use and Management from Latin America* (Cambridge, MA: Cultural Survival, 1988); and Chico Mendes, *Fight for the Forest: Chico Mendes in His Own Words* (London: Latin America Bureau, 1989).

Finally, some works have sought to highlight successful policies or detailed the history of forest extraction development schemes: Judith Gradwohl and Russell Greenberg, *Saving the Tropical Forests* (Washington, DC: Island Press, 1988); and Susanna B. Hecht and Alexander Cockburn, *The Fate of the Forest: Developers, Destroyers, and Defenders of the Amazon* (London and New York: Verso, 1989).

6. *UPI News Wire Dispatch*, 8 June 1987, 6:20 pm.

7. Elizabeth Love, "Panama Canal's Water Supply Threatened, Report Says," *UPI News Wire Dispatch*, 13 April 1987, 7:47 am.

8. Love, 7:47 am.

9. "Protesters Say World Bank Ruins Forests," *UPI News Wire Dispatch*, 29 September 1986, 2:31 pm; and Brad Smith, "Preserving Rain Forests: Conservationist Coalition Seeks to Save Rain Forests," *UPI News Wire Dispatch*, 24 February 1987, 2:44 pm.

10. Smith, 2:44 pm.

11. Tyler Bridges, "The Rain Forest's Road to Ruin?; Ecologists Decry World Bank Role in Building Brazilian Highway," *Washington Post* (24 July 1988).

12. Craig Webb, "World Bank Launches New Pro-environment Campaign," *UPI News Wire Dispatch*, 5 May 1987, 4:41 pm. See also, Constance Holden, "The Greening of the World Bank," *Science* 240 (17 June 1988): 1610; and Constance Holden, "A Heretic Amid Economic Orthodoxy," *Science* 240 (17 June 1988): 1611.

13. See: *UPI Newswire Dispatch,* 8 June 1990, 1:44 a.m. The news report refers to the latest volume issued by the World Resources Institute, *World Resources, 1990-91* (New York: Oxford University Press, 1990): 102.

14. See: Constance Holden, "Multidisciplinary Look at a Finite World," *Science* 249 (6 July 1990): 18-19.

15. Goldsmith, 210-19.

16. See: Stockholm International Peace Research Institute, *Warfare in a Fragile World: Military Impact on the Human Environment* (London: Taylor and Francis, Ltd., 1980); and Arthur H. Westing, ed., *Herbicides in War: The Long-Term Ecological and Human Consequences* (London: Taylor and Francis Ltd., 1984).

17. See: "Ecological Damage, Aggravated by 10 Years of Civil War," *Reuters Newswire* 15 (5 June 1990): 51.

ANNOTATED BIBLIOGRAPHY FOR CHAPTER III

GENERAL

* 3.1 *

The Earth As Transformed by Human Action: Global and Regional Changes in the Biosphere, edited by B. L. Turner, II. Cambridge: Cambridge University Press with Clark University, 1990. LC 89-22362. ISBN 0-521-36357-8.

Three forces—population growth, technological capacity, and sociocultural organization—drive the global transformation of the biosphere. Countervailing these are the mitigating forces of authoritative regulation, market adjustment, and informal regulation. Underlying the forces of drive and mitigation are the cultural rationales, both conditions and choices, that give rise to them.

World population change in the period of 1950-1985 has been unique. Over the course of that thirty-five-year period world population increased—in millions—from 1,650 in 1900, to 2,515 in 1950, to 4,853 in 1985. The annual rates of increase for these time periods, 50 and 35 years respectively, were .84 and 1.88. The annual rates of increase for the periods of 1700-1750, 1750-1800, 1800-1850, and 1850-1900 were .25, .44, .55, and .54 respectively. These data irrefutably establish the uniqueness of the 1950-1985 period with its unprecedented annual rate of increase of 1.88.

After 1985, the rate of increase is expected to decline to 1.45—as it has in fact declined during the last six or seven years, reflecting lower fertility rates worldwide. But even with this reduced rate, the projected world population for 2020 is 8,061 million. Annual rates of increase will show regional variability over the period of 1985 to 2020. Europe will have a .1 rate; North America, a .6 rate; and Latin America, a 1.6 rate. Africa will have a 2.7 rate of increase, up from its 1950-1985 rate of 2.6. Given these marked regional differences in rates of increase, two conclusions emerge: 1) "A gradual moderation of the rate of growth can be anticipated with confidence" and 2) "Almost certainly, in terms of absolute increases, the brunt of the global population explosion is yet to come."

The prevailing assumption of the West has always been that technology is the means that human beings use for their own benefit in the pursuit of their goals of acquiring power over nature and power over people. In their dedication to technology, humans have consumed, often depleted, natural resources and have produced wastes, depletion and wastes being the unintended side-effects of the effort to produce, which is technology's reason for being.

> The consequences of technology do not stop at original intentions, however, but form cycles and feedback loops. In our own lifetimes, technology has become so powerful that we now feel and measure the feedback in the form of resource depletion, environmental degradation, and threats to life itself. It is the growing chasm between the intended purpose and the actual consequences of technology that promotes the fear that technology may be running amok. This is true not only of the nuclear arms race, but also of the exponential increases in resource depletion and environmental pollution that have marked our times.

Western industrial society is now in that stage where it is becoming a world system. As do all societies of whatever developmental stage, industrial society has certain assumptions about resources and natural phenomena; these assumptions the authors characterize as:

> dominance, control, and exploitation with few exceptions made for natural phenomena. Little regard for environmental limits.

The authors conclude that "the current momentum of centralized institutions toward a world system is unlikely to be sustainable." This is so for several reasons which I paraphrase in these terms: 1) fossil fuels supporting these institutions will become scarcer and more expensive, leading to eventual collapse; 2) if current patterns of energy use are continued, there will be increased threats of global environmental disruption, "whether from climate change, acid rain, soil exhaustion, or the loss of genetic diversity." "On the other hand," the authors continue:

> the continued externalization of the social and economic costs of these systems through international trade and financial structures will likely feed back in the form of a global debt crisis, a depression, or major social disorders. The closing of feedback loops that is occurring now is thus generating a new and significant set of risks and threats that logically call for a fundamental rethinking and restructuring of current industrial models and patterns.

International trade and financial structures are responsible for creating an increasing separation of production and consumption. Dependency analysts, with whom chapter author Michael Chisholm does not entirely agree, tend to equate trade with exploitation. They fasten on the multinational company as the villain:

> The driving force for these companies, it is said, is the maximization of profits, which are transferred to the location that gives the greatest fiscal advantages, in order to maximize the value of profits retained. Such firms will have no compunction in transferring their productive facilities from one location to another if they perceive more profitable opportunities—often equated with wages that are lower for a given level of labor efficiency.

This view of the villainy of multinational companies, Chisholm argues, assumes the absence of countervailing forces, a state of affairs which is contrary to fact.

> Since 1945, especially in the exploitation of minerals and fuels, most governments all over the world have sought to put the screws on multinational companies, with a view to extracting better terms. The final sanction, expropriation, has been used. Although it may well be the case that too small a proportion of the benefits from development has been and is retained by the host countries, the balance undoubtedly has shifted toward the host nations, and may well shift further.

Aside from the ability of governments to exert countervailing power on multinational companies, Chisholm relies on the improvement of humankind's scientific capability "to predict the effects of particular forms of exploitation and to devise remedial measures where these are necessary." Chisholm's summary judgment is that: "If the increasing separation of production and consumption implies that there are greater risks that ecologically unsound practices will be employed, the growth of scientific knowledge provides the potential to find partial or complete remedies."

Next Brian Berry takes up the question of the effects of urbanization, or the concentration of population in a relatively small area, on the atmospheric environment. He finds three geographic scales of atmospheric modification: the local scale; the regional scale; and the global scale, which is the most menacing because it involves "urban contributions to the sulfur budget or to CO_2, and thus to the greenhouse effect, to global warming, and to sea-level changes that are likely to be of greatest consequence for major coastal cities." Berry points out, however, that in

North America and Europe a counter process is now unfolding. This process Berry calls "counterurbanization." He defines counterurbanization as "deconcentration," or a movement from a state of more concentration to a state of less concentration.

He attibutes the emergence of patterns of dispersal of populations, in part, to a general recognition that urban concentrations entail disadvantages, inconveniences, and detriments in the quality of life for those who live in them. Berry calls these "disamenities." He even suggests that what may be emerging are urban civilizations *without cities*. Berry uses the term global "polycenter" to characterize the emerging system of population deconcentration in the First World.

To whatever extent the new pattern of urban dispersal may lessen the sulfur budget and diminish the greenhouse effect regionally throughout the First World, there is still no reason for long-term optimism. This is so for the reason that in the Third World urban areas, where dramatic increases in population continue, there is no tendency toward deconcentration and dispersal. Hence it is that

> [I]t is in these massive urban agglomerations, peripheral to the main channels of global interdependence, that the greatest modifications of the biosphere will occur, changing the regional environments within which a growing proportion of the world's population will live marginal lives, pressed to the threshold of subsistence. The scale of Third World urban growth is such that even if First World environmental impacts are significantly reduced, the reductions will be swamped by the increases occurring elsewhere. It is from the Third World's economic growth and urban concentration that the most serious regional threats to the global environment will come.

After considering the many points of conflict and interaction between politics and environmentalism, David Lowenthal concludes in the eighth chapter of this book that "the majority shun radical cures." He therefore views such environmental gains as the banning of DDT and formulation of emission standards as little more than band-aid remedies. He does believe, nonetheless, that there have been a few conceptual advances since the day when the benignity of humankind's intervention in nature went virtually unquestioned. First, there is now a softening of the managerial bent toward growth. "Environmental control is now so clearly fragile and worries about risks are so widespread that the most troglodyte industrialist could no longer celebrate mastery over nature as an unalloyed good." This attitudinal change can be characterized as a loss of entrepreneurial hubris. Second, there has been a loss of scientific hubris in the form of uncertainty about what the consequences of an ecological intervention will be. There is a growing realization that ecology is not, and will not be, a predictive science. Third, there is a loss of moral and religious hubris.

> The moral fervor that once justified assaults on nature is now passé. The need to prove superiority has lost its force. Dogmas enthroning our position above nature have lost their sanction. They are replaced by ethical doctrines emphasizing kinship with other living things. Lynn White's ascription of ruthless Western exploitation to a Christian creed that enthroned man above the rest of creation has aroused intense debate. But what is significant is not whether Scripture proves White's point; it is that *both* sides take for granted that the notion of conquest is deplorable. We may enjoy the benefits of technology's mastery of nature, but we no longer morally justify that mastery.

We have confined our detailed annotation of *The Earth As Transformed By Human Action* to the introduction by Kates, Turner, and Clark, to the seven chapters that constitute Part I entitled "Changes in Population and Society," and to Robert Sack's fortieth chapter—in Part IV—entitled "The Realm of Meaning: The Inadequacy of Human-Nature Theory and the View of Mass Consumption." Two additional parts complete the volume. Part II, which is entitled "Transformations of the Global Environment," examines the sub-topics of land, water, oceans and atmosphere, biota, and chemicals and radiation. Part III, entitled "Regional Studies of Transformation," has the following sub-parts: Long-Term Perspective, Tropical Frontiers, Plains, Populous South, and Populous North.

In "The Realm of Meaning ... " Stack proposes a map of the intellectual terrain of social theory. His map consists of three overlapping circles representing the spheres of Nature, Social Relations, and Meaning, with the inner shaded area labeled "place and context from mass consumption." These spheres correspond to the biological and physical sciences, the social sciences, and the humanities. The root problem that Stack considers is the ancient philosophic one of humankind's own reflexivity or, in more traditional terms, of free will versus determinism. If humans are reflexive agents, then they cannot be the kind of objects of study that are found in the bio-physical sciences—nor even in the social sciences, to the extent that they have adopted the paradigms of physical science.

Theories of human ecological behavior can be formulated within the framework of any of these spheres or modes. Stack elaborates on this point:

> We can, for example, reduce human actions to physical ones, and trace the results within the environment. We could even draw attention to the severity of such impacts and describe how they can be life-threatening. And all the time, the analysis would take place within just one mode of inquiry, and in this case the least philosophically controversial one, the natural mode.

* 3.2 *
Cross, Douglas. "The Politics of Poisoning: The Camelford Aluminum Sulphate Scandal." *The Ecologist* 20:6 (November/December 1990): 228-33.

In July of 1988 there occurred an accidental contamination of the public water supply to the town of Camelford in the county of Cornwall in southwest England. The initial discharge consisted of 20 tons of a 27.8 percent aqueous solution of aluminum sulphate. About four months after the contamination, local physicians began to investigate reports of unusual symptoms in affected people. They found evidence of impaired memory consistent with minor brain injury. Other symptoms included significantly increased blood aluminum levels as well as aluminum deposition in patients' bones.

Local medical findings were smugly denied or belittled by officers of the Ministry of Health and the Ministry of the Environment. An official report from the Ministry of Health precipitated outrage in Camelford because it was nothing less than a cover-up of scientific facts in order to protect the policy of privatization of the Conservative government. Thatcher's government was in the process of "privatizing" local water supply companies. If responsible ministries in London had acknowledged reports of adverse effects on public health in Camelford, then not only this water company but other water companies nationwide would have had to invest in alternative methods of water treatment. "Such investment would have threatened the British Government's flagship policy of selling the publicly-owned water industry of England and Wales to the private sector.

* 3.3 *
Ehrlich, Paul A., and Anne H. Ehrlich. *The Population Explosion.* New York: Simon and Schuster, 1990. LC 89-48263. ISBN 0-671-68984-3.

A few numbers and formulas are sufficient to circumscribe the global population crisis arithmetically. The birthrate is the average number of children born to each 1,000 people in a population. In 1989, the global population of approximately 5.2 billion, or 5,200 million, produced 144 million children. The birthrate was therefore 28 children per 1,000 people. The death rate is defined as the number of deaths per 1,000 people. In 1989, there were 51 million deaths in the population of 5.2 billion, yielding a death rate of 10 per 1,000 people. Because the growth rate equals the birthrate minus the death rate, 1989's growth rate was 18 [28 - 10 = 18]. Birth and death rates are conventionally given as rates per thousand and growth rates are given as rates per hundred. Converting to hundreds, the growth rate of 18 per thousand becomes the percentage of 1.8.

A clarifying way of describing the exponentiality of population growth is to track its "doubling" periods—past, present, and future—assuming a continuation of the current fertility (birth) rate as well as the current death rate. Because "the last decade or two has seen a slight slackening" in the growth rate, from 2.1 in the early 1960s to the present 1.8, the doubling period has been extended from thirty-three to thirty-nine years. In fact, the population did double in the thirty-seven years from 1950 to 1987. Given no further reduction in the birthrate or increase in the death rate, the world population could reach or exceed 10 billion by 2027. Although we could avert this fate through immediate intelligent choice, it is likely that we will not avert it because neither the people nor their leaders are persuaded of the urgency of population control. The Ehrlichs warn us bluntly:

> Nature may end the population explosion for us [emphasis theirs]—in very unpleasant ways [emphasis ours]—well before 10 billion is reached.

The Ehrlichs adduce disturbing evidence of a wide-spread misunderstanding of the idea of overpopulation on the part of people who should know better. Thus, a pillar of the American business establishment, Forbes magazine (20 March 1989), offered the following observation: "If all the people from China and India lived in the continental United States (excluding Alaska) this country would still have a smaller population density than England, Holland, or Belgium." The Ehrlichs' response to Malcolm Forbes is, "So what?" Density of population is irrelevant to the concept of overpopulation.

> The key to understanding overpopulation is not population density but the numbers of people in an area relative to its resources and the capacity of the environment to sustain

human activities; that is, to the area's *carrying capacity* [emphasis theirs].

The Ehrlichs elaborate on the idea of carrying capacity in this manner:

> When is an area overpopulated? When its population can't be maintained without rapidly depleting nonrenewable resources (or converting renewable resources into nonrenewable ones) and without degrading the capacity of the environment to support the population. In short, if the long-term carrying capacity of an area is clearly being degraded by its current human occupants, that area is overpopulated. *By this standard, the entire planet and virtually every nation is already vastly overpopulated.*

Adopting T.S. Eliot's antithesis, the Ehrlichs forewarn that the world may end either with a bang or with a whimper. Given the dramatic improvement in the chances for world peace brought about by Mr. Gorbachev, the Ehrlichs are hopeful that the world may well not end with the bang of nuclear holocaust, but they are less hopeful that the whimper of progressively augmenting environmental degradation can be avoided. A whimpering end may be our fate because overpopulation compounds, and is compounded by, every other source of environmental distress. The sheer pressure of excess numbers is implicated in all forms of ecological degradation. Examples are legion: erosion and salinization of the soil, loss of soil texture and fertility, and desertification; greenhouse warming; acid rain; depletion of the ozone layer; and loss of genetic diversity.

The Ehrlichs propose a formula whereby they clarify the relationships between three key variables: population, affluence, and technology. Their formula reads: $I = PAT$. Expanded, this is to be construed as Impact = Population (X) Affluence (X) Technology. The formula can be illustrated by the millions of cars in Los Angeles spewing forth huge quantities of carbon dioxide to increase the greenhouse effect. In Los Angeles, there is a large population of rich and technically advanced people, working assiduously to degrade the earth's climate. A comparable group of poor and technically less advanced people could not inflict the same degree of severe and irreversible damage on the planet. Whatever the precise interrelationships between these three variables may be in any particular case of negative impact, population size is always a factor of importance.

With full approval and obvious enjoyment, the Ehrlichs quote an observation of Kenneth Boulding's, to wit, "Anyone who believes exponential growth can go on forever in a finite world is either a madman or an economist." The essence of the doctrine of indefinite growth can be expressed as, "If we stop growing, we will grow old." A stable population is one in which there are relatively fewer children and more old people. This is not necessarily harmful. While an older society may have to spend more on the care of the elderly, it will spend less on education of the young. The argument from "youthful innovation" is likewise fallacious. There is no hard evidence that only the young are innovative, and clearly the suggestion that huge numbers alone are the precondition for creativity is nonsense. If it were so, India and China would have to be richly innovative societies, which they are not. And if huge numbers were the fount of creativity, how could one explain the dazzling creativity of miniscule Athens or Elizabethan England? The doctrine of perpetual growth is the "creed of the cancer cell." Instead of the economist's "cancer cell" view of uncontrollable human population growth, the Ehrlichs, as biologists, consider growth to be a stage on the way to maturity.

The arithmetic of replacement reproduction and average completed family size is necessary to an understanding of zero population growth (ZPG). A completed family size of slightly more than two will assure that each couple will be replaced with just two descendants. The "slightly more than" is necessary because in every population there are children who die before reaching reproductive age. In countries where there are high infant mortality rates, replacement values are higher. Thus in the United States, replacement completed family size is 2.1; in India, it is 2.4. The contrast between these replacement values and actual completed family sizes for these two countries, 1.9 and 4.3 respectively, shows that the United States is below replacement level and India faces the most ominous demographic crisis of any country on the planet.

To prevent nature from bringing the population explosion to a very unpleasant whimpering end, there are several courses of action, political and ideological, that concerned citizens can take. Political action in the form of direct appeals to elected governmental leaders is one possibility. Beyond that, there is the slow, steady work of persuasion that the concerned can carry out in their communities. Essential to the task of averting the ultimate disaster is bringing people who are just beginning to plan their families to a realization of what responsible parenthood is. Responsible prospective parents should know that they must have no more than two children whom they are to educate to the fullest extent of the children's capacities. The doctrine that the large family has any social, economic, or genetic virtue must be utterly discredited.

* 3.4 *

George, Susan. *A Fate Worse Than Debt: The World Financial Crisis and the Poor.* Rev. and updated ed. New York: Grove Weidenfeld, c.1988, 1990. LC 87/8-35733. ISBN 0-8021-1015-0. ISBN 0-8021-3121-2 (pbk.) First published in Great Britain in 1988 by Penguin Books, Ltd., London.

In the physical and natural sciences, practitioners have criteria for validating and refuting claims made within their prevailing world view or paradigm. Although paradigms may and do change, a discipline's mechanisms of validation and refutation must be functional at all times. "Mainstream development theorists and practitioners, unlike scientists, have so far been *unable to or unwilling to establish criteria for recognizing, correcting, and avoiding error.* For this reason, development theory hews closer to astrology than to astronomy." The reigning development model has been in effect for decades, during which time it has not only not alleviated human suffering and oppression, but actually intensified them. George characterizes the reigning development model thus:

> For the past thirty years the dominant escape-from-poverty paradigm has been bounded on the north by "growth," on the east by "trickle-down," on the south by "comparative advantage" in trade and on the west by "modernization" or "transfer of technology."

She concludes her indictment with these words:

> Three decades have passed during which its magic should have operated but has all too visibly failed to do so. We witness, rather, a fiasco: unmanageable debts, stagnant trade, a permanent slump in commodity prices, tragic hunger and poverty on a hitherto unheard-of-scale. Even the terminally myopic can see that the emperor has no clothes.

The phrase "terminally myopic" is typical of the sardonic language George uses in referring to the two principal international financial agencies, the International Monetary Fund and the World Bank. Also typical is the phrase "hit squads," as in: The IMF's hit squads no sooner disembark from their plane than they order a debt-ridden Third World country to accept a regimen of severe austerity, euphemistically called "adjustment." To avoid distracting contention, George does use the standard nomenclature of development economics; she does distinguish between "developed" versus "undeveloped" countries. She suggests, however, that these terms are also euphemistic. Far more apt would be the antithesis of "dominant" versus "dominated" countries.

The prevailing development program depends on loans from the First World's largest banks (e.g., the Chase Manhattan Bank), operating under the general supervision of the IMF and the World Bank. Should any Third World debtor nation be late in making payments, or, worse still, threaten to default on payments, that nation immediately learns the meaning of the word "dominated." Total default is impossible in the modern world of international finance; the IMF has so many sanctions at its command that it can stifle any threatened default and force compliance with a "rescheduling" agreement. Rescheduling is another euphemism. For the debtor nation, it means being forced to take out new loans in order to pay the interest on old loans. As the price of new loans, such nations are obliged to accept strict IMF control of their national economies.

The IMF prescription for regained solvency always has the same components: increase exports; decrease imports; reduce the national bureaucracy; impose deep cuts on social services; and make these adjustments no matter what ramifying ill effects any of them may unleash and no matter how many self-defeating contradictions they may engender. If six African debtor nations are ordered to increase exports and decrease imports, they are effectively barred from trading with each other. If on the other hand, a debtor nation elects to increase exports of a mineral commodity like copper to dominant nations, it could well find that the price of copper on the world market has sharply declined because advanced technology has learned to substitute fibre optics for copper wire. Product substitution has on many occasions devastated the economies of debtor nations that have been taught to place an extreme reliance on substitutable natural commodities.

Just as the development program depends on loans, so does the development paradigm rest on readily identifiable presuppositions. The first presupposition concerns the idea of growth. The assumption is that economic growth can and should be indefinite and that the purpose of a development plan is to nurture growth at all costs. Development planners need not, however, be concerned with the distribution of wealth internally, for wealth at the top, that is, in the hands of an elite, will always "trickle-down" to enrich those on the bottom rungs of the society. Nor need they be concerned with either the forms or essence of political democracy. Tyranny is acceptable if it promotes economic growth and national solvency.

The next set of presuppositions in the reigning development paradigm centers around products of "comparative advantage." Planners have consistently urged each developing national economy to "forge the strongest possible links with world markets, selling those goods that it can supposedly produce better and more cheaply than other countries and buying those that are better and more cheaply produced elsewhere."

The last set of assumptions centers around "technology transfer" and modernization:

> Agriculture, industry and economic life in general must
> be transformed using techniques and technology originating
> in the now industrialized countries, generally through sales
> or investments of transnational corporations, supervised by
> expatriate experts or nationals trained in their methods.

The so-called Green Revolution aptly illustrates the dangers of asymmetrical technology transfer. The new "green" agriculture contains within it a high degree of dependence on fossil fuels and consequently a high degree of vulnerability to an interruption of accessible supplies. When OPEC has raised the price of crude petroleum on the world market, developing nations, with their newly acquired vulnerability to fluctuations in the prices of fossil fuels, have suffered acutely, some of them unrecoverably.

The extreme hazards of First World bankers promoting the principle of comparative advantage can be seen in the recent history of Morocco. After acquiring independence from France in the early 1960s, Morocco needed help from Western sources of finance. IMF "experts" decided that the country should adopt orchard products as its comparative advantage. Accordingly, the full apparatus of the "green revolution" was put into place, with the usual consequences. In Morocco's semi-arid land, intensive cultivation of citrus fruits for export meant a complex system of expensive irrigation works. This, in turn, tended to concentrate all the most fertile lands in the control of an affluent agricultural elite who profited from the export trade in citrus fruits, while concurrently the country's former self-sufficiency in grains and cereals vanished. In a chapter entitled "Morocco—A Meddlesome Model and a Bitter Harvest," George describes Morocco's bitter harvest. Spain and Portugal, both major producers of citrus fruits, joined the European Economic Community. In so doing, they pre-empted the European market for citrus fruits. The prices that Morocco could command for its citrus fruits declined sharply. Morocco's bitter harvest consisted of plunging revenues and a famine that resulted from its abandonment of its former cultivation of grains.

"There are two debt/environment connections. The first is borrowing to finance ecologically destructive projects. The second is paying for them—and all the other elements of debt-financed modernization—by cashing in natural resources." Large, expensive irrigation dams create a host of difficulties for a fragile environment. Even the best designed irrigation systems—and very few qualify as such irrespective of cost—conduce to increased salinization, siltation, and loss of soil fertility. Salinization in particular is a key factor in desertification.

Some development plans produce nothing less than ecocide. A case in point is the transmigration program being carried out in Indonesia. The plan envisaged the relocation of seventy million people from Java and Bali to the outer islands. The fatal flaw in the plan is that the outer islands are in no way capable of absorbing seventy million additional cultivators. It is estimated that only about two percent of these soils are capable of sustaining systematic cultivation. The plan will have two major consequences: the relocated farmers will suffer acute famine and the outer islands will be reduced to wastelands.

Were development economics a science, as its practitioners pretend that it is, the dominant paradigm would have come crashing to earth long ago. It would have been seen "as worse than useless—murderous."

* 3.4 *

Goldsmith, Edward. "Is Development the Solution or the Problem?" *The Ecologist* 15:5/6 (1985): 210-219.

Peoples of the Third World have been encouraged by the World Bank and other developmental agencies to exchange that which is indispensable to them—their forests, their soil, their water, their culture, and, in the long term, their physical survival—for the gadgetry, the tawdry mass-produced goods, the junk foods, and the rest of the paraphernalia of the modern way of life. "If this is so, then never in the history of mankind, has a more cynical confidence trick been perpetrated on so many people."

The first requirement for the cynical confidence trick to take effect is that the recipients of development "aid" acquire something to exchange for it. They must, therefore, transmute their natural resources into commodities that are capable of immediate commercial exploitation. Often their most obvious resource consists of their forests. They then "cash in" on their forests, which are subjected to disastrous over-exploitation. The inevitable results of this are soil erosion, loss of fertility, increased aridity.

A development plan that calls for a great expansion of cash crops for export invariably concentrates the best land in the hands of the richest farmers, leaving only the marginal land, usually the driest land, to the poor farmers who must struggle to grow food for their own consumption. Over-exploitation of marginal lands greatly augments the likelihood of serious erosion. In San Salvador, all the prime land has been engrossed by plantation owners. Therefore, 350,000 campesinos are left to scratch out the meagerest living from severely eroded slopes. The degree of erosion is so advanced that the campesinos are compelled to abandon their slopes after a single year's harvest. Severe malnutrition, and often famine, are the result. It should also be noted that the marginalized peasants cannot afford to purchase the food grown for export on the prime land plantations. Such food is totally beyond their financial reach.

Prime land was never intended to grow food to feed the local population. Under the development scheme of things, Third World countries must augment their exports of commodities needed on the global market. In Costa Rica, the commodity exported in vast quantities is beef. This does not mean that the average Costa Rican is eating more beef. Quite the contrary, during the 1960s and 1970s when beef production more than tripled, the amount of beef Costa Ricans consumed declined markedly until today they eat less than the average North American house cat. North American house cats and North American hamburger eaters are the only clear beneficiaries of the enormous "development" of Costa Rican beef production, if we discount McDonald's, Wendy's, and other fast-food chains.

Marginal, and usually arid, lands that remain to the use of poor peasants are further degraded through the agency of grazing animals. Cattle grazing on arid or even semi-arid lands are pernicious in that they compact the soil dangerously, especially around watering holes. Compaction leads to salinization and the growth of the desert. Salinization, added to severe erosion, means the destruction of soils and, as in Ethiopia, to famines that can only be called genocidal.

Supporters of the World Bank and other development agencies believe that development reduces population growth, the belief being based on an analogy with Europe where, after the industrial revolution, population tapered off to, or close to, replacement levels. Whatever demographic drama may have been played in Europe is not being replayed in the Third World. The reasons that expectations are not being fulfilled can be summarized in the following way. The transition from a peasant to an industrial economy is characterized by feelings of extreme insecurity. The extended family is undermined; traditional cultural values are attenuated; and the environment from which they earn their livelihood is degraded. In such conditions people will tend to produce *more* children, not *fewer*. Goldsmith elaborates on this crucial point:

> The truth is that birth control is not a technological problem but a *social one*. Thus even in the absence of sophisticated birth-control technology, our tribal ancestors succeeded in maintaining the stability of their populations for hundreds of thousands of years.
>
> To do so, they exploited all sorts of strategies that were built into their cultural patterns, such as taboos against sexual activity during lactation, and during the first years of

widowhood, the prohibition on widow remarriage among certain castes in India, and many more.

The trouble is that once a society's cultural pattern is disrupted by development, such built-in cultural controls—the only ones we know to work—cease to be operative, and population growth, among many other things, is out of control.

Goldsmith concludes that development in the sense that the World Bank uses the term is an economic impossibility, and that all loose analogies to Europe before and after the industrial revolution are beside the point. He reminds his readers that when Britain industrialized, conditions could not have been more favorable. Britain's empire provided both a seemingly limitless supply of raw materials and a captive market for her manufactured goods. Such historical considerations as these lend support to Goldsmith's harsh judgment that the industrialized North is perpetrating a cruel and cynical confidence trick on the undeveloped South.

* 3.5 *
Goldsmith, Edward. "Editorial—The Uruguay Round: Gunboat Diplomacy by Another Name." *The Ecologist* 20:6 (November/December 1990): 202-204.

Although they were sometimes pleased to ascribe their empire building to altruism, in fact the European powers proceeded on unashamedly economic motives. They often annexed countries outright, but usually they did so only when economic penetration through trade was denied them. The Chinese emperors denied the right of trade to the British in the mid-nineteenth century. Because the Chinese disdained British manufactures, the British chose opium as the one product the Chinese people did not scorn, despite its being prohibited under Chinese law. The British determination to force opium on the Chinese as an exchange for the products they wished to import led to the infamous opium wars. "To open up the Japanese market did not require a war." In 1854, Commodore Perry of the U.S. Navy—supported by a powerful squadron of warships in Tokyo Bay—compelled the Japanese to enter the orbit of world trade.

In 1944, the Bretton Woods Conference fashioned two international financial institutions, the International Monetary Fund and the World Bank. Four years later came GATT. These three creatures of the principal trading countries then ushered in a new era of colonialism under the apparently benevolent guise of "development." The three work together as "a single integrated structure, dominated by US interests and effectively in control of the world economy." The role of GATT is and has been to require that Third World countries satisfy certain conditions, among which these are the most important:

Scrap import quotas and reduce import tariffs to a minimum, thereby preventing Third World countries from protecting their own fledgling industries against competition from the established and highly-capitalized enterprises of the industrial world.

Devalue their currencies to make exports more attractive to the North—which has also meant that Third World countries must pay more for their imports.

Cut expenditure on social welfare, in particular on food subsidies which are often critical to protecting the mass of the population from the disruptive effects that rapid socio-economic change inevitably brings about. Such expenditure, according to the IMF, is better spent on western imports or on building up a country's industrial infrastructure.

Undertake to mechanize agriculture, thus providing an important market for northern agricultural machinery and agro-chemicals.

Third World countries that defy the economic commandments of GATT quickly learn "that the gunboat mentality of the colonial era is far from dead."

* 3.6 *
Gray, Andrew. "Indigenous Peoples and the Marketing of the Rainforest." *The Ecologist* 20:6 (November/December 1990): 223-27.
The marketing of rainforest products is a double-edged sword. Industrial society has frequently returned destruction and ecological devastation in exchange for the natural products it has taken from the indigenous peoples of the Amazon. During the rubber boom of 1894 to 1914, indigenous peoples lost up to 90 percent of their populations through "displacement, disease, and murder." The history of indigenous contacts with the markets of the First World demonstrates that it is dependency of indigenous peoples on the marketing system that has led to the destruction of their cultures and societies.
"There are examples, however, of Amazonian peoples who have managed to deal with the market economy on their own terms." The Amarakaeri of Peru have gained control of their territories with recognized land titles. They have continued to maintain a traditional

subsistence economy along with participation in a gold marketing economy. Essential to the continuance of a subsistence economy is control over the marketing process. Such control entails: 1) control over the processing of products before they go to the market; 2) control over the transportation of commodities to market; and 3) control of their own contacts through their national and international organizations to gain marketing outlets.

The World Resources Institute proposes to enhance biodiversity combined with measures to encourage sustainable development. Such an approach is not necessarily culturally appropriate.

> Prohibitions, social production patterns and cosmological questions could all affect how a community reacts to being persuaded to sell rainforest produce.

We must not try to force our economic priorities on the indigenous peoples of the Amazonian rainforest.

> The days when indigenous peoples' problems are solved paternalistically should be over. They are capable of facing these difficulties themselves and we should be listening to their voices. If we do not, we will turn the marketing of rainforest products into a commercial side-show as we witness the destruction of the rainforest and the extinction and assimilation of the indigenous and forest peoples who have been custodians of the diversity of species there for thousands of years.

* 3.7 *

Holden, Constance. **"The Greening of the World Bank."** *Science* 240 (17 June 1988): 1,610.

In response to criticism of its neglect of environmental imperatives, the World Bank has added environmental positions to its staff and created a new environmental department. Skepticism of an authentic policy change continues among environmentalist activists although there is some evidence of revised economic thought whereby the traditional emphasis on growth economics has been modified to accommodate a moderate acceptance of a biologically based theory of economics.

* 3.8 *

Holden, Constance. **"A Heretic Amid Economic Orthodoxy."** *Science* 240 (17 June 1988): 1,611.

The heretic is Herman Daly in the World Bank's Latin American section. Daly is a supporter of steady-state economics. His argument rests on a major premise: the earth's resources are finite and will remain so no matter how ingenious and efficient technology may become. It follows that growth must stop and a steady state be achieved to supersede the fantasy of indefinite growth. Advocates of indefinite growth ignore a central task of economic thought, which is to determine the optimal economy of a country. Daly observes: "There is something fundamentally wrong in treating the earth as if it were a business in liquidation."

* 3.9 *
Peng, Martin Khor Kok. "The Uraguay Round and the Third World." *The Ecologist* 20:6 (November/December 1990): 208-13.

Affirming Raghaven's thesis, Peng says flatly that the industrialized countries, through GATT, are attempting to tighten and extend their control of Third World economies. They propose to achieve control by pressing their current advantages in three domains of economic penetration.

1) Services
The U.S. and other industrial countries argue that foreign firms in Third World countries must have *right of establishment*. Further the Third World governments must grant *national treatment* to such foreign firms. Still further, the governments of the foreign firms must be able to retaliate in the event that they are discriminated against. Retaliation can be simple or it can be what is known as *cross-retaliation*.

2) Trade-Related Investment Measures
Among the existing measures that, to some extent, protect Third World countries are the following: a) local contents requirements; b) export requirements; c) trade balancing requirements; d) local equity requirements; e) limits on the remittances of profits abroad; and f) manufacturing limitations.

> Third World governments argue that these measures are needed to protect their countries' balance of payments position, to prevent unethical TNC [Transnational Corporations] practices such as transfer pricing or monopolistic market allocation and to put a limit to TNC ownership of key sectors of national economies.

Developed countries are seeking, as the main purpose of the Uruguay Round, the removal of most of these protective measures.

3) Trade-Related Intellectual Property Rights

Industrialized countries are using the Uruguay Round to press for agreement to the following proposals: 1) uniform property rights laws will apply for all countries; 2) these rights will be enhanced in most Third World countries; 3) enhanced rights are not to be counterbalanced by obligations; 4) patent rights should apply to all products without exception—this is the U.S. position; the EC position is somewhat less draconian; 5) rights should be granted for a relatively longer period of time than prevails at the present; 6) rights fall under GATT jurisdiction; 7) once such rights are securely under the GATT umbrella, then delinquent countries will face retaliatory and cross-retaliatory actions for non-compliance.

* 3.10 *

Raghavan, Chakravarthi. "Recolonization: GATT in its Historical Context." *The Ecologist* 20:6 (November/December 1990): 205-07.

The GATT was designed as a replacement for nineteenth-century gunboat diplomacy. As such it serves the interests of trans-national corporations (TNCs), all of which are centered in, and controlled by, the industrialized countries of the world. In every one of GATT's "rounds," including the current Uruguay Round, TNCs have demanded greater freedom for their operations throughout the world where greater freedom means, essentially, freedom from restrictions on market access.

In the Uruguay Round, the United States is attempting to incorporate into the GATT framework intellectual property rights, services, and investments, areas that have not traditionally been thought to be "trade" issues.

> If the US-led effort succeeds, Third World countries may find themselves obliged to reduce or eliminate conditions regulating the investments and operations of foreign companies on their territories—in mining, manufacturing, and services such as banking, insurance, transport, wholesale and retail trade and professional services like accounting, advertising and legal practices. Under penalty of retaliatory measures against their exports, Third World countries would be obliged to introduce laws protecting and enhancing patents and other industrial property rights.

* 3.11 *

Ritchie, Mark. "GATT, Agriculture and the Environment: The US Double Zero Plan." *The Ecologist* 20:6 (November/December 1990): 214-20.

It is the purpose of the Bush administration's "double zero" plan to force a sharp reduction in, or elimination of, domestic farm support programs throughout the world. Such reductions or eliminations would put an end to various programs of environmental protection which governments around the world have instituted.

The loss of environmental protections will, in turn, entail many grave detrimental consequences. Among these are: 1) an increase in the land under cultivation; 2) more intensive cultivation of land through the use of more chemicals and fertilizers; 3) loss of income among small and medium-sized farmers; 4) the elimination of programs designed for conservation of resources; 5) absentee landlords and corporations increasingly replacing individual owner-farmers; 6) diversified livestock producers being replaced by feedlots and confinement operators; 7) small specialty producers increasingly being pushed out of the market by large corporate producers; 8) farmlands being increasingly converted to industrial and commercial uses.

The U.S. further proposes that nations no longer be allowed to limit the volume of agricultural and other raw material products which they import. This in turn will lead to local farmers being forced to resort to more intensive and environmentally damaging methods of production. "Those farmers not able to intensify will be eventually pushed off their land, leading to the consolidation of small holdings into huge corporate-style farms." Another U.S. proposal would weaken the right of nations to set environmental and health safety standards, as for example on pesticide residue levels.

U.S. proposals for changes in GATT requirements and standards have engendered some opposition in the U.S. itself. A coalition of environmental groups calling itself the Working Group on Trade and Sustainable Development has come into being. The Group has become cognizant of the fact that the doctrine of free trade could, at some time in the near future, undermine democracy itself. The rights of the states and the federal government to enact protective environmental laws could be sacrificed in the name of free trade.

THE GLOBAL COMMISSIONS

* 3.12 *

Hayter, Teresa. *The Creation of World Poverty: An Alternative View to the Brandt Report.* London: Pluto in association with Third World First, 1981. LC 81-188225. ISBN 0-86104-339-1 (pbk.)

Hayter begins her rebuttal of the Brandt approach to the North-South crisis by quoting a few lines from Jorge Luis Borge's *A Universal History of Infamy*, as follows:

> In 1517, the Spanish missionary Bartolomé de las Casas, taking great pity on the Indians who were languishing in the hellish workpits of Antillean gold mines, suggested to Charles V, king of Spain, a scheme of importing blacks, so that they might languish in the hellish workpits of Antillean gold mines. To this odd philanthropic twist we owe...endless things....

The difference between Hayter's socialist view of the deepening crisis in the Third World and the view of the Brandt Commission turns on the question of whether national and international developmental institutions of capitalism can arrest, let alone reverse, the growing disparity in the wealth of North and South. Hayter argues that inequality is inherent in capitalism, that the Brandt approach to development aid can only aggravate existing disparities. Hayter does agree that there have been changes in the last twenty to thirty years in the relationships between developed and undeveloped countries. Manifestly industrialization of Third World countries has increased, but she insists that it has not redounded to the benefit of these countries. "They are, much as before, doing the dirty work of the West, and they are being unmercifully exploited."

> The increase in export-processing activities in underdeveloped countries is a special phenomenon; it is not a balanced process of industrial growth. As before, the economies of the underdeveloped countries are appendages of those of the metropolitan owners and function in their interest. There are some who ask themselves how it is that, say, an apparently decent Canadian manager of a multinational company can treat his workers with such ruthless disregard. The answer is that he does it because he is able to do it: the reserve army of workers is there and waiting, because for the time being they have no other way of surviving. In addition, in most underdeveloped countries, the supposedly blind forces

of the market are, in reality, much helped by the repressive apparatus of the state, which in turn is aided by the West.

Also inherent in the capitalist world system are waste, pollution, squalor, the promotion of useless consumption through advertising and unemployment. Hayter's position is that the neo-colonial nations of the developed North have poured the old colonial wine into new bottles. Once again, the countries of the South are doing the "West's [North's] dirty work" in new hellish workpits. For Hayter, we have a forced option between socialism or barbarism.

* 3.13 *

Independent Commission on International Development Issues (The Brandt Commission). *North-South, a Programme for Survival.* Cambridge, MA: MIT Press, 1980. LC 80-50086. ISBN 0-262-52059-1.

According to the introduction of the chair, Willie Brandt, this first report of the Independent Commission was finished in late December of 1979. A comparison of it with the 1983 report indicates that in 1980 the members of the commission did not have their later vivid sense of the deleterious effects of development on the environment. Deeply impressed with the pervasive disparities in wealth, health, and quality of life that separate the developed nations of the North from the undeveloped nations of the Southern hemisphere, the Brandt Commission urged that diverse measures be adopted by the prosperous North to build up the industry, agriculture, and trade of the South.

A major recommendation was that special attention be given to "irrigation, agricultural research, storage and increased use of fertilizers and other inputs, and to fisheries development." The proposal that fertilizers be used more intensively is flatly contradicted by the 1983 report, which found that the incautious use of fertilizers was implicated in ecological degradation. Furthermore, the 1983 report specified that agricultural research be rigorously adaptive.

* 3.14 *

Independent Commission on Development Issues (The Brandt Commission). *Common Crisis North-South: Co-operation for World Recovery.* Cambridge, MA: MIT Press, 1983. LC 83-60614. ISBN 0-262-52085-0.

The Brandt Commission's 1983 report was occasioned by the failure of its 1980 report on the dangerous North-South polarity of the world's developed versus developing nations to produce satisfactory results. Furthermore, the publication of *The Global 2000 Report*, which had been commissioned by the Carter administration and published in late 1980, was even more explicit in its warnings of future threats to the world's welfare. Accordingly, the Brandt Commission's second examination of the North-South crisis was more somber and less optimistic than its first one had been. Specifically, it found the threat to the global environment to be much graver than it had previously supposed. It called upon the world's developed nations to halt and reverse the processes of anthropogenic ecological degradation, processes that it proclaimed had in 1983 assumed "emergency proportions." The processes the commission specifies are deforestation, soil erosion, and desertification. An agricultural practice singled out for special attention includes the incautious use of fertilizers and chemicals.

The commission urged the necessity for a vigorous and generously funded program of adaptive agricultural research. By adaptive, it meant research designed to ascertain the crop varieties and animal breeds that are most suitable to given local soil and climatic conditions. Furthermore, it argued that research was needed to devise methods of production that are least vulnerable to the high cost of energy. Governments of developed nations must make greater provision for adaptive research and they should not be put off by the tendency of results to be indirect and slow to become manifest. An augmented program of adaptive agricultural research will produce the indirect benefit of an increased intellectual and scientific capacity among native investigators in the developing world.

The authors of the report point out that adaptive research costs tens of millions, not billions, of dollars. The failure of governments in the developed world to produce such relatively modest sums is "reprehensible neglect."

Unaccountably the report did not consider the damaging effects of excessive population growth, as the first report did, despite the fact that the *Global 2000 Report to the President* laid a major stress on this topic. It should be emphasized that both Brandt Commission reports were primarily concerned with complex questions of the financing of international aid.

* 3.15 *
United States. Department of State and the Council on Environmental Quality. *The Global 2000 Report to the President.* 3 vols. Washington, DC: U.S. Government Printing Office, 1980. New York: Pergamon, 1980. LC 80-20264. ISBN 0-08-024618-4.

If the present rates of degradation of the environment continue unabated, by the year 2000 the earth's ecosystems will certainly have suffered irreversible damage. Whether that damage will be fatal is an open question. The consequences for agriculture, water resources, forests, diversity of animal species, and the earth's atmosphere and climate will be of the utmost gravity. *The Global 2000 Report* envisages a deeply troubled future for the planet as it enters the twenty-first century:

> The environment will have lost life-supporting capabilities. By 2000, forty percent of the forests still remaining in the less developed countries in 1978 will have been razed. The atmospheric concentration of carbon dioxide will be nearly one-third higher than pre-industrial levels. Soil erosion will have removed, on the average, several inches of soil from croplands all over the world. Desertification (including salinization) may have claimed a significant fraction of the world's rangeland and cropland. Over little more than two decades, fifteen to twenty percent of the earth's total species of plants and animals will have become extinct—a loss of at least 500,000 species.

Global 2000 continues: there will be increased vulnerability to natural disasters and to disruptions from human causes. Food production will be even more dependent on fossil fuel supplies as development projects sponsor and encourage petro-intensive monocropping. Monocropping will lead in turn to an accelerated loss of genetic diversity.

Central to the study's method and approach is the perplexing question of the earth's carrying capacity. It accepts the National Academy of Science's figure of a maximum world population. In 1969, the Academy concluded that 10 billion people "is close to—if not above—the maximum that an *intensively managed* world might hope to support with some degree of comfort and individual choice." At present and projected rates of growth, the world's population will reach 10 billion in 2030. Before the end of the twenty-first century, the global population will be 30 billion. This estimate presupposes a concerted effort on the part of the world's governments to reduce fertility levels. Without such efforts, the figure will be much higher than 30 billion. Population, however, may decline without fertility controls. As the earth's population outpaces its capacity to grow food on a steadily deteriorating planet, infant mortality rates will soar among the world's severely malnourished women of childbearing years. The study concludes on a somber note:

> The time for action to prevent this outcome is running out. Unless nations collectively and individually take bold and imaginative steps toward improved social and economic conditions, reduced fertility, better management of resources, and protection of the environment, the world must expect a troubled entry into the twenty-first century.

The numerical data above have been taken from Volume I of the study: *Entering the Twenty-first Century.* Volume II is the *Technical Report.* Volume III contains the documentation of the government's global model.

* 3.16 *

World Commission on Environment and Development [Brundtland Commission]. *Our Common Future.* Oxford and New York: Oxford University Press, 1987. LC 87-7853. ISBN 0-19-282080-X.

The Secretary General of the United Nations charged this commission to place the environment at the center of its deliberations on development. To re-inforce its environmental primacy, the secretary appointed as the commission's chair Gro Harlem Brundtland, Prime Minister of Norway and formerly her country's Minister of the Environment. The commission is thus the first international deliberative agency to be chaired by a person of Brundtland's ministerial experience and environmental knowledge. In its remarkably well-integrated report, one quest unifies the commission's deliberations: the search for patterns of sustainable development that do not imperil the environment.

Sustainable development is defined as that development "that meets the needs of the present without compromising the ability of future generations to meet their own needs." Contained within this definition are the further ideas, that "needs" are the essential needs of the world's poor; and that the capacity of the environment to provide for the present and the future is limited. Restated, the Brundtland Commission rejects the premise of unlimited growth. The commission postulates six challenges to our common future. These are population and human resources; food security—sustaining the potential; species and ecosystems—resources for development; energy—choices for environment and development; industry—producing more for less; and the urban challenge.

In addition to the obvious aesthetic, ethical, and scientific importance, species and ecosystems have incalculable economic value. It is therefore imperative that they be preserved and their extinction be not just arrested but reversed. The loss to humanity of the genetic diversity that still abounds in animal and plant species could seriously threaten further progress in agriculture, industry, and medicine. As an example of an improved source of food, the report cites one very clarifying illustration of the economic value of a plant. A primitive species of maize was recently discovered in a mountain forest in Mexico. This species is a perennial whereas all other established species of maize are annuals that require annual plowing and planting. When cross-bred with existing commercial varieties, this plant, which was almost extinct, will bestow genetic benefits on agriculture worth millions of dollars.

The nations of the world must adopt an anticipatory and preventive policy with respect to rapidly vanishing species. No longer can any nation afford to wait until grave damage has been done before restorative action is taken. Restoration is vastly more difficult to achieve than is the creation of safeguards for species under threat. Remedies the commission advocates include improved species monitoring programs, enlarged protected areas, and better international structures to ensure the enforcement of existing wildlife treaties.

"Future development crucially depends on ... [the] long-term availability [of energy] in increasing quantities from sources that are dependable, safe, and environmentally sound." Unfortunately at the moment there is no such source. Fossil fuels are not environmentally sound. In fact, the burning of fossil fuels is responsible for concentrations of carbon dioxide into the atmosphere. This, in turn, has led to the gravest possible threats to the environment, increasing acidity of precipitation and a gradual global warming, the so-called "greenhouse" effect. The acidity of rain is responsible for much of the destruction of forests, which in turn is responsible for much of the threat to species. Furthermore, fossil fuels are clearly non-renewable. Therefore they do not meet minimal requirements for a path to an environmentally sound plan for global development.

Since the occurrence of disastrous accidents in nuclear power plants around the world, nuclear power can no longer be considered a credible alternative or supplement to fossil fuels. Nuclear power plants cannot be made either safe or dependable. They pose the gravest threats to the environment on two fronts: the ecologically devastating effects of radiation released in the course of accidental malfunctioning, and the intractable problem of the disposal of nuclear wastes.

After ruling out an increased reliance on wood as a primary fuel, which is of course implicated in disastrous deforestation, the commission argues that there should be a major effort to improve and augment energy retrieval from wind, solar, and geothermal sources. Beyond this, the world's prime reliance must be on energy conservation. The commission is more pessimistic about the prospects for an energy plan than it is about any other part of its task. At present, no conceivable energy plan meets the commission's three-fold requirements: safe, dependable, and environmentally sound.

GLOBAL ASSESSMENTS

* 3.17 *

State of the World 1992; A Worldwatch Institute Report on Progress toward a Sustainable Society, edited by Linda Stark. Project Director: Lester R. Brown. New York: W.W. Norton, 1992. ISBN 0-393-30834-0 (pbk.)

Hilary F. French examines the need for strengthening global environmental governance in Chapter 10. Countries find themselves unable to mount effective environmental action on problems that transcend national boundaries and national sovereignties. If the metaphor of "guarding the commons" is adapted to our present circumstance, then the sea and the ozone layer can be considered as parts of the global commons. In both these areas, there has been spotty progress in the last decade, particularly in efforts to limit ozone depletion. The progress attained, however, is disappointingly limited and much remains to be done in securing compliance with existing regulations.

Above all, strengthening global governance requires reform of the legal assumptions underlying the United Nations system. In the spring of 1989, seventeen heads of state from such countries as Brazil, France, India, Japan, and West Germany, believing that enforcible solutions to problems of ozone depletion and global warming required a new institution within the UN system, signed the Declaration of the Hague. The Declaration specified that the new institution was to be empowered to act "even if, on occasion, unanimous agreement has not been achieved." French amplifies on its startling implications:

> The Hague Declaration is revolutionary because it goes beyond existing concepts of international law, which are based on the notion of a compact between sovereign states that cannot be bound to an international agreement without their express consent.

Unfortunately, three years after the Declaration was issued, it had "slipped from sight." Its principal supporters, among whom is Gro Harlem Brundtland of Norway, appear to have given up in the face of the intransigent resistance of member states like the United States and the Soviet Union. However, the Hague initiative has not been entirely futile in as much as it has given rise to a widespread sense among world leaders that something like it must be reinvented and put in place in the UN's legal machinery.

In Chapter 11, Lester R. Brown examines the requirements for launching the environmental revolution. Strong worldwide iniatives are needed to "reverse the degradation of the planet and restore hope for the future." Although he acknowledges that action by individuals, organizations, and corporations is important, Brown stresses that the role of governments in implementing new initiatives is pivotal, indispensable, for only governments have the power to set in motion effective mechanisms of change. A key governmental prerogative is the power to tax.

> Taxing environmentally destructive activities, such as carbon emissions, the generation of hazardous waste, and the use of virgin materials, permits the market to operate unimpaired, taking advantage of its inherent efficiencies while steering it in an environmentally sustainable direction.

Today Europe is in the forefront of governmental experimentation with tax policy for environmental purposes. In September 1991, the EC proposed that its member governments levy a new energy tax equal to $10 a barrel of oil. The new proposed tax is designed to both reduce carbon emissions and encourage investment in energy efficiency and in the development of renewable resources. The EC's Council of Ministers, however, has yet to approve the new proposed tax, although it is expected to do so. This new initiative will render the EC a catalytic agent for change at a level above the traditional nation-state.

In Chapter 9, Michael Renner investigates how industrial countries might restructure their economies by creating sustainable jobs. Widespread unemployment is not the inevitable result of significant restructuring. Indeed, restructuring may generate more jobs than it eliminates. This is so for the reason that the industries that an environmentally sustainable economy needs are more labor-intensive than are those in today's resource-based industries. Renner concentrates on three broad divisions of an advanced economy: transportation, energy efficiency and renewables, and forestry.

Transportation by cars and trucks as it now exists is a major user of fossil fuels and "therefore an important source of urban air pollution, acid rain, and global warming." For years, governments in the industrial countries have been giving precedence to motor vehicles and thus creating a pernicious dependence on them. Renner argues that we will have to reverse this dependence by giving priority to railroads, subways, light rail, and buses. A shift to these modes of transportation would employ "part of the work force that now assembles, operates, or services cars and trucks." The development of the efficiency of energy systems and of renewable sources of energy will absorb—to what precise degree cannot be determined—most of the workers previously employed in resource-based industries, such as the extractive industries. The purely extractive industry of forestry will have to give way to a "stewardship of forests."

Renner does not suggest that any of this will be easy or painless. On the contrary, he concedes that transitions to a sustainable economy will produce "many losers," but, he adds:

> the evidence is strong that the winners will outnumber them: more jobs will be created in energy efficiency, recycling, and public transportation than will be lost in the oil and coal industries, car manufacturing, and waste disposal.

Although in "Shaping Cities" (Chapter 8) Marcia D. Lowe also stresses the central importance of urban rail transport systems, she is primarily concerned with the question of how they can be made economically sustainable. The answer she returns is the wise implementation of urban land-use policies in "shaping cities." Such policies are, she says, transport's "missing link." Lowe points out that for rail transport systems to become economically feasible, the populated areas they serve must be reasonably compact and uniformly dense. This situation is the exact opposite of the pattern of American cities today which can be characterized by such terms as "central cities," "edge cities," and "endless sprawl of suburbia." Therefore Lowe argues persuasively that our cities must be re-shaped to meet the requirements of cities that are susceptible of being served by rail transport systems.

When Lowe refers to "humane cities," she means cities that are fit for pleasant and satisfying human existence. This idea also figures in Chapter 2, John C. Ryan's "Conserving Biological Diversity." Ryan argues that the single most effective means of conserving biological diversity is the protection of habitat. Ryan explains the connection between a city's humanity and its capacity to be biologically benign in this way:

> But even concrete jungles can support some diversity. Most urban areas have waterways running through them or corridors of unused land such as steep ravines; if their use as waste receptacles is reduced, these can be maintained or restored as wildlife habitat. A number of European and U.S. cities have moved to establish greenway corridors along rivers, old railroad tracks, and urban perimeters. Although created primarily for recreation, these greenways have great biological potential to help *reconnect increasingly fragmented and dysfunctional enclaves of nature beyond city limits*.

In "Confronting Nuclear Waste" (Chapter 4), Nicholas Lenssen considers the perplexities of disposing of irradiated fuel. Two methods that scientists once proposed have already been abandoned: 1) burial in

Antarctica ice; and 2) disposal in space. A third method, long-term storage, is no longer being actively studied by governments. This leaves four remaining methods that governments are still actively studying. Lenssen characterizes these methods as: 1) geologic burial—burial in mined repositories hundreds of meters deep; 2) reprocessing—the chemical separation of uranium and plutonium from fission products in irradiated fuel; 3) seabed burial—burial in deep ocean sediments; and 4) transmutation—the conversion of waste to shorter-lived isotopes through neutron bombardment.

The magnitude of the risk of nuclear contamination can only be assessed when the duration of the risk is understood. The duration of radioactivity is measured in "half-lives," with a half-life being the amount of time required for fifty percent of the original activity to decay. Lenssen particularizes for plutonium-239:

> This means that the isotope plutonium-239, for example, with a half-life of 24,000 years, is dangerous for a quarter of a million years, or 12,000 human generations. And as it decays it becomes uranium-235, its radioactive "daughter," which has a half-life of its own 710,000 years.

Geologic burial is, at best, a calculated risk. The central scientific difficulty is that, in the present state of geologic knowledge, it is impossible to predict that a repository of nuclear waste will be immune against even the common hazards, such as rock shifts and seepage of underground water. And earthquakes and volcanoes create hazards of nuclear contamination of catastrophic proportions.

Because worldwide the politics of geologic burial have become increasingly acrimonious, no government has achieved a consensus on it as a means of disposal, with the result that projected dates of opening of new deep burial sites have been repeatedly postponed. As of now, most nuclear countries expect to have deep burial sites in operation no earlier than 2020. The intractability of the disposal problem has led Sweden to a national decision to phase out nuclear power by the year 2010.

Some proponents of nuclear power who call for a worldwide six-fold increase in the number of nuclear reactors do not even mention the fact that this number of reactors would require opening a new burial site every two years. George Bush's 1991 National Energy Strategy illustrates the point precisely.

> [Bush] proposed a doubling in the number of nuclear power plants in the next 40 years, *but did not discuss the need for future waste sites.*

Other chapters in this volume are

- "Denial in the Decisive Decade," by Sandra Postel;
- "Building a Bridge to Sustainable Energy," by Christopher Flavin;
- "Reforming the Livestock Economy," by Alan Thein Durning and Holly B. Brough;
- "Improving Women's Reproductive Health," by Jodi L. Jacobson; and
- "Mining the Earth," by John E. Young.

* 3.18 *

State of the World 1991; A Worldwatch Institute Report on Progress toward a Sustainable Society, **edited by Linda Starke. Project Director: Lester R. Brown.** New York: W. W. Norton, 1991. ISBN 0-393-30733-6 (pbk.)

Lester Brown's lead article, "The New World Order," states the theme that integrates the ten essays composing this progress report. Noting that the collapse of the cold war between East and West makes it possible to build a new world order, Brown considers that there are two sharply divergent views concerning the form that new order should take. The first view is that of traditional capitalist economics, a guardedly optimistic view. Financial papers and business weeklies regularly announce that the world is "in reasonably good shape."

> Even those predicting a severe global recession in 1991 are bullish about the longer term economic prospects for the nineties.

And yet that the world is not in reasonably good shape is obvious to anyone who reads ecological literature. In fact, with respect to global ecology, "the situation could hardly be worse."

> Every major indicator shows a deterioration in natural systems: forests are shrinking, deserts are expanding, croplands are losing topsoil, the stratospheric ozone layer continues to thin, greenhouse gases are accumulating, the number of plant and animal species is diminishing, air pollution has reached health-threatening levels in hundreds of cities, and damage from acid rain can be seen on every continent.

Re-stated, the two views are those of the economist and the ecologist. Economists believe in the possibility of unlimited growth. Advances in technology can push back any limits, they argue. Ecologists, on the other hand, from their studies of living things in relation to each other and their environments, know that growth always follows an "S"-shaped curve.

> Ecologists think in terms of closed cycles—the hydrological cycle, the carbon cycle, and the nitrogen cycle, to name a few. For them, all growth processes are limited, confined within the natural parameters of the earth's ecosystem. They see more clearly than others the damage to natural systems and resources from expanding economic activities.

The new world order of which Brown speaks is an ecological order. Nowhere is the ecological requirement for limitation and reversal of growth more important than it is in population policy. In "Coming to Grips with Abortion," Jodi L. Jacobson demonstrates an ebb and flow of legislation pertaining to abortion throughout the world. In the 1950s, many nations of the world, including three of the most populous, began to liberalize their laws relating to abortion. By 1989, there were ten nations that set no conditions for abortions during the first trimester of pregnancy. Other nations authorized abortions under varying sets of conditions. The United Kingdom and West Germany, for example, authorized abortion for both social and socio-medical reasons, while seven other countries authorized it only for reasons of maternal health. Ireland, among eleven other countries, limited abortions to cases in which the mother's life is in imminent danger should the fetus be carried to term.

In the nineteen-eighties, a reaction set in. Right-wing politicians sought to re-impose various crippling restrictions on previously liberal laws. Often this took the form of a refusal to fund. When national legislators and executives "re-criminalize" abortion, they do not lessen the number of abortions. All they achieve is a great increase in the numbers of women who are killed at the hands of inexpert operators working under surreptitious, and therefore medically hazardous, conditions.

As Jacobson establishes beyond doubt, abortions are essential, particularly in the Third World, to terminate unwanted pregnancies and to prevent what would otherwise be an inexorable growth of population. In other words, a widespread availability of abortion does slow population growth rates. Furthermore, nations wishing to reduce population growth to less than one percent cannot expect to do so without abortion.

There is only one way to reduce the number of pregnancies and of abortions and that is to increase access to family planning information and supplies. The experience of Denmark is very revealing.

Danish family planning programs focus on preventing unwanted pregnancies to the greatest extent possible by making contraceptive services universally available, even to teenagers. The results are clear. Today, pregnancy rates among Danish teens are less than half those in the United States. Abortion rates among women age 15-19 fell by nearly half between 1977 and 1985.

Alan Durning in his essay, "Asking how much is enough", considers why it is that members of the vast consuming society, that is, citizens of all the industrialized countries, think that endless acquisition and consumption are the roads to happiness. People persist in this belief despite the fact that every religion has rejected it and despite the fact that the doctrine of unlimited growth it entails wreaks grave damage on an already overburdened environment. Ecology fastens the major share of responsibility for environmental destruction on greed, while religion and philosophy uniformly condemn greed as a way of life. Despite this, philosophic thinkers have always acknowledged that the roots of greed run deep in the human psyche. Aristotle, among many other thinkers, said that human appetites are insatiable. If Aristotle was right, then there is very little hope for a reversal of the course of ecological destruction.

Durning does not consider that Aristotle said the last word on human greed. He believes that what appears to be insatiability is the result of a consumerist ethos, an ethos that is itself amenable to deliberate change. Basic values do change. As proof of that, he points to what has happened to the once almost universal habit of cigarette smoking. Forty years ago, smoking enjoyed widespread acceptance; now after forty years of elaborate scientific education in the baneful effects of tobacco on human physiology, it has, for the most part, been relegated to the least-well educated segments of our society. Durning infers from this that scientific education can be effective.

He proposes to use the very instruments of consumerist greed to inculcate a new sense of environmental ethics and a new sense of moderation and restraint in purchasing. Chief among these instruments is television. Some of his remarks on this point are worth quoting in full.

At the grassroots level, the Vancouver-based Media Foundation has set out to build a movement boldly aimed at turning television to anti-consuming ends. The premiere spot in their High on the Hog campaign shows a gigantic animated pig frolicking on a map of North America while a narrator intones: "Five percent of the people of the world consume *one-third* of the planet's resources...those people are us." The pig belches.

In "Rethinking Urban Transport," Marcia Lowe begins with the observation that the automobile "makes a good servant but a bad master." That the automobile is dominant in the cities of the consuming society is incontestable. It is also the single largest contributor to the haze of smog over our cities.

> The main component of car-induced smog is ozone, a gas formed as nitrogen oxides and hydrocarbons react with sunlight....Automobiles also emit carbon dioxide, the greenhouse gas responsible for over half the global warming problem.

We need a rational approach to the automobile, an approach that relegates it to the status of being just one transportation option out of many. By dethroning the automobile from its present tyrannical position, we make it once again a good servant. The other mechanized transportation options are rapid rail, light rail, transit bus, van pool, and car pool. There are only two non-mechanized options, but they are of the utmost importance to a rational transportation scheme: walking and bicycling.

An acceptable transportation system is one in which the need for travel has been reduced to far below its present levels and the need for travel by automobile has been held to a minimum. Obviously, then our workplaces and our places of residence must be brought closer together, and the distance between them should ideally be bridged by the least polluting forms of transit, rapid, and light rail. Travel that is not related to work should be accomplished to the greatest possible extent by means of walking and cycling.

But our cities as currently constituted are not hospitable to pedestrians and cyclists who find that they cannot move through automobile congestion with safety and comfort. Work now being done in the Netherlands and Germany is designed to abolish the tyranny of the private car. Dutch and German urban planners of re-designed streets call automobiles the "guests" of pedestrians and cyclists. The re-design of city streets deliberately slows traffic by the method called "traffic-calming," known in German as *Verkehrsberuhigung*. The Dutch call an area of calmed traffic *woonerf* or "living yard".

> In the *woonerf*, cars are forced to navigate slowly around carefully placed trees and other landscaping. Since motor traffic cannot monopolize the entire breadth of the street, much of the space becomes more open to walking, cycling, and children's play.

In the country recently known as West Germany, Verkehrsberuhigung was originally instituted only in residential areas, but it is now being adopted throughout whole cities.

> Traffic calming greatly improves the quality of life in neighborhoods where it is implemented, and so is gathering popularity in many countries, including Italy, Japan, Sweden, and Switzerland. Such restraints are so well-received in Denmark that local residents themselves are often willing to pay for measures.

Christopher Flavin's and Nicholas Lenssen's contribution, "Designing a Sustainable Energy System," begins with the contention that we are rapidly approaching the end of the petroleum era. The evidence for this contention consists of current estimates of production years of the remaining oil reserves worldwide, at 1989 production rates. According to the *BP Statistical Review of World Energy*, worldwide no more than 44 production years remain. This is, of course, a world average. The estimate for the Middle East is 110 years; for North America, it is 10 years; and for Western Europe, it is 13 years. Because nuclear power will not be a major source of energy—the development of nuclear reactors has slowed almost to a halt in the past 10 years in countries around the world—the only alternative to petroleum is energy from the sun.

Under energy from the sun, Flavin and Lenssen subsume those renewable energy sources that are immediately or ultimately derived from the sun. They are wind, geothermal, photovoltaic, solar thermal, and biomass.

> Renewable energy resources are available in immense quantity. The U.S. Department of Energy estimates that the country's annual influx of accessible resources is more than 200 times its use of energy, and more than 10 times the total reserves estimated for fossil and nuclear fuels.

The costs of the various forms of energy from the sun are steadily declining, and they can be expected to decline further, particularly if renewable energy development programs receive the degree of support from government funding they require. The pace of technological advance will be determined by government policy.

Spokespeople for the petroleum industry allege that conversion to energy from the sun will inevitably result in massive unemployment among fossil fuel workers. Flavin and Lenssen deny this.

To the contrary, a sustainable energy economy would likely have more jobs than one based on fossil fuels—primarily because improving the efficiency of energy use creates more jobs than supplying energy. In the future, the number of jobs in energy will probably grow, and the skills in demand will shift dramatically.

The remaining essays in the volume are

- "Reducing Waste, Saving Materials," by John E. Young;
- "Reforming Forestry," by Sandra Postel and John C. Ryan;
- "Restoring the East European and Soviet Environments," by Hilary F. French;
- "Assessing the Military's War on the Environment," by Michael Renner; and
- "Reshaping the Global Economy," by Sandra Postel and Christopher Flavin.

* 3.19 *
State of the World 1990; A Worldwatch Institute Report on Progress toward a Sustainable Society, **edited by Linda Starke. Project Director: Lester R. Brown.** New York: W.W. Norton, 1990. ISBN 0-393-30614-3 (pbk.)

Beginning with its first volume covering the year 1984, the World-watch Institute has issued an annual ecological assessment of Earth in each succeeding year. In the 1990 volume's lead article, entitled "The Illusion of Progress," Brown calls attention to an anomaly. Whereas key economic indicators show that the world is prospering, in fact, biological production is demonstrably shrinking, biological production being the produce of croplands, forests, and grasslands. Standard economic indicators create an illusion of progress when they fail to distinguish between uses of resources that sustain progress and uses that undermine it. A fatal weakness in the gross national product formula, the traditional economic measure, is that it does not take into consideration depreciation of biological capital. Biological capital consists of nonrenewable resources like oil and topsoil, and renewable resources like forests. By the recommended re-calculation of global economic performance, progress during the last few years can be shown to be illusory.

In "Picturing a Sustainable Society," Brown and assistant project directors Flavin and Postel propose five assumptions about sustainability. Their first assumption is that, if the world is to achieve sustainability, it will need to do so within the next forty years. "If we have not succeeded by then, environmental deterioration and economic decline are likely to be feeding each other, pulling us into a downward spiral of social disintegration. Our vision of the future therefore looks to the year 2030." Next, they assume that new technologies will have been developed within the forty-year period. However, they do not rely on them; they prefer to be conservative and limit their sketch of sustainability to existing technologies and foreseeable improvements in them.

Their third assumption is that the world economy of 2030 will not be powered by *coal, oil, and natural gas*. The rationale for this assumption is the clear evidence linking carbon emissions to global warming. "It is now well accepted that continuing reliance on fossil fuels causes catastrophic changes in climate." Stabilizing the climate requires that global carbon emissions be limited to two billion tons per year.

Their fourth assumption is that, by the year 2030, birth rates worldwide will have been reduced to that level that produces a stable or declining population. As of 1990, 13 European countries have such populations. If birth rates elsewhere are lowered to replacement levels or below, then the total population will be at most eight billion. If rates are not lowered in such countries as Ethiopia, India, and Nigeria, then the United Nations prediction of nine billion by 2030 will be fulfilled. "Either these societies will move quickly to encourage smaller families and bring rates down, or rising death rates from hunger and malnutrition will check population growth." The only humane path to sustainability is a systematic reduction of birth rates.

Lastly, Brown *et alia* assume that the world economy of 2030 will be more equitable and more secure. Preeminently, this means a reduction of Third World debt to the point that the net flow of capital from industrial to developing countries is restored.

Ultimately the creation of a sustainable society presupposes a fundamental shift in individual values away from the acquisitive materialism so characteristic of modern affluence to a broader, more humane view of the good life, one based on richer human relationships, stronger communities, and greater provision for aesthetic expression.

A few points of major interest can be excerpted from one other chapter in the 1990 volume: "Slowing Global Warming," by Christopher Flavin. From September 1988 through November 1989, the parliaments of six national governments considered legislation to curb global warming by limiting carbon emissions. The United States Congress held hearings on a proposal to cut carbon emissions by 20 percent in late 1988. The bill ran into stiff opposition, however, and its main provisions "failed to move forward." The Netherlands, Norway, Sweden, the United Kingdom, and West Germany all debated legislation similar to that contained in the U.S. bill. Sweden alone actually approved a freeze of carbon dioxide emissions at current levels. The other countries have adopted a holding pattern. Thus, the legislative record was one of unrealized promise.

The remaining chapters in the volume are

- "Saving Water for Agriculture," by Sandra Postel;
- "Feeding the World in the Nineties," by Lester R. Brown and John E. Young;
- "Holding Back the Sea," by Jodi L. Jacobson;
- "Clearing the Air," by Hilary F. French;
- "Cycling into the Future," by Marcia D. Lowe;
- "Ending Poverty," by Alan B. Durning; and
- "Converting to a Peaceful Economy," by Michael Renner.

* 3.20 *

State of the World 1989; A Worldwatch Institute Report on Progress toward a Sustainable Society, edited by Linda Starke. Project Director: Lester R. Brown. New York: W.W. Norton, 1989. ISBN 0-393-30567-8 (pbk.)

The 1989 volume, the sixth in the series, looked back on the year 1988 and saw a deepening crisis. "A World at Risk" was the lead article, written by Lester R. Brown and the assistant project directors, Christopher Flavin and Sandra Postel. It was a decisive year for the public's consciousness of the immediacy of environmental danger. It was also a year of heat waves, drought, and declining agriculture. Medical wastes washed up on the Atlantic Coast; thousands of seals died in north European waters; there was news that deforestation of the Brazilian rain forest was proceeding at a faster pace than had previously been supposed; and, as a result of the deforestation of the Himalayas, there were catastrophic floods in Bangladesh.

The authors ask whether the greater public awareness of environmental stress will be transmuted into political action. They do not answer their own question. Earth is at a greater risk than ever before for one overriding reason: global warming.

> Indeed, climate change, like no other issues, calls the whole notion of human progress into question. The benefits of newer technologies, more efficient economies, and improved political systems could be overwhelmed by uncontrolled global warming. Some warming is inevitable. But unless trends are reversed, tragic changes could occur in just the next two decades. The challenge is to act before it is too late—which means *before the scientific evidence is conclusive* [emphasis ours]. The longer society waits, the more radical and draconian the needed responses will be.

Many of the chapters in the 1989 volume deal with the implications and effects of global warming. In "Halting Land Degradation," Sandra Postel identifies the albedo effect as a consequence of denuding of vegetation and as a cause of further global warming. "Albedo" is defined as the ability of a land surface to reflect light back into the atmosphere. A dense forest has low reflectivity whereas a desert has high reflectivity. Land in the process of being desertified or degraded (Postel considers the two terms to be synonymous) has a steadily rising level of reflectivity. Therefore, albedo functions as an aggravating agent that reinforces the effects of over-grazing, over-cultivation, salinization, and deforestation.

Meteorologist J. G. Charney first advanced the albedo hypothesis in 1975. Postel gives this account of it:

> According to Charney's hypothesis, less of the sun's radiation is absorbed at the earth's surface as albedo increases, so surface temperatures drop. This in turn fosters greater subsidence, or sinking motion in the atmosphere. Since subsiding air is dry, rainfall would decline. The degraded area would feed on itself, becoming ever more desert-like.
>
> Tests of Charney's hypothesis using climate models generally confirmed it: large increases in albedo did indeed reduce rainfall.

Global warming assumes central importance in Jodi L. Jacobson's chapter entitled "Abandoning Homelands." Recent estimates of global temperatures rising by 5 degrees Celsius would precipitate a rise in sea level of 1.4 - 2.2 meters by 2100. The areas in greatest danger are, of course, low-lying coastal areas like Bangladesh and Egypt. Rising global temperatures set in motion a chain of baneful effects. Not only would there be inundation of low areas but tropical storms would increase in intensity and in their destructiveness of life and property. As the toll in human lives increased, people would abandon their homes and flee inward.

> Eventually, the combination of rising seas, harsher storms, and degradation of the Bengal delta may wreak so much damage that Bangladesh as it is known today may virtually cease to exist.

The waves of environmental refugees fleeing from inundations of coastal areas will aggravate and reinforce every existing source of environmental distress. The refugees will be relegated to the least desirable, least productive, and most fragile agricultural lands. They will then proceed to destroy these lands by radical over-cultivation. Other problems of unparalleled magnitude will ensue, such as epidemic disease, political turmoil, and war.

Other chapters in this volume are

- "Re-examining the World Food Prospect," by Lester R. Brown;
- "Protecting the Ozone Layer," by Cynthia Pollock Shea;
- "Rethinking Transportation," by Michael Renner;
- "Responding to AIDS," by Lori Heise;
- "Enhancing Global Security," by Michael Renner;
- "Mobilizing at the Grassroots," by Alan B. Durning; and
- "Outlining a Global Action Plan," by Lester R. Brown, Christopher Flavin, and Sandra Postel.

* 3.21 *

State of the World 1988; A Worldwatch Institute Report on Progress toward a Sustainable Society, edited by Linda Starke. Project Director: Lester R. Brown. New York: W.W. Norton, 1988. ISBN 0-393-30440-X (pbk.)

In this fifth annual assessment of the earth's condition, the Worldwatch Institute has again taken its vital signs and found that they are not reassuring. "The earth's forests are shrinking, its deserts expanding, and its soils eroding—all at record rates." Moreover, thousands of plant and animal species are disappearing annually, many before they can be named or cataloged. The ozone layer is thinning and the temperature of the earth is rising and dangerous pesticides are engaged in a race with the rapid evolution of crop pests. These threats to our future on the planet are so grave that they may conduce to feelings of either apathy or despair. Neither emotional response is justified, for we can still take steps to restore the earth's health. Among the combattable threats discussed here are some of the topics treated in the 1988 volume.

In "Avoiding a Mass Extinction of Species," Edward C. Wolf, the associate project director, identifies an important causal component in the endangerment and extinction of species. That component is variously called the Minimum Critical Size of habitats or "the equilibrium theory of island biogeography."

First proposed to explain species changes observed on islands, the theory is being tested in many different ecosystems, and studies have confirmed that reducing habitat size increases species' risk of extinction. Thus data on the distribution and abundance of known species can be analyzed

using biogeographic theory to anticipate the disappearance
of plant and animal species as natural habitats shrink.

In accordance with the theory of minimum critical size, censuses of
wildlife species and individuals in natural parks confirm that the smallest
parks have lost the greatest share of their original mammalian species.
Thus, in Bryce Canyon Park, with an area of 144 square kilometers, 36
percent of its original large animal species have been lost; in Grand
Teton-Yellowstone, with an area of 10,328 square kilometers, four
percent of its species have been lost. To avoid a mass extinction, it is
imperative that we reverse our longstanding policy of fragmenting
ecosystems.

In "Controlling Toxic Chemicals," Sandra Postel analyzes the steps
that are being taken, and that can be taken in even greater measure, to
minimize the baneful effects of the widespread use of pesticides. The
case against pesticides is two-fold. They are the most pervasive polluting
and contaminating agents now found throughout the world. Their
residues pollute soil, groundwater, rivers, lakes, and streams and oceans.
Some of them are known, while others are suspected, to be carcinogenic.
Moreover, the wastes incident to their manufacture are second only to
nuclear wastes as contaminants of ground and ocean disposal sites.

Pollution and contamination pose deeper threats in the Third World
than they do in developed countries. The reason for this is that, while the
governments of developed nations have banned domestic sales of some
pesticides they allow their nationals to export those same pesticides to the
overseas markets. DDT and benzene hexachloride are both banned in the
United States and most of Europe and yet they account for about three-
fourths of the total pesticide use in India.

> Residues of these compounds, both suspected carcino-
> gens, were found in 75 samples of breast milk collected
> from women in India's Punjab region. Through their
> mothers' milk, babies daily were ingesting 21 times the
> amount of these chemicals considered acceptable. Similarly,
> samples of breast milk from Nicaraguan women have shown
> DDT levels an astounding 45 times greater than tolerance
> limits set by the World Health Organization (WHO).

The second charge against pesticides is that, over time, they lose their
effectiveness. Pests have evolved mechanisms to detoxify and therefore
to resist the chemicals designed to kill them.

> In 1938, scientists knew of just seven insect and mite
> species that had acquired resistance to pesticides. By 1984,

that figure had climbed to 447, and included most of the world's major pests. Resistance in weeds was virtually non-existent before 1970. But since then, with the growth of herbicide use, at least 48 weed species have gained resistance to chemicals.

Because of nature's ingenuity in blocking human chemical intervention, we are witnessing a race between farmers and pesticide producers on the one hand and the rapid evolution of crop pests on the other. This is a race that farmers and chemists cannot win.

There is an alternative to an exclusive reliance on pesticides and herbicides. That alternative is known as integrated pest management (IPM). Under integrated pest management, "farmers use chemicals selectively and only when necessary, rather than as the first and primary line of attack." The first line of attack is centered on natural predators of pests (biological controls). Another line of attack consists of genetic manipulation of crop varieties to produce those that exhibit resistance to pests. Pesticides are used only to stabilize crop production, their purpose not being to eradicate insects and weeds but to hold them at the level where they cannot inflict damaging economic losses.

In "Planning the Global Family," Jodi Jacobson asks whether governments can successfully encourage reductions in fertility "in the face of extensive poverty." "What mix of policies is likely to promote smaller families, thereby reducing fertility and raising living standards?" The Peoples Republic of China adopted a combination of incentives and deterrents in its program to hold its population to 1.2 billion by the year 2000. The Chinese program contained many coercive features that only a totalitarian government can impose. It was, however, a rarity in the history of concerted drives to reduce fertility. It was a qualified success. That is sufficient reason to study it closely.

Initially, Chairman Mao did not perceive danger in his country's rapidly expanding population. In 1953, the first census under the communist regime revealed a population of 582 million, but Mao did not understand population arithmetic in a country where infant mortality was low and maternal health was good. The Chinese population almost doubled in thirty years, to reach one billion in 1983. By the early 1970s, the reigning Chinese leaders had become far more sophisticated arithmetically than Mao had been. They realized that the population could not be allowed to double again, to reach two billion by the year 2012. In the 1970s, the Chinese leadership instituted a program of Wan Xi Shao, which can be translated as: Later— Longer—Fewer; or Marry later—wait longer between children (longer birth intervals)—and have fewer children. The Chinese came to view this palliative as a case of band-aid therapy where major surgery was indicated. They therefore decreed and enacted the one-child family.

To achieve the goal of holding the population to 1.2 billion by 2000, the program used a classic carrot-and-stick approach. The carrots offered were substantial pay increases, better housing, longer maternity leaves, and priority access to education. The stick consisted of heavy fines and social criticism for couples who defied the state and had more than one child.

The rigor of the Chinese program has been modified so that some segment of the total population are permitted two children.

Other chapters in the 1988 volume are

- "Creating a Sustainable Energy Future," by Christopher Flavin;
- "Raising Energy Efficiency," by Christopher Flavin and Alan Durning;
- "Shifting to Renewable Energy," by Cynthia Pollock Shea;
- "Reforesting the Earth," by Sandra Postel and Lori Heise;
- "Assessing SDI," by William U. Chandler; and
- "Reclaiming the Future," by Lester R. Brown and Edward C. Wolf.

* 3.22 *

State of the World 1987; A Worldwatch Institute Report on Progress toward a Sustainable Society, **edited by Linda Starke. Project Director: Lester R. Brown. New York: W.W. Norton, 1987. ISBN 0-393-30389-6 (pbk.)**

In their fourth annual assessment of earth's condition, Brown and the staff of the institute examined 1986 as a year in which various perceptual thresholds were crossed. The phrase "perceptual threshold" they adapted from Harvey Brooks of Harvard. For them it means roughly the following: "Enough people must perceive the threat for a cogent response to emerge. Information is the key to crossing such thresholds. Once public concern is aroused, it becomes possible and indeed necessary for politicians to act."

The concept of the perceptual threshold applies with particular force to the events of 1986 as Brown and his staff describe them in the 1987 volume. Clearly the hazards of nuclear power were a major perceptual threshold in 1986, for on 26 April two large explosions destroyed one of four power reactors at Chernobyl in the Soviet Union. A groundswell of anger and resentment swept Europe, particularly Scandinavia where the radiation fallout was most intense and most contaminating. In "Reassessing Nuclear Power," Christopher Flavin analyzed political fallout as a consequence of radiation fallout. For many years, nuclear power had been losing favor among energy advocates in every country except France. France had proclaimed its intention to secure 90 percent of its energy from nuclear power. Despite modest resentment on the part of the French people about contamination from clouds of radioactive material from the Ukraine over France, the government did not modify its official policy. Elsewhere the reaction was different. Thus, Austria's foreign minister, when he addressed the 1986 meeting of the International Atomic Energy Authority, plainly stated the need to abandon dependency on nuclear power.

> For us the lessons of Chernobyl are clear. The Faustian bargain of nuclear energy has been lost. It is high time to leave the path pursued in the use of nuclear energy in the past, to develop new alternative and clean sources of energy supply, and, during the transition period, devote all efforts to ensure maximum safety. This is the price to pay to enable life to continue on this planet.

Other manifestations of post-Chernobyl political fallout in Europe were

1) Finland—Opposition to nuclear power doubles; the government postpones new orders for power plant.

2) Italy—100,000 protest in Rome; all parties turn against nuclear program.

3) Sweden—Heavy fallout redoubles opposition; government establishes a commission to consider detailed plans for previously agreed phaseout.

4) United Kingdom—Opposition to new plants up 18 points; the Labour and Liberal parties call for phaseout, although the ruling Conservatives re-affirm the government's nuclear course.

5) West Germany—Large demonstrations; Green Party makes gains in state elections; government establishes cabinet-level post for nuclear safety; Social Democrats call for phaseout.

In "Analyzing the Demographic Trap," Lester R. Brown calls attention to a gap in the demographer's understanding of population growth, stability, and decline. The standard theory is Frank Notestein's theory of demographic transition. Notestein postulated three stages. In the first stage, birth and death rates are high and population is stable. In the second stage, health conditions improve and food production expands, and, although birth rates remain high, death rates decline; the result is rapid growth in the population. In the third stage, economic gains combine with lowered infant mortality rates to reduce the desire for large families. In this stage both birth and death rates are in equilibrium. Brown comments on the Notestein theory:

> This remarkably useful conceptualization has been widely used by demographers to explain differential rates of growth and to project national and global populations. But as we approach the end of the twentieth century, a gap has emerged in the analysis. The theorists did not say what happens when developing countries get trapped in the second stage, unable to achieve the economic and social gains that are counted upon to reduce births.

The theory also fails to explain why second stage population growth rates of three percent per year—which means a twenty-fold increase per century—continue indefinitely. They soon begin to overwhelm local life-support systems.

The Notestein theory was an undue and improper generalization from European data and experience of recent centuries. Moreover, it makes no provision for the ramifying effects of ecological deterioration.

> Once populations expand to the point where their demands begin to exceed the sustainable yield of local forests, grasslands, croplands, or aquifers, they begin directly or indirectly to consume the resource base itself. Forests and grassland disappear, soils erode, land productivity declines, water tables fall, or wells go dry. This in turn reduces food production and incomes, triggering a downward spiral.

Other chapters in the 1987 volume are

- "Assessing the Future of Urbanization," by Lester R. Brown and Jodi Jacobson;
- "Electrifying the Third World," by Christopher Flavin;
- "Realizing Recycling's Potential," by Cynthia Pollock;
- "Sustaining World Agriculture," by Lester R. Brown;
- "Raising Agricultural Productivity," by Edward C. Wolf;
- "Stabilizing Chemical Cycles," by Sandra Postel;
- "Designing Sustainable Economies," by William U. Chandler; and
- "Charting a Sustainable Course," by Lester R. Brown and Edward C. Wolf.

TROPICAL FORESTS

* 3.23 *

Gradwohl, Judith, and Russell Greenberg. *Saving the Tropical Forests.* London: Earthscan Publications Ltd.; Washington, DC: Island Press, 1988. LC 88-13267. ISBN 0-933280-815-0.

In his preface to this volume, Michael Robinson invokes the strategic and tactical concept of environmental triage and labels it a suboptimal solution to the destruction of the world's tropical forests. By triage, he means saving only the most vital forest habitats while letting those that are beyond hope die. Gradwohl and Greenberg do not develop this idea, but instead concentrate on measures of prevention and restoration that have already been tried with some degree of success in various specified locales. The authors arrange their case studies under four rubrics: forest reserves, natural forest management, tropical forest restoration, and sustainable agriculture.

Swidden-fallow, or shifting, agriculture, the practice most widely followed in the tropics, is the single most significant cause of deforestation. Swidden-fallow is not inherently destructive, however; it is possible to practice it, as many indigenous peoples have done and do, in an ecologically responsible manner. The difficulty arises when too many people attempt to farm too little land. In this increasingly prevalent situation, the fallow periods during which the land recovers are shortened or sometimes eliminated completely. One remedy is the successional scheme, which roughly imitates the natural forest succession. Gradwohl and Greenberg explain the sustainability of successional farming:

> The plot begins as a small opening in the forest, similar in size to a large tree fall; the farmer plants to imitate normal forest regrowth. For the first few years, root crops and annuals are tended before they are allowed to be overtaken by weeds. Perennial shrubs are tended and harvested for fruit, nuts, medicine, firewood and other household products. This system, and the agricultural yield, lasts in the fallow until it is cut again. As for pests and weeds, by the time invading weeds begin to choke understory crops, trees are developing and the closing canopy makes it difficult for them to grow.

Other characteristics of ecologically sound forest agriculture are high crop diversity, tree crops, nutrient enhancement, small plots, integrated domestic animals, and cash crops.

"Upon closer examination, however, it becomes apparent that erecting a large fence around most tropical forests is not only impractical, but probably ineffective and unnecessary." There are legitimate economic uses of forests; some economic uses may even be helpful in preserving forests. All forest reserves must be as large as possible if they are to be effective in ensuring the survival of plants and animals. As with sustainable forest agriculture, successful multiple-use forest reserves have certain uniform characteristics and functions. Local people initiate and manage them in a manner that benefits indigenous peoples. They have research functions; they provide watershed protection, environmental education, and clear land ownership provisions. It is even possible to allow limited tourism in forest preserves.

Natural forest management depends on devising techniques for sustainable wood extraction. Many current programs of forest management in South America seek to simulate natural gap formation. "Cutting cycles range from thirty to forty years, and gaps are formed near intact forest, which then provides the seed for regeneration." Because heavy machinery compacts the soil, it is advisable to use draft animals and overhead cables to move sawn logs out to collection points.

"The restoration of degraded land is different from regenerating natural forest. The primary goal of most restoration projects is to take degraded land and make it productive. It is a strategy that is adopted in areas of severe erosion and soil compaction, where quick action is needed. Normally fast growing exotics, rather than native trees, are planted. Regeneration of natural vegetation, by contrast, is a protracted process. And while restoration projects generally get funding for implementation, regrowth of natural vegetation is still largely a focus of research." Fast growing exotics do not tend to support indigenous wildlife and they are more subject to pests and diseases. Research into the question of using exotic versus native trees indicates that the best results are achieved by using an innovative combination of native species.

* 3.24 *

Myers, Norman. *The Primary Source: Tropical Forests and Our Future*. New York and London: W. W. Norton, 1984. LC 83-13494. ISBN 0-393-01795-8.

Tropical forests are a primary source of genetic diversity and of complex and intricate interactions between life forms. They are also a primary source of congruity between human and nature when it is recognized that people and forests are "equal occupants of a communal habitat."

The defining characteristics of tropical forests are to be found in temperature, rainfall, and seasonality. Thus, tropical forests are "forests that occur in areas that have a mean annual temperature of at least 75 degrees Fahrenheit and are essentially frost-free—in areas receiving 2,000 millimeters or more of rainfall per year and not less than 100 millimeters in any month for two out of three years." Generally such forests occur at altitudes below 1,300 meters.

The diversity of species in a tropical lowland forest is a function of its moisture. As moisture increases, the number, ecological complexity, and subtlety of tree species, and their parasitic and symbiotic life forms, all escalate dramatically. It is the unparalleled richness of life forms to be found in tropical forests that makes them nature's indispensable "powerhouses"—powerhouses that must be safeguarded against every influence that enervates them, sometimes fatally. It is important to ask why tropical forests contain proportionately more biologically active compounds than do other biomes. The answer turns on the relationship between numbers and complexity. The greater the numbers, and there are greater numbers of life forms here than anywhere else, the more intricate become the interactions. There follows a form of "biological warfare" in which competition becomes intense, in response to which species engender unique biocompounds in their tissues.

In considering responsibility for threats to tropical forests, some blame the forest farmer, virtually to the exclusion of all other. This indictment is unwarranted. Myers summarizes the evidence in this fashion: "In short, the forest farmer deserves to be regarded as an unwitting instrument, rather than a deliberate agent, of forest destruction. He is no more to be blamed for what happens to the forest than a soldier is to be blamed for starting a war. The root causes of his lifestyle lie in a set of circumstances often many horizons away from the forest zones. Far from being an enthusiastic pioneer of forest settlement, he finds himself pushed into the forest by circumstances beyond his control."

Commercial logging threatens the survival of tropical forests to a greater extent than any other intrusive danger. The developed world has an insatiable lust for fine hardwoods for houses, furniture, and industrial products, Japan and the United States being the worst offenders. Logging in a tropical forest wreaks enormous damage on trees that are not themselves under attack. The felling of a single tree will fatally wound ten others. Cattle raising in tropical lands, such as Central America, is a dire threat, and the hazards are totally out of proportion to the net potential gain. Irreplaceable forests are being squandered in order to gratify the North American's lust for cheap beef.

All modern plants require an infusion of new genetic material to increase productivity, enhance nutritive content, improve taste, and resist emergent diseases. Because tropical forests are the primary source of genetic diversity, they are nature's indispensable powerhouses. During the past several decades, genetic resources from tropical forests have saved cocoa, bananas, and coffee. Forest resources thus make enormous contributions to agriculture.

Tropical forests represent nature's main pharmaceutical storehouse of raw materials for modern medicine. Plants alone offer a host of analgesics, antibiotics, heart drugs, enzymes, hormones, diuretics, antiparasite compounds, ulcer treatments, dentifrices, and laxatives. There are three main applications of forests to medicine. First, extracts from organisms can be used directly as drugs. Second, the chemical structures of forest organisms offer templates, or blueprints, to permit biochemists to synthesize drug compounds. Third, forest organisms advance the development and testing of drugs and pharmaceutical.

In the control of the environment, tropical forests serve several salutary functions of the first order of importance. Among these are flood and sedimentation control, erosion abatement or prevention, and mitigation of the disruptive effects of landslides, rockfalls, and earthquakes.

> When forest cover is maintained, climate tends to persist with the predictable patterns established through hundreds of thousands, if not millions, of years. We know what we can expect from climate: generally speaking, the same as before, with perhaps some marginal trends that may take millennia to express themselves. Whenever climate changes are in the making, tropical forests serve to modulate their shifting course, smoothing out the "wrinkles." But when tropical forests are eliminated, we can find that climatic changes swiftly ensue, some of them so abrupt and sizable that we have next to no time to adapt to their arrival.

* 3.25 *

Myers, Norman. *Conversion of Tropical Moist Forests.* A report by Norman Myers for the Committee on Research Priorities in Tropical Biology of the National Research Council. Washington, DC: National Academy of Sciences, 1980. LC 80-12477. ISBN 0-309-02945-7.

Myers' report contains three detailed regional surveys of: 1) Southern and Southeast Asia and Melanesia; 2) tropical Latin America; and 3) tropical Africa. Southern and Southeast Asia and Melanesia comprises fifteen countries: Australia, Bangladesh, Brunei, Burma, India, Indonesia, Kampuchea (Cambodia), Laos, Malaysia, Melanesia, Papua New Guinea, the Philippines, Sri Lanka, Thailand, and Vietnam. Tropical Latin America comprises twelve countries and regions: Bolivia, Brazil, the Caribbean, Central America, Colombia, Ecuador, French Guinea, Guyana, Mexico, Peru, Suriname, and Venezuela. Tropical Africa comprises thirteen countries: Cameroon, Congo, Gabon, Ghana, Ivory

Coast, Kenya, Liberia, Madagascar, Nigeria, Sierra Leone, Tanzania, Uganda, and Zaire.

In his analysis of the forest conversion data in each country, Myers uses whatever subdividing terms he needs to designate existing threats to tropical forests in that country. In his section on Indonesia, he cites shifting cultivation, timber exploitation, and the transmigration program. In the Ivory Coast, he attributes rapid conversion to timber exploitation and agricultural expansion. In Brazil, he adds cattle raising as a major cause.

Indonesia

Indonesia is composed of more than 13,000 islands, of which 3,400 are inhabited. The islands, constituting a 5,000-km chain, lie astride the equator between Asia and Australia. They link two biogeographic zones with two distinctly different continental biota. The country's total remaining forested area cannot be measured accurately, but, circa 1978, there were "probably as little as 850,000 square kilometers, conceivably as low as 800,000 square kilometers." Much of its remaining lowland forest, primarily rain forest, is undergoing broadscale conversion at a rapid rate as a result of the inroads being made by shifting cultivation, timber exploitation, and transmigration. Very little will be left in Sumatra and Sulawesi by 1990; in Kalimantan by 1995; and in Irian Java by 2000.

Shifting cultivation is a dominant land-use pattern in most of Indonesia. "At least 12 million people are believed to be involved, not only traditional tribal groups but also landless peasants." It is probable that "between 280,000 and 370,000 square kilometers of former forest land have now been accounted for through shifting cultivation, of which 160,000 square kilometers are considered to be in critical condition."

Indonesia has encouraged broadscale timber exploitation since the mid-1960s. National commercial legislation offered generous incentives to foreign corporations to cut and export the country's forest resources at the rate of at least ten to fifteen trees per hectare. This level of harvest fatally damages between one-third and two-thirds of the residual forest. Moreover, such intensive harvesting leaves 30 percent of the ground exposed. "In these circumstances, there is little prospect of the forest regenerating itself within a harvest cycle of thirty-five years, which is supposed to allow a forest to be sustained."

The government of Indonesia designed its transmigration program to move some of the excess population from Java, Madura, and Bali to more sparsely populated outer islands. The ultimate goal is to relocate two million families, or twelve to fifteen million people. The land that has been and is being allocated to these new settlers on the outer islands is not fair quality agricultural land. The government is therefore compelling the settlers to become shifting cultivators.

Ivory Coast

In the Ivory Coast, it is a combination of timber exploitation and agricultural expansion that has resulted in a rapid conversion of the country's moist forests. The government has allowed its capital stock of moist forests to be exploited on a once-and-for-all basis, without any consideration being given to sustainability of harvest. The pattern of conversion works in the following manner: for every five square meters of logs removed, one hectare of residual forest will be eliminated through follow-on cultivators.

Brazil

Brazil's commitment to the expansion of its cattle-raising strategy for Amazonia compels ranchers to steadily encroach on the adjacent forest. As the soil becomes exhausted of its nutrients, the owner can pre-empt a tract of undisturbed forest and hence start the process of soil degradation and soil replacement anew, at the expense of the moist forest. The position of the government is that this kind of development is legitimate because the supply of forest is inexhaustible.

* 3.26 *

Myers, Norman, and Richard Tucker. "Deforestation in Central America: Spanish Legacy and North American Consumers." *Environmental Review* 11 (Spring 1987): 55-71.

In 1500, forests covered about 500,000 square kilometers of Central America; in 1950 about 400,000; today only 200,000 square kilometers remain forested. Myers and Tucker ascribe this extensive deforestation to a convergence of the Spanish legacy of the *hacienda*, the land hunger of the *campesinos*, and the explosive growth of cattle ranching in Central America in response to an insatiable North American appetite for cheap imported beef. The colonial Spanish administrators introduced into the area the hacienda system, which concentrated huge blocks of land in the hands of a land-owning oligarchy. Before the triumph of the Sandinistas in Nicaragua in 1979, the Somoza family alone owned about one-quarter of the country's agricultural land.

Although this was an extreme example, the situation was almost as bad in the other five republics of Central America. Such inequity in land ownership relegated the independent peasant to an increasingly marginal economic position. With the best agricultural land pre-empted by the land-owning elite, the peasants retreated to the forested hillsides where they practiced a form of "slash and burn" agriculture. They would clear a section of the forest, cultivate it intensively for a few years until unscientific farming techniques exhausted and eroded the soil, and finally abandon it for still further reaches of the forested slopes. When they abandoned previously farmed sections, these would revert to second forest growth and become excellent cattle pasturage lands. These in turn were added to the haciendas.

The peasants became the agents for the steady enlargement of the cattle ranching haciendas at the expense of the shrinking forest, as a vast new export market for cheap, grass-fed beef provided the stimulus to accelerated cattle raising. "For two decades 1955 beef exports soared from 20,000 to almost 150,000 tons a year, most of it shipped to the United States." In the 1980s, exports of beef to the United States began to decline. "Although the connection between North American hamburgers and deforestation in Central America is greatly reduced for the present, its twenty-year history is a salient reminder of how marketplace pressures from the developed world have influenced the environment, most notably tropical forests, in the developing world."

Central American forests possess an extraordinarily rich diversity of genetic resources. The wanton destruction of this diversity of phytochemicals produces an irreversible loss of numerous species that might have been of great value in the treatment of cancer and other life-threatening diseases.

* 3.27 *

World Resources Institute. *Tropical Forests: A Call for Action, Pt. I, The Plan; Pt. II, Case Studies; and Pt. III, Country Investment Profiles.* Washington, DC: World Resources Institute, 1985. LC 85-51864. ISBN 0-915825-10-4.

"World Resources Institute gratefully acknowledges the financial support provided for this project by the World Bank, the United Nations Development Programme, the U.S. Agency for International Development, the Canadian International Development Agency, the Netherlands Government, and the W. Alton Jones Foundation."

The Institute's plan recommends to national governments and development assistance agencies six proposals for accelerated action: 1) Strengthen the capabilities for policy formulation and planning by national forestry administrations; 2) Improve integration of agriculture and forestry in research, training, and extension through collaborative research programs, revised curricula, and restructuring of extension programs; 3) Emphasize agroforestry, socioeconomic factors in forestry and land use, low-cost technologies for rural forestry programs, and extension techniques in training programs; 4) Strengthen national research, training, and education institutions and develop stronger links between national and regional institutions; 5) Concentrate on a few high-priority research topics with high potential impact on rural poverty; 6) Involve local people in extension and outreach programs.

Part II, Case Studies reports on numerous encouraging experiments in conservation of tropical forest ecosystems, forest management for industrial uses, watershed management, and agroforestry. Agroforestry is the systematic exploitation of trees for multiple purposes, such as fodder, fruit, and building poles in addition to fuelwood. It entails the use of the silvicultural techniques of pollarding, coppicing, and pruning. Their successful use in Bangladesh, Burkina Faso, the Philippines, and India has meant the lifetime yield of a tree is much greater than it would have been if the tree had been allowed to grow and then felled for its stem volume. In China, the Northwest Institute of Soil and Water Conservation was able to use aerial seeding to reclaim a wasteland that was inaccessible by road. "In the 400-millimeter grassland zone, 30 indigenous species and some exotics were tested. By far the most successful was common alfalfa/lucerne when sown at 2.25 kilograms per hectare. Striking results were obtained just 3 years after aerial seeding."

Mexico's biosphere reserves, Mapini and La Michilla, contain examples of the world's tropical forest ecosystems. They illustrate how "an area can be used for long-term environmental monitoring, research and education, while also encouraging sustainable development that fosters the support and participation of local people." At the center of both reserves is a core zone that is devoted exclusively to scientific research. Around the core zones, farming and other uses of the land are permitted. Mapini lies within a semi-desert basin while La Michilla has "a central core of relatively unmodified, mountainous terrain covered in evergreen vegetation."

Part III summarizes the investment needs of eleven to thirty-three countries in four categories. These are: 1) fuelwood and agroforestry; 2) land use on upland watersheds; 3) forest management for industrial uses; and 4) conservation of tropical forest ecosystems.

* 3.28 *

Shiva, Vandana. "Forestry Myths and the World Bank: A Critical Review of Tropical Forests: A Call for Action." *The Ecologist* 17:4-5 (1987): 142-149.

The World Resources Institute (WRI) plan revives, propounds, and perpetuates four myths about the causes of deforestation: 1) "That people, not profits, are the primary cause of tropical deforestation; 2) That the 'developed' world has protected its forests and must teach conservation to the Third World; 3) That commercial forestry, based on private ownership, can solve the fuelwood crisis for the poor; 4) That commercial afforestation can guarantee ecological recovery."

Shiva denies the allegation of the World Bank that Ethiopia's poor are responsible for the degradation of the highlands of that country. She sketches an alternative view of a tragic chain of events. The government of Ethiopia opted for a rapid development of the Awash Valley for the cultivation of cotton and sugar as export commodities. To make way for large plantations in the lowlands, Afar pastoralists were driven from their traditional lowland pastures and forced to flee into the fragile uplands. These fragile uplands were then overgrazed and degraded.

She summarizes the Ethiopian case: "The degradation of the Ethiopian highlands thus needs to be viewed in the context of the introduction of commercial export agriculture in the lowlands, and the consequent displacement of nomads and peasants. It is not local ignorance but the exploitation of land and forests by commercial companies that is responsible for the tropical forest crisis."

Shiva is even harsher in her critique of the WRI's concept of "scientific forestry." She says of the Institute that it is engaging in a form of Orwellian double-speak in which "ecological destruction is called environmental protection." The Institute's view of forest development is centered on the reductionist economic ideas of productivity and profit, unmediated by, and without reference to, two necessary ecological ideas: multiple use—as opposed to all forms of monocropping—and sustainability of yield. The multiple functions, which forests should and must serve are soil and water stabilization and the provision of food, fodder, fuel, and fertilizer.

Shiva denies that commercial tree planting can ensure ecological recovery, citing India's Nayer Watershed project, which was funded at $6,912 million. This project introduced intensive chemical farming, while ignoring traditional techniques of soil conservation. As a result of the chemical pollution thus produced, there has been severe degradation of the water in the watershed.

Shiva contrasts two opposing views on the most effective mechanism of ecological recovery. The View from Washington holds that: "Profitability criteria can be an exclusive and effective guide to ecological rehabilitation." The View from the People holds that: "Exclusive concern with profitability has caused ecological destruction and therefore cannot reverse it. Afforestation programmes based on profitability alone can become ecological hazards in themselves."

* 3.29 *

Renner, Magda. "A Critical Review of Tropical Forests: A Call for Action." *The Ecologist* 17:4-5 (1987): 150.

The World Resources Institute (WRI) plan fails to go to the root of the problem, which is, the ruthless exploitation of tropical forests by transnational corporations and national government departments, financed by the destructive international aid agencies. The plan makes no reference to these agents of destruction and, instead, blames the rural poor for disastrous deforestation. Renner is emphatic in her categorical rejection of the plan, particularly as it applies to the Amazonian rain forest of Brazil. The authors of the plan have allowed considerations of economic return to negate "social and long-term ecological imperatives." She charges that the authors of the plan confuse that which is technically feasible and economically rewarding today with progress and sustainable development. Its principal aim is economic and industrial growth and not the conservation of the Amazonian rain forest.

WARFARE AND UNDERDEVELOPMENT

* 3.30 *

Herbicides in War: The Long-Term Ecological and Human Consequences, edited by Arthur H. Westing. [Prepared by] Stockholm International Peace Research Institute. London: Taylor and Francis Ltd., 1984. LC 84-2468. ISBN 0-85066-265-6.

Herbicides in War is an outgrowth of an independent "International Symposium on Herbicides and Defoliants in War: The Long-Term Effects on Man and Nature" that was held in Ho Chi Minh City on 13-20 January 1983. Herbicides used in the Second Indochina War were the final result of secret experiments in chemical warfare that the governments of the United States and the United Kingdom carried out during World War II. The discovery of phenoxy and other chemicals that mimic plant hormones made during those experiments led ultimately to "agents orange, white and blue" used by the United States military in Vietnam, the first extensive use of such chemical agents in war. During the eleven-year period of 1961-1971, the United States sprayed 44,338 hectoliters of agent orange, 18,835 hectoliters of agent white, and 8,182 hectoliters of agent blue for a total of 72,354 hectoliters of herbicides. "The damage to nature involved the death of millions of trees and often their replacement by grasses, maintained to this day by subsequent periodic fires." Other long-term effects of the chemical spraying include: 1) deep, lasting inroads into the mangrove habitat; 2) widespread site debilitation via soil erosion and loss of nutrients in solution; 3) decimation of terrestrial wildlife primarily via destruction of their habitat; 4) losses in freshwater fish, largely because of reduced availability of food species; and 5) a possible contribution to declines in offshore fishery. Harmful effects on human populations include "long-lasting neuro-intoxications as well as the possibility of increased incidences of hepatitis, liver cancer, chromosomal damage, and adverse outcomes of pregnancy from exposed fathers." Westing elaborates on these baneful effects, whether verified, probable, or merely possible, in Chapters 2 through 9 of the book, which are detailed below.

Chapter 2) Terrestrial Plant Ecology and Forestry

Herbicides severely damaged the dense semi-evergreen (seasonal) forests of South Vietnam. Aerial photography shows that early estimates of damage were too low. Fire is a continuing source of danger to grass-dominated areas. Fires must be controlled if recovery within decades rather than centuries is hoped for.

Chapter 3) Terrestrial Animal Ecology

In order to advance recovery of forest habitat for animals in the sprayed areas of Vietnam, the report recommends that those in charge of the work of restoration make changes in their programs and research plans. Animal ecologists should develop land-use policies for the inland forests. Research is urgently needed in the dynamics of faunal change in forests that are subjected to chemical disruption.

Chapter 4) Soil Ecology

"Nguyen Hung Phuc, et al., have recently found arsenic in the soil in areas treated by cacodylic acid (Agent Blue) roughly 15 years earlier. Although they pointed out that organic arsenic compounds may not be toxic as such, they may be transformed at some time into trivalent arsenic that is toxic. They also found chlorophenol degradation products of Agent Orange sprayed during that period still present in the soil."

Chapter 5) Coastal, Aquatic, and Marine Ecology

The consequences of herbicides on Vietnam's coastal, aquatic, and marine ecology include, *inter alia*, barren and degraded mangrove soils; loss or deformation of aquatic species; and reduction in fishery yields.

Chapter 6) Cancer and Clinical Epidemiology

"The most convincing evidence of a causal link between phenoxy herbicide exposure and increased risk of malignancy in humans is that of Hardell and colleagues. These authors discovered that workers (agricultural and forestry sprayers) occupationally exposed to these compounds suffer from a markedly elevated incidence of soft-tissue sarcomas and malignant lymphomas."

Chapter 7) Reproductive Epidemiology

"There is sufficient apparent evidence of adverse reproductive effects in Viet Nam following exposure to herbicides to indicate the need for continued and expanded investigation."

Chapter 8) Cytogenetics

"Some *in vitro* tests suggest that dioxin, a contaminant associated with the phenoxy herbicide 2,4,5-T, is a mutagen and thus perhaps as well a mammalian carcinogen." Direct tests for dioxin carcinogenicity using rodents have confirmed that the chemical does cause cancer in animals, but whether it does so in humans has not yet been established.

"Disturbing indications exist from Viet Nam that exposure to phenoxy herbicides will cause chromosome aberrations."

Chapter 9) Conclusions on Dioxin Chemistry.

"It is highly recommended that further research on critical samples from Viet Nam be performed."

* 3.31 *

Nietschmann, Bernard. "Battlefields of Ashes and Mud." *Natural History* (November/December 1990): 35-37.

"The environment has always been both a military target and a casualty of war." Though attacks on the environment are old—the first use of chemical warfare occurred 3,000 years ago when Abimelech's forces spread salt on the conquered city of Shechem—the intensity and magnitude of environmental destruction rose to unparalled heights in Vietnam when U.S. forces pioneered the technique of "bomb the haystack." Looking for guerrillas in a forest or community is like looking for a needle-in-a-haystack; therefore, forget the needle and bomb the haystack. According to R. Kipp, chief historian of the Strategic Air Command, "Guerrillas are not fought with rifles, but rather are located and then bombed to oblivion." A celebrated commander of SAC once said that he proposed to "bomb Hanoi back into the stone age."

It is not only wars themselves that wreak immeasurable devastation; preparations for future wars run a close second, and especially is this so with respect to the production and testing of nuclear weapons. The United States, Great Britain, and France have detonated more than two hundred nuclear devices on or near the Pacific Ocean alone. The French record of testing violence has attained horrendous proportions.

> Beginning in 1966, France detonated 132 nuclear weapons on Moruroa and Fangatuafa atolls in the South Pacific. On Moruroa the bombing created fissures a half mile long and eighteen inches wide in the coral base, blew large pieces out of its sides, collapsed the entire atoll until it is barely awash above the sea, and produced more than one million leaking bags and barrels of radioactive waste.

Furthermore, the collapse of the coral reef may have caused the proliferation of single-celled, toxin-producing organisms that many species of fish devour. The result of this food chain is that "ciguatera fish poisoning is now a public health and economic problem on many Pacific islands where people depend on fish for food and income." And on Johnson Island:

> The United States is planning to incinerate expired-date chemical and biological weapons materials despite the protests of island peoples living downwind and downstream.

* 3.32 *

Nietschmann, Bernard. "Conservation by Conflict in Nicaragua." *Natural History* (November 1990): 42-48.

In the mid-1970s the Sandinistas launched their first serious efforts to subvert the Somoza dictatorship. From that time to February 1990 Nicaragua suffered large scale casualties and deep impoverishment from intermittent civil war. Anomalously civil war relieved the pressure that a peace economy placed on the country. As war waged between the Sandinistas and Somocistas and then between the Sandinistas and the Miskitus and the U.S.-supported Contras, the threat to the country's natural resources receded. Ecological relief was effected in several ways. During sixteen years of civil war, insurgencies were carried on by guerrillas operating in the forests, and the government in power would infiltrate the forests to capture the armed guerrillas. Hunters could no longer safely shoot game for fear of disclosing their positions and of being taken for guerrillas. Animal populations, therefore, quickly rebounded. Ecological relief also came about through the decline of deforestation. Ranches were no longer profitable, and therefore there was no pressure to expand into surrounding forests. Also the cattle populations declined sharply as warring factions slaughtered cattle for immediate food.

* 3.33 *

Pfeiffer, E. W. "Degreening Vietnam." *Natural History* (November 1990): 37-40.

For ten years beginning in 1961, U.S. air forces sprayed about ten million gallons of herbicidal chemicals on South Vietnam. Herbicides are chemicals that either defoliate or mimic and accelerate the action of plants' growth hormones, causing their leaves to drop off. Mangrove forests were particularly vulnerable to agent orange, a prime weapon in the U.S. chemical arsenal.

The mangrove forest is a transition zone between land and sea. As a coastline accretes, mangroves invade the new soil and hold it against the erosive action of wind, wave, current, and tide.

The mangrove tree is equipped with a special filtering system that filters out most of the salt of seawater that enters the tree from its roots. It is the presence of a highly effective filtering membrane that enables the mangrove to flourish in brackish or sea water and thereby to solidify the coastline against erosive forces. This is not the mangrove's only ecological function.

Mangrove leaves, decomposing in the mud or tidal water, supply an enormous amount of nutrients and thus support a great variety of life—especially invertebrates such as snails, crabs, and mollusks.

The consequences of the chemical destruction of mangrove forests were predictable. It could have been predicted that there would be enormous loss of animal and plant populations, including the extinction of some species. There has been at least as much loss as anyone predicted. It could have been predicted that severe erosion of the exposed tidal soils would ensue. There has been such erosion of the coastline.

After the cessation of chemical spraying, there has been slow, very slow, recovery. Dr. Arthur Westing, a noted authority on the ecological effects of warfare, states that: "Substantial recovery can [will] take more than a century."

* 3.34 *

Quy, Vo. "On the Wings of Peace." *Natural History* (November 1990): 40-41.

During the Vietnam War, in order to drive the Viet Cong out of one of its major bases, U.S. forces attempted to drain all the water out of the Plain of Reeds in the Mekong Delta. The American program of systematic ecological devastation proceeded through a series of steps. First, canals were dug; then because the soil dried out, sulfur rose to the surface, producing sulfuric acid. This, in turn, cut the pH down to 3.9 or lower, with the consequence that crops, especially rice, could no longer be grown. "The residual water in the canals was affected even more than the soil, having a pH of about 2.8. Freshwater fish and floating rice, once rich and important sources of food for local wildlife, gradually disappeared."

During the dry season, this area now had virtually no water to accommodate water-dwelling animals. Flocks of birds, including cranes, greater adjutants, Asian openbills, and cormorants, had to find their habitats elsewhere. Besides digging the drainage canals, U.S. troops sprayed the plain with toxic chemicals and napalm to destroy all cajeput forests.

After the war, the people of the Mekong Delta, working closely with scientists from Hanoi University, made tremendous efforts to revive the ecology of the devastated area. Those efforts have resulted in partial recovery. The cranes are returning. By May 1989, 1,000 cranes had been counted. The Vietnamese have a saying: "Birds only stay in good lands."

The crane, a symbol of happiness and longevity, whose image can be found in stylized forms in almost all pagodas, temples, and other places of Buddhist worship in Vietnam, has returned to Vietnam, the beautiful land of peace.

* 3.35 *
Renner, Michael G. "Military Victory, Ecological Defeat." *World Watch* 4:4 (July-August 1991): 27-33.

In assessing the ecologically destructive consequences of the recent war against Iraq, it is convenient and appropriate to distinguish the environmental effects of desert warfare *per se* from the consequences of Hussein's torching of the Kuwait oil fields. Although Renner does not, I shall deal with his analysis of the first set of consequences first. The territory over which the war was fought—Saudi Arabia, Kuwait and Iraq—is a fragile desert ecology. In such an ecology, vegetation, though sparse, is essential to stabilize and protect the soil. When tanks and other military vehicles of the coalition forces maneuvered in large numbers over the desert, they disrupted and then compacted the soil. In so doing, they destroyed plants whose root systems lie close to the surface. The result of such extensive plant loss is most probably an accelerated rate of erosion. This in turn may lead to lengthening of dry spells and ultimately to long-term ecological decline. John Cloudsley-Thompson, a University of London expert on desert ecology, predicts that it may take hundreds of years for the desert to recover from the Persian Gulf War. This prediction is supported by the observation that the Libyan desert still bears deep scars from the tank warfare of World War II, warfare that occurred more than fifty years ago.

The war's intrinsic destructiveness was not limited to the compaction of desert soils by tanks. Other destructive effects followed from the armed forces' use of highly toxic materials "to maintain and operate their tanks, jet aircraft, and other pieces of equipment." The blistering heat of Saudi Arabia required the use of special lubricants that are intensely toxic. Exposure to even trace amounts of these chemicals in drinking water, or through skin absorption, or by inhalation "can cause cancer, birth defects, and chromosome damage, and may seriously impair the function of the liver, kidneys, and central nervous system." Furthermore, the bombing of Iraq's chemical and petrochemical facilities "generated a variety of deadly toxins, including cyanide, dioxin, and PCBs."

As a result of Hussein's maniacal decision to torch Kuwait's oil fields, those fields resembled a towering volcanic eruption emitting unprecedented amounts of pollutants into the atmosphere.

> Roughly 10 times as much air pollution was being emitted in Kuwait as by all U.S. industrial and power-generating plants combined.

And by no means does this massive concentration of pollutants pose a merely local threat, for the geography of pollution is vast in extent.

> As far as 1,000 miles away—in parts of Bulgaria, Romania, Turkey, and the Soviet Union that border on the Black Sea—smog levels caused by the fires are as serious as the smog found anywhere in Europe under normal conditions.

Although in the short term the pollutants from Kuwaiti oil fields may contribute to a cooling effect, in the long-term they are making an enormous contribution to global warming. "It may add as much as 240 million tons of carbon to the atmosphere in the course of a year—about 4 percent of the current global annual carbon release." Augmenting the global carbon release at a time when we should be moving to reduce carbon emissions is potentially catastrophic.

Before the war, Hussein repeatedly threatened to torch Kuwait's old fields. The U.S. government even commissioned environmental impact studies of such a contingency, proving that it took the threat very seriously. Despite the virtual certainty that Hussein would deliver on his threats, the government went to war. Obviously it then considered the ecological disaster that has in fact ensued to have been an acceptable risk. Renner does not agree. If the government had resolved to press its earlier policy of economic sanctions against Hussein, that policy, though it would have been less swift and certain than military force, "would likely have spared many lives and avoided the tragic environmental effects." Environmental disaster is not an acceptable risk.

It was after the dawn of the atomic age that nations gradually came to realize that nuclear arsenals, if used, would destroy what they were supposed to defend. Now, in the wake of the Gulf War and its immense environmental toll, conventional warfare, too, may come to be seen as a less-acceptable means of settling conflicts.

* 3.36 *

Seager, Joni. "Assessing the Environmental Costs of the Gulf War: Operation Desert Disaster." *Ecodecision: Revue Environnement et Politiques/Environment and Policy Magazine* 2 (Septembre/September 1991): 42-46.

The ecologically destructive effects of the war in the Persian Gulf unfolded in three stages. In the first stage more than a half million soldiers of the coalition forces assembled in the fragile environment of Saudi Arabia. The sheer size and mass of this soldiery produced a "staggering amount of garbage." The coalition governments responsible for assembling them made no provision whatever for the disposal of liquid and solid wastes. When Seager queried the Pentagon on this point, she received the curt bureaucratic reply that, by arrangement, garbage disposal was the responsibility of the "host country" (e.g., Saudi Arabia). No one, apparently, considered that, because of the extreme aridity of the atmosphere, the bio-degradation of non-plastic garbage takes a long time in a desert. "The waste that is being dumped in the desert today will sit undisturbed and undegraded literally for decades. We may be witnessing the creation of a true 'wasteland'."

Still during the preparatory stages of build-up leading to war, the manuevering of coalition tanks and armored vehicles across the fragile ecosystem of Saudi Arabia wreaked incalculable damage on desert vegetation and wildlife. Whether engaged in actual combat or merely massing and assembling, a huge military force is a polluting and contaminating force of the worst imaginable kind.

> Not only do they manufacture and consume vast quantities of chemicals of all descriptions—solvents, paints, PCBs, cyanides, acids, radioactive materials and poisons—but most militaries are protected polluters. Using national security as a shield, their flagrant polluting practices have gone unchecked for decades.

And further on the protected military polluter:

> Even if environmental regulations are zealously applied to domestic military facilities, which has generally not been the

case, regulation still stops at the border. U.S. military
facilities and activities located overseas are not subject to
American environmental laws. Even where they apply, in
practice host regulation of foreign military forces is really
no regulation.

Operating with a suspension of all meaningful regulation and behind
the impenetrable shield of military censorship, invoked in the name of
national security, the huge U.S. military machine has created a threat of
chemical contamination of underground water supplies in Saudi Arabia.
Moreover, these water supplies, urgently needed for irrigated agriculture, are diminishing at an alarming rate.

The oil spills in the Gulf and the torching of the Kuwait oil wells,
both predictable consequences of waging war in the region, have
immeasurably augmented the dangers of global warming. Seager refers
to the oil fires as:

[A]n unprecedented catastrophe, and with few predictive
tools at our disposal and virtually no ameliorative ones, we
can do no more than witness the unfolding of the tragedy.

Perhaps the most deplorable consequence of the war has been the
stimulus it has given to the arms trade which is now flourishing. Seager
concludes with a sombre warning:

As more and more governments rush to buy more and more
weaponry, there can be no doubt that we will witness an
escalation in the environmental damage caused by any future
conflict, regional or global.

* 3.37 *

Stockholm International Peace Research Institute. *Warfare in a
Fragile World: Military Impact on the Human Environment.* Preface by
Frank Barnaby, Director of SIPRI. London: Taylor and Francis, Ltd.;
distributed in the United States by Crane, Russak, 1980. LC 79-20421.
ISBN 0-85066-187-0.

This book was written by Dr. Arthur H. Westing while he was a
senior research fellow at SIPRI. Westing systematically examines the
disruptive effects of warfare on temperate regions, tropical regions,
desert regions, arctic regions, islands, the ocean, and finally on the
global ecology. He construes warfare or military action as a special case
of people abusing their environment, the standard case being civil abuse,
examples of which are soil erosion and degradation, deforestation, and
all forms of chemical pollution. These abuses have rendered the fragile

global environment exceedingly vulnerable to the compounding effects of military abuse.

The first generalization about military abuse of the environment that must be made is that it has become progressively more devastating as science and technology advance. The consequences are that, over time, military casualties decline and civilian casualties increase. To confirm this, one exercise will suffice. Compare the civilian deaths in the U.S. Civil War as a proportion of total deaths, with the civilian deaths in World War II, again as a proportion of total deaths. Presented in tables, charts, and appendixes, Westing's statistical documentation of the case against warfare is exhaustive and persuasive.

1) Temperate Regions

All of the world's major powers are located within the temperate regions and 90 percent of the world's military expenditures are incurred by temperate nations. Moreover, it is precisely the temperate nations that have been responsible for most of the global environmental degradation through routine civil abuse. When civil abuse is compounded by massive military depredations, as it has been in the twentieth century's monster wars, the results are devastating.

2) Tropical Regions

The tropical habitat today is subject to grave ecological threats from deforestation, soil degradation, excessive cultivation, and over-population. These existing threats augment the area's vulnerability to the devastation wrought by technological warfare. The use of herbicides and defoliants during the Second Indochina War obviously hastened and compounded the damage being done through civil abuse.

3) Desert Regions

"The desert is only sparsely populated with plants and animals, many unique to this habitat, and both the biomass and the productivity of desert ecosystems are exceedingly modest. Moreover, this living community is easy to disrupt and its recovery is slow. Large areas of the world's desert and semi-desert ecosystems are currently becoming degraded owing to agricultural (livestock) over-utilization and other forms of cultural mismanagement. The plight of the people caught in this situation is a terrible one. Damage to the desert brought about by military activities in war and peace thus exacerbates this already disastrous process of desertification."

4) Arctic Regions

The Arctic regions support some of the earth's most unstable ecosystems. Moreover, they are among the slowest to recover from damage. Despite its extreme fragility, the region was a theater of military operations during World War II. After the war, recovery was not only slow but only partial in extent. Some of the damage inflicted has proved to be irreversible.

5) Islands

The ecologies of most small islands are unique in some respects. "Once such an island is substantially disrupted and a fraction of its endemic plant and animal species driven to extinction, its ecosystem has been irreversibly harmed."

6) The Ocean

Deliberate or accidental underwater explosions, always a possibility when the military operates on or near the oceans, prove lethal to marine life either from the over-pressure of the shock wave or the toxic or radioactive properties of the chemicals released. Such explosions occur with a high degree of regularity. Battles at sea produce other underwater explosions that further threaten the fragile ecology of the oceans. "The over-all pressure of the shock wave of an underwater explosion travels outward in all directions and can therefore be expected—under ideal conditions—to diminish as an inverse function of the cube of the distance travelled." It can readily be seen that the area of lethal effect is extensive.

7) The Global Ecology

Beyond the fact that warfare severely debilitates the earth's varied habitats and ecosystems is a further fact that it is a voracious consumer of natural resources, both renewable and non-renewable. Warfare, humankind's most frivolous activity, significantly adds to the global ecological crisis by taking renewable resources at rates exceeding the natural rates of renewal and recovery and by bringing reserves of non-renewable materials to the point of exhaustion. Westing concludes on a note of deep pessimism:

> He (man) is introducing pollutants into the environment at levels increasing above the point at which they can dissipate and decompose to insignificance—among them radioactive isotopes from weapon-testing and carbon dioxide from the burning of fossil fuels. Facing an inevitable shortage of fossil fuels and the present lack of safe alternate-energy systems, he is turning increasingly to nuclear fuels, which are unavoidably linked with the spread of nuclear-weapon competence and other intractable problems. He is becoming poorer by the day; that is to say, despite continued advances

in science and technology, the world-wide average standard of living—already unconscionably low—continues to decline; and his ability to cope with over-population and other root causes of his many-sided predicament is not improving.

* 3.38 *

Weinberg, Bill. *War on the Land; Ecology and Politics in Central America*. London and Atlantic Highlands, NJ: Zed Books Ltd., 1991. LC 91-13782. ISBN 0-86232-946-9. Address of Zed Books in the U.S. is: 165 First Avenue, Atlantic Highlands, NJ 07716.

By using the words, "war on the land," Weinberg intends to call attention to an ambiguity and a compound truth. Ecologically considered, the phrase is to be construed literally. Agri-business in Central America is waging war on, or against, the land. The creation of huge agri-businesses in Central America has resulted in a large-scale dislocation of people from the countryside to the slums of the cities and to the rainforests where they engage in relentless deforestation. Displaced people are politically unstable and prone to support revolutionary and anti-imperialist movements. They are therefore the occasion for conservative politicians to form harshly repressive military regimes. This is the other sense of "war on the land." It means war waged over the land, over an already ecologically devastated land. Just one example of a harsh military regime will suffice. The Somoza dynasty in Nicaragua remained in power for forty-five years. So entrenched did it become—it was supported by every U.S. administration since Franklin Roosevelt's in 1934—that the Sandinistas had to wage a protracted war, lasting from 1963 to 1979, to dislodge it.

Pointing to the mutual re-enforcement of ecological degradation and militarily repressive regimes in Central America, Weinberg advises that the traditional rationale of U.S. involvement in the region be reversed. Traditionally, U.S. imperialists have demanded that Central America be made safe for U.S. interests. The time has come for a new approach and a new policy. We must make the U.S. safe for Central American interests. Weinberg is explicit about the implications of such a revolutionary approach.

> This means calling a halt to military interventions and CIA escapades. It means seeking and implementing a new solution to the debt crisis in which "austerity" will be imposed not on the poorest in the poor nations but on the wealthiest of the rich nations, the corporate elite who can best afford it. It means restructuring the North American

(and European) economy so that consumers are not dependent on globe-spanning corporations for food and employment.

Weinberg leaves no doubt that the needed restructuring will have sweeping consequences for American and European life styles.

Coffee may have to become a special treat for rare occasions rather than the psychic fuel that wakes us up in the morning and gets us through the workday. Bananas will become less plentiful and more expensive. Hamburgers will be consumed less frequently, and will be made from domestic beef.

Chapter IV

Environmental Decline in

Post-War Africa:

A Case Study

To provide a brief illustration of how the circumstances of economic underdevelopment and ecological decline are reciprocally linked, we can begin by tracing the post-World War II history of Africa. Political histories of the post-war period abound for almost all parts of the continent, since it was during this era that many African colonies struggled for and won political independence. Detailed ecological histories of colonialism and the post-colonial states, however, are just beginning to be researched and written. Nevertheless, several broad patterns and general trends of this history are now becoming apparent, and they can be set forth in rough narrative form even though detailed histories have yet to be compiled.[1]

Throughout Africa and much of the rest of the Third World during the colonial period, rural regions had come to depend upon imported manufactured goods for their household needs or their agricultural activities. Axes, machetes, hoes, pots, cotton cloth, and a whole sundry of petty manufactured goods from matches to kerosene lanterns had penetrated into rural regions during the early years of colonial rule. At the same time, these regions had become accustomed to producing agricultural commodities like peanuts, coffee, cocoa, and cotton to earn the money to purchase these petty manufactures.

During World War II, however, two phenomena occurred simultaneously: first, the supply of European manufactured imports was cut off by scarce or non-existent shipping under wartime conditions. This raised the price of imports considerably, and for some time many goods simply were not available at all. The need for the goods upon which local households had come to depend remained pronounced, however, and in the process a pent-up demand for European goods began to grow throughout the Third World. The second major phenomena, again due in part to wartime stringencies and problems of shipping, was that agricultural commodities produced for sale exceeded shipping capacity, and thus their price dropped in local markets. These combined phenomena created considerable pressure for change in colonial economic circumstances in the immediate post-war period.

With the removal of the wartime shipping problems in the late 1940s and 1950s there ensued a boom period of economic expansion without precedent in previous colonial history. The colonial administrations usually contented themselves with building roads and public works infrastructure while maintaining public order, but apart from these roles they needed to do little positive planning to encourage economic growth in this period. The peasants' pent-up demand for manufactures and their capacity to expand their own production to earn more cash for these purchases were by themselves sufficient to enable most colonial regions in Africa to witness a remarkable trading bonanza fueled by this rapid cash-crop expansion.

The cash-crop boom, although sustained for several years, remained nevertheless an inherently unsustainable phenomenon, ironically because of its very success. So many peasants in the Ivory Coast, Ghana, Nigeria, and the Cameroons turned to cocoa and coffee production that the mounting supply exceeded world demand, and the prices for these commodities began to fall in real terms during the 1950s. As Brazil and East African countries like Kenya entered the ranks of coffee and cocoa producers, the purchase prices of these commodities declined even further over time.

This engendered the classic syndrome known to economists as the "primary producer's squeeze." The dilemma went something like this. Oversupply was at the root of the declining purchase price for these commodities, and it could be argued that the peasants should refrain from producing further cocoa or coffee or the like until the supply declined and the prices came up to a level of their liking. While this might be a theoretical possibility, in practical terms it was never really an option for most peasants.

The reasons for this were simple: peasants had already made the infrastructural investment in the cocoa and coffee plantations. The trees could not simply be turned on or off like a faucet when prices proved favorable. On the contrary, cocoa and coffee were harvested annually and would be wasted entirely if not sold within a fairly short time of the annual harvest. If the weather and pest problems were manageable and a region experienced a particularly good production year, they were faced with the irony of a locally glutted market at harvest time and a correspondingly depressed purchase price. In the face of a depressed price, peasants with fixed or escalating costs or other demands upon their income had basically two options open to them. Either they could choose to expand the scope and scale of their production to maintain or enlarge their income to meet their growing needs, or alternatively they could leave cash-crop farming and go to the city in a search for non-agricultural work. Such was the squeeze most peasants faced in one form or another.

A third option, that of engaging once again in foodstuff agriculture, was largely precluded at the time by the impact upon Africa and other Third World areas of the pattern of agricultural overproduction from the Western countries, particularly the United States. In the post-war era, farmers in the United States began to mechanize agriculture, purchasing tractors, fertilizers, and pesticides to substitute for the declining manpower engaged in on-farm production. The initial results of this petro-subsidized agriculture were very impressive in volume output, and, since oil prices at the time reflected only minimal extraction and transport costs, surplus agricultural production from the United States began to appear to the world at large as an answer to momentary or even more long-term shortages in local food production. Through both aid and trade channels, the United States sought actively to export its agricultural surpluses. Since most capital cities of Third World countries were constructed as ports or trans-shipment centers during the colonial period, it became very easy and even appeared wise to purchase American grain surpluses to feed growing urban populations in the Third World. When disasters like floods, earthquakes, or typhoons hurt the remaining local agricultural systems, U.S. aid agencies provided relief supplies of food at cost through PL 480 funds and the "Food for Peace" program. In the face of the massive arrival of food surpluses from the industrial world, it became clear that peasant farmers—often situated in remote rural areas with poor transportation links to the cities—were not generally able to engage in profitable competition with Western farmers and the state apparatus of industrial nations, which together had the power to pursue agricultural "markets" in the Third World.[2]

The cyclical and self-perpetuating nature of the problem started to become apparent by the early 1960s. Peasants, trying to stay afloat economically, began to devote more and more of their arable land to cash-cropping, which, in turn, provided less and less in relative terms, the more they produced. In the process, with relatively less land and labor devoted to foodstuff agriculture in Africa, not only its urban areas, but also major rural regions became dependent from the 1960s onward on substantial imports of foreign surpluses. According to one observer, "food imports rose from 4 million to 24 million tons during the 1970s. By 1985 the continent was importing two-fifths of its food supply and about a third of its people depended wholly or partly on imported food."[3] Meanwhile, those peasants or their children who had left the village began to swell the ranks of the urban areas with no real prospects for steady wages. Urbanization is occurring at rates that exceed population growth in most of Africa, and at current rates experts estimate that fully

45 percent of Africa's population will live in urban or semi-urban areas of 4,000 or more by the year 2010.[4]

Rapid urbanization produces a politically volatile situation, for hungry urban populations could prove to be explosive. Quite understandably, then, urban-based political elites tended to continue to buy political tranquility in the short run by purchasing food from the cheapest source—the surpluses of Western industrial countries. In order to purchase this foreign food, the state exhorted its cash-cropping peasants to produce ever greater quantities of export commodities so that it could obtain the foreign exchange for the increasingly necessary food-purchase transactions. While exports expanded, commodity prices dipped with oversupply, and foreign exchange became scarce, despite expanded output. In this circumstance the states concerned either had to seek food aid or incur foreign debt to purchase the food upon which they had come to depend. Indebtedness proved to be only a short-term solution for, with the increase and unsteady fluctuation of interest rates, many African countries soon found themselves having to devote much of their foreign exchange earnings to servicing these debts. The overall debt burden for the continent rose from $14 billion in 1973 to an estimated $125 billion in 1987.[5]

The rapid rates of urbanization that contributed to the pattern of collapse in local agriculture had yet another demographic impact on the rural areas. Faced with the departure of the young, able-bodied members of their households, families often resorted to having several children in the hope that some would remain to undertake the ever more demanding cash-crop work.[6] Collectively this translated itself into a rapid spurt in population growth, particularly as this period also witnessed the arrival of rudimentary medical facilities and the equipment for clean water supplies in rural areas. Both of these latter phenomena contributed to the decline in infant mortality, and the result over time was a rapid rise in absolute numbers in rural areas. During the 1950s and 1960s, those portions of these growing populations that remained on the land greatly expanded the areas devoted to agricultural activity without substantially changing the technologies applied to production. The result was enormously taxing upon the land itself and the environment in general. In bush-fallow systems of land usage, fallow periods were shortened or eliminated altogether. On the thin and nutrient-poor soils, the new usage rapidly exhausted arable lands.

In addition, previously undisturbed forests began to be cleared under a two-fold pressure. First, the relative decline of commodity prices for coffee and cocoa left the state short of foreign exchange, and it began to extend rights to timber concessions for cutting and exporting tropical hardwoods as a means of shoring up sagging trade balances. Secondly, peasants hoping for new cash-cropping opportunities or those in search of fertile land for growing food began to encroach upon remaining zones of uncut forest.

Removal of large portions of tropical forest cover and conversion of whole regions to cropland and grassland had the effect of changing the nature of the local hydrological regime. Water which previously was held in the canopy or locked in the root systems of vegetation in the forest ran off at accelerated rates with little or no ground cover left to hold it. Dramatic flooding became a feature of the rainy season in many parts of Africa, and considerable topsoil was lost to sheet and rill erosion, thus further depleting the agricultural potential of the land. The deterioration became particularly acute in those areas subject to annual foodstuff production. By comparison, the land devoted to plantation cash-crop agriculture largely retained and in some cases enhanced its fertility. Over time the disparities between the land devoted to export production and those remaining for food production became all the more pronounced. Some regions of rural Africa have been so overgrazed, over-cropped, and eroded that it is doubtful that agriculture can continue on these soils for much longer without considerable imported subsidies to rebuild soil structure and fertility.

Soil fertility is not all that is involved in this cycle of decline. The rainy season floods are not infrequently followed in local areas by dry season droughts. The water in the annual hydrological cycle is not maintained in watersheds to be drawn upon over the full year. Instead, it rushes through the region, often taking all before it in the rainy season, only to leave sunbaked clays and dried up wells in the ensuing months. In areas where soil depletion and the change of ground cover has proceeded to decline for decades, it is even possible that local weather patterns can shift over time.

While the global climate fluctuates over periods and with dynamics that are not yet fully understood, it seems nonetheless the case that regional weather patterns or micro-climates can be significantly altered in a matter of generations or even decades if major shifts in land and water use are engendered by new patterns of resource exploitation. Humankind can foster the processes of desertification by pursuing unwise development strategies or by encouraging peasants to overtax their land and water resources. While there seems to be a periodic pattern to drought in Africa, there may well be an anthropogenic component to the weather anomalies that the continent has witnessed over the last two decades.[7]

Circumstances in the 1990s do not present a promising picture for countries that have become irreversibly dependent upon North American agricultural surpluses, and agricultural analysts are wary about the prospects for long-term food security on a global scale.[8]

In cases of local or regional drought, populations that have become dependent upon purchasing food in exchange for cash can find themselves short of food for reasons well beyond their control. Fluctuations in the price of oil affect both international shipping and internal transport costs of food as well as the total foreign exchange profile of individual countries. Thus, fitful increases in oil prices have been translated in Africa into an increase in the price of imported food and a pattern of seasonal or chronic shortage. This is compounded as the world market in grains fluctuates with the purchasing and consumption habits of major industrial countries. When Soviet, Chinese, or Indian harvests are poor and Western grain surpluses are bought up on the international market, African countries find themselves in the face of prices beyond their purchasing power.[9] As we have seen in recent years, food shortages can become acute and famine widespread. Crash efforts to develop "modernized" agriculture based on "green revolution" technology are offered by Western agricultural experts in the wake of these famines to meet the urgent and evident need for expanded food production, but in ecological terms these kinds of development projects should be examined carefully before they are adopted. Generally these technological packages are based upon "high-yield-varieties" (HYVs) of crops that have been selected to respond well to a combination of fertilizers and pesticides designed for their needs. In this regard the HYVs are more appropriately labeled "high response varieties" (HRVs). They respond well to the petro-chemical subsidies that they were engineered to use, but on their own their performance may well not even equal that of traditional varieties.[10] When one considers the probable rise in cost of the petro-chemical additives needed to make them produce, along with the infrastructural investments required for irrigation systems, storage systems, and mechanized equipment associated with the "modernized" agriculture, it is not clear that the choice of these technologies is a wise one for the Third World in the long run.

On the contrary, similar investments in roads, marketing facilities, or land directed towards traditional crops may well prove over the long run to be better spent than the money devoted to the alluring promise of "miracle" crops. The real costs of HRVs become apparent only over a period of several years or decades as it becomes clear that adopting this kind of agriculture amounts to transforming bio-sustainable solar-based agricultures to petro-subsidized systems of production.[11] In the face of declining petroleum supplies it is questionable whether agricultural development schemes based upon increasingly energy-intensive technologies can be sustained much longer.

Another element of the underdevelopment spiral leading to chronic environmental degradation in Third World rural areas is the problem of undernutrition, malnutrition, and resulting spread of chronic and epidemic disease among the population. Undernourished and malnourished populations generally experience higher infant mortality rates than well-fed populations.[12] Increased infant mortality can lead to the impulse to have more, not fewer, children if it engenders a generalized anxiety on the part of peasant parents to be able to supply their labor needs and means of support in their elderly years.

In general, fertility rates decline among peasant populations only after mortality rates have continued to decline for a noticeable period of time. As long as disease patterns or economic hardships assure that mortality remains high or actually increases, fertility itself is likely to remain high as well. There now seems to be no assurance that the Third World as a whole will be likely to experience the same kind of "demographic transition" that characterized the population history of Europe during the last several centuries of its economic development precisely because deteriorating conditions in the Third World may keep mortality levels high. Chronic famine in Africa has made this dramatically apparent.

Beyond the question of mortality, however, and its indirect effects upon fertility, there is the problem of endemic morbidity—the debilitating phenomenon of chronic or epidemic disease. In agricultural societies dependent upon manual labor, chronic levels of disease seriously reduce productivity over time. This is particularly true at serious labor demand periods when food is in short supply. Poorly fed populations can be either too sick or too weak to undertake the necessary extra work needed to adopt conserving measures in their cultivation practices or even to assure a proper preparation of their fields for planting.[13] Nearly all the peasants I have worked with would like to be able to plant on larger surfaces than they do, but they are either not able to mobilize the labor or not capable of undertaking the extra work themselves. A peasant who repeatedly becomes sick or incapable of planting his own food is in a dangerously precarious position.

As the colonial regimes recognized, investments that improved public health were well worth their expense because of the benefits to rural production they would engender. Conversely, the post-colonial governments that are short on investment funds and do not provide adequately for maintaining public health in rural areas are likely to witness a measurable decline in agricultural productivity over time. In regions of East Africa now struck by AIDS, agricultural production has been reduced appreciably.[14] More pervasively a drug-resistant form of malaria is beginning to gain hold in parts of Kenya, weakening populations and reducing work capacity.

As circumstances in rural areas become more desperate, some peasants may leave their regions in search of better conditions elsewhere. When this is done individually it often takes the form of rural-urban migration. In areas where urban employment is not promising, however, this can take the form of rural-rural migration of laborers, either as seasonal or permanent workers in new lands. When large changes occur in the development potential of whole regions due to drought or irreversible ecological deterioration, whole communities have been seen to move. At the height of the drought in Chad, 500,000 people were said to be on the move with all their possessions and livestock from northern regions to southern regions of the country.

These massive migrations of population were at one and the same time a symptom and a cause of environmental degradation. The movement of cattle stock into more restricted ranges threatens the accommodating territory with overgrazing and places pressures on the available water supply. Once populations in this migrant state become dependent upon relief supplies of food aid in order to eat, the major problem becomes how to design agricultural systems that can help them re-establish their agricultural autonomy, usually on a severely impoverished resource base. Often this cannot be done, and today there are more than 5,000,000 people on the African continent who live in refugee or relief camps of some sort.

Whether in refugee camps or in the expanding shanty towns surrounding major urban agglomerations, the growing populations, uprooted from productive agricultural activity, strain the ability of the state to deliver even the most elementary of services. Demand for housing, clean water, electricity, and food outpaces the supply provided through state or authorized private sector channels. The result is often the emergence of an "underground" economy or "black market" in everything from local consumer goods and foreign imports to foreign currency and food itself. Official exchange rates between Western and local currencies are frequently subverted, sometimes by government employees charged with enforcing them.

As the gap between the "haves" and the "have-nots" increases in this situation, government officials come under increasing pressure to use their office or influence to obtain whatever state-controlled perquisites are within their reach. These goods or favors can be sought for friends, for closely related kin, or equally for frustrated international businesspeople merely seeking to get something done in the face of the near total collapse or unpredictable availability of public amenities like water, electricity, permits to do business, foreign exchange, and so on.

The net effect is the same. As income disparities grow, corruption can become rampant, and a career in "public service" can appear to be merely a means of diverting state money for private gain. Arresting, regulating, or even assessing environmental deterioration in developing countries under these circumstances can become very difficult. Local government officials cannot always be counted upon for complete cooperation or support in preserving or restoring resources if programs designed to do so threaten their customary patterns of providing for themselves and their clients.

Widescale corruption in public office is often offered as an explanation for Africa's sad state of affairs, particularly by journalists.[15] On balance, corruption is far better understood as a symptom of systemic malfunction rather than as its basic cause. Nevertheless, the amassing of private fortunes in public office and their expatriation into foreign bank accounts result in massive "capital flight" from many developing countries, and thus exacerbates the underdevelopment spiral.

NOTES

1. For a more extended discussion of a particular case study of West African ecological history see: Timothy C. Weiskel, "Toward an Archaeology of Colonialism: Elements in the Ecological Transformation of the Ivory Coast," in *The Ends of the Earth*, ed. by D. Worster (Cambridge: Cambridge University Press, 1988), 141-71.

2. Alain Revel and Christophe Riboud, *American Green Power* (Baltimore: Johns Hopkins University Press, 1986). For a critique of the impact of U.S. surplus exports see: Frances Moore Lappé, Rachel Schurman, and Kevin Danaher, *Betraying the National Interest* (San Francisco: Institute for Food and Development Policy, 1987). For a discussion of the various impacts of foreign food dependence see: Timothy C. Weiskel, "A Public Policy for Plant Genetic Resources," *Worldview* 23:10 (October 1980); and "Food, Famine and the Frontier Mentality," *Worldview* 12:12 (December 1981): 14-16.

3. Jennifer Seymour Whitaker, *How Can Africa Survive?* (New York: Harper & Row, 1988), 18.
   During the 1980s there was a veritable flood of published analyses concerning these interrelated aspects of food policy, focusing particularly upon how in the postwar period Africa lost its capacity to feed itself. Each study seemed to offer a set of possible solutions to "develop" Africa's agricultural potential, ranging from revitalizing state-organized production systems to allowing greater latitude for the operation of "free market" principles. See: Robert H. Bates, *Markets and States in Tropical Africa: The Political Basis of Agricultural Policies* (Berkeley: University of California Press, 1981); Economic Research Service, United States Department of Agriculture, *Food Problems and Prospects in Sub-Saharan Africa* (Washington, DC: USDA/ERS, 1981). Foreign Agricultural Research Report No. 166; The World Bank, *Accelerated Development in Sub-Saharan Africa: An Agenda for Action* (Washington, DC: The World Bank, 1981); Keith Hart, *The Political Economy of West African Agriculture* (Cambridge and New York: Cambridge University Press, 1982); Dharam P. Ghai and Samir Muhammad Radwan, *Agrarian Policies and Rural Poverty in Africa* (Geneva: International Labour Office, 1983); Office of Technology Assessment, *Africa Tomorrow: Issues in Technology, Agriculture, and U.S. Foreign Aid: A Technical Memorandum* (Washington, DC: Office of Technology Assessment, 1984); Per Pinstrup-Andersen, Alan Berg, and Martin Forman, *International Agricultural Research and Human Nutrition* (Washington, DC: International Food Policy Research Institute; Rome: UN Administrative Committee on Co-ordination, Sub-Committee on Nutrition, 1984); Peter Lawrence, ed., *World Recession and the Food Crisis in Africa* (London: James Currey/Review of African Political Economy, 1986); John Ravenhill, ed., *Africa in Economic Crisis* (New York: Columbia University Press, 1986); Dharam P. Ghai and Lawrence D. Smith, *Agricultural Prices, Policy, and Equity in Sub-Saharan Africa* (Boulder, CO: L. Rienner, 1987); John W. Mellor, Christopher L. Delgado, and Malcolm J. Blackie, eds., *Accelerating Food Production in Sub-Saharan Africa* (Baltimore: The Johns Hopkins Press, 1987); Prabhu L. Pingali, Yves Bigot, and Hans P. Binswanger, *Agricultural Mechanization and the Evolution of Farming Systems in Sub-Saharan Africa* (Baltimore: Published for the World Bank, Johns Hopkins University Press, 1987); Donald

Curtis, Michael Hubbard, and Andrew Shepherd, *Preventing Famine: Policies and Prospects for Africa* (London: Methuen, 1988); Per Pinstrup-Andersen, *Food Subsidies in Developing Countries: Costs, Benefits, and Policy Options* (Baltimore: Published for the International Food Policy Research Institute [by] the Johns Hopkins University Press, 1988); Jean-Francois Bayart, *L'Etat en Afrique: la politique du ventre* (Paris: Fayard, 1989).

While there seems to be no shortage of academic expertise concerning Africa's food policy alternatives, not enough has been implemented to avert famine in large parts of the continent. For example, severe food shortages are present in Liberia, Angola, and Sudan. In each of these areas civil strife has been both the cause and the effect of food shortages. On 25 October 1990, Roger Winter, director of the U.S. Committee for Refugees, told the House Foreign Affairs subcommittee on Africa that Sudan was on the verge of witnessing a famine of "biblical proportions" that would affect millions of people if food relief were not mobilized quickly by the international community. See: Ruth Sinai, "Sudan Famine," *AP Newswire* 25 October 1990, 10:41 aes.

4. The massive expansion of urban areas is not uniquely an African phenomenon. Mexico City is already the largest city in the world and growing at a rate of 1 million per year. Asia will have 23 cities with populations of 5 million or more by the year 2000. See "Population Boom for Asian Pacific," *UPI News*, 7 June 1988, 17:47 pm.

5. Whitaker, 19.

6. Anthropologists have long noted the correlation between high birth rates and the potential value of child labor. As one recent study phrased it: "there is a phase in the commercialization and intensification of agriculture in conjunction with industrial and urban growth during which the value of children as a source of labor and family income is enhanced." See: Marvin Harris and Eric B. Ross, *Death, Sex and Fertility: Population Regulation in Preindustrial and Developing Societies* (New York: Columbia University Press, 1990), 172.

7. On the interaction of human activity and climate see particularly Michael H. Glantz, *Desertification: Environmental Degradation in and around Arid Lands* (Boulder, CO: Westview Press, 1977); Richard W. Franke and Barbara H. Chasin, *Seeds of Famine: Ecological Destruction and the Development Dilemma in the West African Sahel* (Montclair: Allanheld, Osmun, 1980); Alan Grainger, *Desertification: How People Make Deserts, How People Can Stop and Why They Don't* (London: International Institute for Environment and Development, 1985); Independent Commission on International Humanitarian Issues, *Famine: A Man-Made Disaster?* (London: Pan Books, 1985); and most recently, Alan Grainger, *The Threatening Desert: Controlling Desertification* (London: Earthscan, 1990).

8. See: "Food Experts Study Hunger in the Midst of Plenty," *UPI News*, 4 June 1988, 16:56 pm.; "Drought May Sink Grain Stocks," *AP News*, 26 June 1988, 15:32 pm. [Sunday].; Food-Threats, USDA Expert Sees Trouble Ahead," *AP News*, 10 July 1988, 4:12 am. [Sunday].; "Soviet-Harvest, Bumper Crop Seen for Soviets," *AP News*, 12 July 1988, 19:17 pm. [Tuesday].; and "Drought Is Boon to S. America," *AP News*, 22 July 1988, 13:13 pm. [Friday].

9. A number of studies have focused specifically on how to avoid further famine in Africa, whether its causes are drought, excessive food dependence, or inadequate government agricultural policies. See: Michael H. Glantz, *Drought and Hunger in Africa: Denying Famine a Future* (Cambridge [Cambridgeshire] and New York: Cambridge University Press, 1987); Donald Curtis, Michael Hubbard, and Andrew Shepherd, *Preventing Famine: Policies and Prospects for Africa* (London: Methuen, 1988); Peter Walker, *Famine Early Warning Systems: Victims and Destitution* (London: Earthscan, 1989).

Clearly variations in weather patterns and climate can have a disruptive impact on food production both locally and globally. This can mean that countries dependent upon foreign food imports can be subject to unpredictable food shortages due to climate anomalies or weather disasters in remote regions of the world. A failure of successive American harvests or a shift in the pattern of output can mean that African populations may be the first to suffer, since surpluses they have come to depend upon may no longer be available. For a consideration of the global implications of climate shifts see: Wilfrid Bach, Jurgen Pankrath, and Stephen H. Schneider, *Food-Climate Interactions* (Boston: D. Reidel, 1981).

10. See Kenneth A. Dahlberg, *Beyond the Green Revolution: The Ecology & Politics of Global Agricultural Development* (New York: Plenum Publishing Corporation, 1979); Tim Bayliss-Smith and Sudhir Wanmali, eds. *Understanding Green Revolutions: Agrarian Change & Development Planning in South Asia* (New York: Cambridge University Press, 1984); Edward C. Wolf, *Beyond the Green Revolution: New Approaches for Third World Agriculture* (Washington, DC: Worldwatch Institute, 1986). Worldwatch Paper no. 73; and Bernhard Glaeser, *The Green Revolution Revisited* (Winchester, MA: Allen & Unwin, Incorporated, 1987).

11. For critiques of the energy costs of petroleum-subsidized agriculture see: Maurice B. Green, *Eating Oil: Energy Use in Food Production* (Boulder, CO: Westview Press, 1978); and John Gever, et al., *Beyond Oil: The Threat to Food and Fuel in the Coming Decades* (Cambridge: Ballinger, 1986). Concerning the deadly impact of pesticides necessary in petro-subsidized agriculture see: David Weir and Mark Schapiro, *Circle of Poison: Pesticides & People in a Hungry World* (San Francisco: Institute for Food & Development Policy, 1981); David Bull, *A Growing Problem: Pesticides and the Third World Poor* (Oxford: OXFAM, 1982); and David Weir, *The Bhopal Syndrome: Pesticide Manufacturing and the Third World* (Penang, Malaysia: International Organization of Consumers Unions, 1986).

12. Even in oil-producing Nigeria, malnutrition is reported to be on the increase. Gordian Ezekwe, minister of science and technology, acknowledged on national radio that despite increases in agricultural production, hunger and malnutrition were increasing in the country. See: "Hunger Increasing in Nigeria," *Reuter Newswire* 24 October 1990, 12:53 aes.

13. Considerably more work needs to be done on the health impact of undernutrition and malnutrition in specific African circumstances, but work done elsewhere suggests that one of the human body's immune systems is affected by poor nutrition. For a popular account of the impact of poor nutrition on the body's ability to resist disease see: Dr. Bernard Jensen and Mark Anderson, *Empty Harvest: Understanding the Link between Our Food, Our Immunity, and Our Planet* (Garden City Park, NY: Avery Publishing Group, 1990). For the general problem in relation to the develop-

ing world see: Margaret R. Biswas and Per Pinstrup-Andersen, *Nutrition and Development* (Oxford and New York: Oxford University Press, 1985).

14. On 2 October 1990 the World Health Organization (WHO) reported that following the United States the countries with the most reported AIDS cases were Uganda (12,444 cases), Zaire (11,732), Brazil (11,070), France (9,718), Kenya (9,139), Malawi (7,160), Italy (6,701), and Spain (6,210). "WHO Reports Increased AIDS Cases," *UPI Newswire*, 2 October 1990, 16:02 pes. The health impact of the disease is probably at least as severe in African cities as it is in the rural regions. In recent months health officials have reported that AIDS has become the leading cause of death among adult males in Abidjan, Ivory Coast.

15. See for example, Xan Smiley, "Misunderstanding Africa," *Atlantic Monthly* 250 (September 1982): 70-80 and Whitaker, 48-52.

ANNOTATED BIBLIOGRAPHY FOR CHAPTER IV

POST-WAR AFRICA: COUNTRIES AND REGIONS

* 4.1 *
Franke, Richard W., and Barbara H. Chasin. *Seeds of Famine: Ecological Destruction and the Development Dilemma in the West African Sahel.* Montclair, NJ: Allanheld, Osmun, 1980. LC 79-52471. ISBN 0-916672-26-3.

When, sometime in the first century A.D., the Romans introduced the camel, the desert's "ship," into Africa, they put in place a precondition for the rise of empire in West Africa, for the camel made possible traversal of the Sahara, previously an ominous and impenetrable ocean of sand. From 500 to 1600 A. D., there were successively three native imperial states in the Sahelian region of West Africa, states that on the whole sustained relative prosperity and ecological balance. European colonialism, which began circa 1600, was economically and ecologically destructive from the very beginning. The European presence in the Sahelian region meant a disruption of the nomadic culture of the region. Europeans, particularly the French, built ports along the Atlantic coast of Africa. Goods and services could then be easily imported and exported to and from Europe by sea, thus nullifying the trans-Saharan camel caravans that had been the mainstay of indigenous Sahelian cultures. European ship-borne commerce was but the first step. In the nineteenth century, railroad lines virtually completed the process of making the camel caravan technologically obsolete.

Severe ecological destruction of the region can be traced to a time relatively late in the colonial hegomony of France. After their defeat at the hands of the Prussians in 1870-71, the French intensified the exploitation of their African colonies in order to compensate for the losses they had sustained on the European continent (Alsace and Lorraine). The economic consequences of the decline of the camel caravans are readily apparent:

> The decline of the caravans brought general impoverishment of the nomads, in particular reducing their capacity to survive periods of bad weather. This decline is evidenced dramatically by the loss in trading values to the nomads. At the beginning of the 20th century, for example, a camel laden with salt from Amadror could be converted into 15 to 20 loads of millet; by 1945-50, the same salt brought only six to ten loads of millet, and by 1974, the salt was worth

only two loads of millet in a good year but often will bring only an equal weight.

With the collapse of the caravan trade, the nomadic societies of the region turned to increasing herd sizes as the only means of safeguarding their futures against bad times.

French colonial administrators decided that the native farmers must raise peanuts as a cash crop. Moreover the French prescribed methods that were far less ecologically sound than the traditional ways of planting peanuts. In pre-colonial days, Sahelian farmers had alternated peanuts with millet. When peanuts and millet were interspersed, the stems and roots of millet, being left in the ground, protected the soil against erosion. Also, peasants had allowed six years of fallow after three years of planting. Under French pressure to produce, these proper agricultural methods were abandoned. The result was that over-exploitation of the land caused organic matter in the soil to diminish. The soil's water retentive capacity lessened and its susceptibility to drought sharply increased. Degradation of Sahelian soils is a classic case of agricultural shortsightedness combining with the greed of a colonial administration to produce ecological disaster.

The famine of 1968-74 that struck West Africa was one of the worst tragedies of the twentieth century. Explanations of the famine have tended to follow the presuppositions of the explaining disciplines. Thus climatologists have stressed climate as a causative factor; agronomists, characteristics of Sahelian soils; forestry experts, deforestation; demographers, over-population, and so forth. Out of this welter of explanations, Franke and Chasin opt for a unifying point of view that is contained in an answer to the question asked by a group of French radical theorists: "Qui se nourrit de la famine en Afrique?" [Who is benefiting from the famine in Africa?]. They summarize their position up to this point in their analysis: "A full understanding of the forces that led to the dramatic crisis of 1968-74 takes one far beyond climate, desertification, overgrazing, mismanagement, population growth, and the like and compels one to study the colonial and post-colonial international economic and political system."

In the wake of the famine, aid organizations of the United Nations and its affiliated agencies joined with those of France and the United States and with regional alliances like the EEC and the OECD to draw up development plans that would rid the Sahel of food shortages and make it an ecologically sustainable environment. In capsule form, the plan proposes enormous increases in crop production to be sustained by greatly augmented irrigation works and with drilling of many additional wells. In this plan, the emphasis on rapid expansion of food production is so strong that it amounts to a *headlong rush to intensify the exploitation of a dangerously degraded environment* [emphasis in the original].

Using data drawn from Southeast Asia, Latin America, and India, the authors point out that drives to achieve food sufficiency in a short period of time result in a tragic loss of genetic variability in plants and their ability to resist local pests. Such a loss leads, ultimately, to greater rather than lesser vulnerability of the ecology of the region and its food supply. This is precisely the result in Africa's Sahel.

In their final chapter, Franke and Chasin ask: "Are all Sahel projects doomed to failure? Does the combination of Western government-multinational interests and the interests of Sahelian elites render impossible the successful tackling of the enormous ecological and production problems in the region? Are there meaningful alternatives to present projects?"

The only meaningful alternative is the small project, six of which Franke and Chasin describe. These are Guidimaka, funded by a British-based charity, War on Want; Tabelot—Tuareg Gardens, maintained by the Church of the Brethren; Timbuktu—The Isle of Peace Project, supported by the dominique Pire Foundation of Belgium; Gao—the herders' co-operatives, financed by the French-based Catholic Committee against Hunger and for Development; a water-retaining dike, supported by the British-based relief organization, Oxfam; the Lake Faguibine refugee camp, maintained by the American Friends Service Committee.

These projects, all organized, directed, or funded by small charitable organizations, are free of the economic and political strings that major donor agencies impose on projects they support. Thus they can bypass the effects of the involvement of Sahelian elites. However, it must be borne in mind that these projects are of very limited scope, and that they operate on the periphery of major local interest groups and are, perhaps, destined to have only a limited effectiveness. The promise of these small efforts lies, more than anything else, in the fact that their sponsors do not require them to be profitable, in either the short or the long term. Returning to the question, "Who is benefiting from the famine in Africa?" the answer is clearly, under the present structure of large-scale aid to famine-ridden African countries, the large donor organizations are benefiting from that famine.

* 4.2 *
Smiley, Xan. **"Misunderstanding Africa."** *Atlantic Monthly* 250, no. 3 (September 1982): 70-79
"The overwhelming reason for Africa's grim failure [since independence] is that the continent is very badly governed by the Africans." Smiley is reluctantly forced to accept this conclusion after having dismissed every possible allowance for misgovernment as the consequence of the lingering effects of European colonialism, the price of oil, market fluctuations in the price of commodities, among other causes.

A major contributing cause of incompetent government in Africa is the artificiality of the borders of its nation states. Conceived and drawn, in the first instance, by colonial map makers, these national frontiers were confirmed after independence "by tiny black elites." Smiley elaborates: "Totally disparate peoples, tribes with less in common than, say, Poles and Spaniards, have been thrown together in arbitrary political entities and told to choose governments." No real national consensus has emerged in any of them. Tribalism has remained "incorrigibly stronger" than the spurious nationalism fashioned by ill-informed colonial geographers and cartographers. African politics are inevitably tribal politics, with high positions being meted out to achieve and maintain tribal balance. In the absence of an authentic nationalism, tribal balancing has had to rely on patronage—with its attendant corruption—and on one-party rule.

"The one-party system has been adopted throughout Africa to counter the divisive tendencies exacerbated by tribalism." Moreover, the idea of a "loyal opposition" is considered by most Africans to be "crazy." Smiley reports that a group of Zimbabwean secondary-school teachers were unanimously hostile to the notion of the secret ballot. Political control becomes rigid and totalitarian and its methods of coercion are often brutal. With rigid control comes an idolatrous worship of the personality of the leader, now rampant in the totalitarian politics of Africa. African idolatry of the leader is strangely reminiscent of old-fashioned Soviet personality cults.

"There is a strange duality in African thinking." On the one hand, Africans think the fruits of the West are desirable, but that Western methods of acquisition are undesirable. "Material glitter is cherished, but the boring, methodical rigor with which nations are built, and the dreary civic obligations that give cement to political decisions, are somehow to be dispensed with."

* 4.3 *

Weiskel, Timothy C. "Toward an Archaeology of Colonialism: Elements in the Ecological Transformation of the Ivory Coast". In: *The Ends of the Earth: Perspectives on Modern Environmental History*, ed. by Donald Worster. Cambridge and New York: Cambridge University Press, 1988. LC 88-15293. ISBN 0-521-34365-8.

In 1889 the French designated their African coastal possessions Les Etablissements Français de la Côte d'Or, perhaps as a deliberate echo of the neighboring British colony of the Gold Coast. In 1893 they renamed the region La Côte d'Ivoire. Four periods of European involvement in the affairs of the region can be distinguished, the period prior to 1889 and three periods of varying degrees of French colonial control: 1) 1890-1925—a period in which French rule was uneven, ambiguous; 2) 1926-1950—the period in which the French solidified their authority,

which they used to encourage European settlers to establish large plantations of export crops; 3) 1950-to the present. At the beginning of this
period the French colonial administrators reached a three-part accord
with the leaders of the native resistance. Weiskel characterizes the accord
as follows:

> First, there was a tacit assurance that African small-holder
> plantations would become the enduring basis for the colony's
> production of coffee and cocoa. Second, in the subsequent
> years the French made provisions to expand research on
> other agricultural crops and develop possible large-scale,
> government-controlled plantations of palm oil and rubber.
> Third, the government envisioned a policy of extending the
> trade and transportation infrastructure to facilitate the expan-
> sion of the import/export economy. All three ingredients of
> this political agreement were to have far-reaching and
> seemingly irreversible ecological implications in the follow-
> ing decades.

Each period had far-ranging consequences for both the human and
plant ecology of the Ivory Coast, although Weiskel is careful to point out
that there can be no exact correlation between the changes in political
control and phases of ecological transformation. Despite this, some
correlations between datable events and ecological changes are confirm-
able through an examination of the archaeological record.

In the days before European penetration into the region, there was
extensive settlement in villages with high population densities. "Concentrations of shell middens along the lagoon areas near Dabou and
Sangon-Dagbé attest to the probable presence of sizable settlements of
foragers or at least to sites of enduring resource exploitation, dating
several thousand years back." Settlement patterns changed after the start
of European slave hunting. There is evidence that the people fled inland
and constructed fortified villages to protect themselves against slavers.

Defensive nucleated settlements of the kind that the people of the
region built required changes in their agricultural practices. They had
only two choices: intensification of agriculture or migration. They chose
to migrate in a pattern called disjunctive; that is, a large number of
people moved over great distances into new and unfamiliar territory.
After the danger from slavers had abated in the early nineteenth century,
settlements again shifted back to the coast.

Of all plants introduced into the Ivory Coast, cocoa has proved to be
economically the most important, and ecologically the most disruptive.
It was introduced into the region in 1859, and although initially it was
the Europeans, primarily missionaries, who tried to cultivate it, African
farmers were the first to prove that cocoa could be grown at a profit as

a cash crop. After they had demonstrated the profitability of the plant, the French responded by setting up agricultural experiment stations to enhance its economic potential as a commodity for export. During the period of strict French rule, 1925-1950, the infrastructure for exporting bulk agricultural produce was firmly laid.

After the 1950 accords allowed African farmers to retain the profits of their agriculture, they accepted the logic of converting forest or fallow lands to cash crop plantations. Conversions spread rapidly without any exhortation from the government. In doing so, the Africans seized control over their own resources. "In 1961 the country produced 93,605 tonnes of cocoa beans on plantations covering a surface of 372,800 hectares." By 1977 the tonnage had risen to 228,328 and the land surface to 896,500 hectares. The figures from the earlier period are telling: 115 and 14,000 tonnes in 1915 and 1928 respectively. These conversions have reduced the twelve million hectares of rain forest in the Ivory Coast in 1956 to an estimated four million in 1979.

"The consequences of this conversion will be clearly visible to future archaeologists, for the loss of forest cover on this scale in regions of heavy seasonal rainfall quickly leads to accelerated rates of soil erosion, alluvial deposition and estuary sedimentation. The muddy residues at the bottom of rivers, lakes, lagoons, and the ocean floor will constitute vital evidence for future archaeologists in understanding the dynamic of colonialism. Indeed, the increase in the soil-erosion rate, registered in large sedimentary deposits, is likely to be so striking for this period that it may well be regarded as the overwhelming diagnostic trait of the 'colonial strata' in future soil profiles. Furthermore, the massive exportation from the local ecosystem of millions of tonnes of biomass in the form of timber permanently removes from these soils important restorative sources of organic and inorganic nutrients, impoverishing them to such an extent that future plant communities will increasingly require supplementary fertilizers to be able to grow on a sustained basis."

* 4.4 *

Whitaker, Jennifer Seymour. *How Can Africa Survive?* New York: Harper & Row, 1988. LC 87-46181. ISBN 0-06-039089.

The future of Africa lies in deep shadows. It is likely that more African countries will fail to survive as countries than will succeed. Sub-Saharan Africa is now in a contracting phase of the post-colonial era that began circa 1960. The exuberance the newly independent Africans felt has all but vanished. With its post-1960 dependence on imported oil to fuel its export-oriented agricultural industries, Africa became the principal victim of OPEC's devastating increases in the market price of petroleum in the early 1970s.

The explosion of the population puzzled observers in the 1970s. Whereas in Latin America and Asia rising health care, education, and personal incomes had been accompanied by falling birth rates, in Africa the reverse was true. To take just one example, the average Kenyan woman in 1960 had 6.2 children; in 1970, she had 7.2 and in 1980, she had an unprecedented 8.3. African leaders and their people still do not understand that excessive population is a major cause of the economic and ecological decline they see around them.

Children have a profound symbolic significance for traditional Africans, both women and men. Children are a blessing because they are needed to carry on reciprocal religious duties implicit in the generational cycle of ancestors, the present generation, and children. Ancestors exert a direct influence on human life.

> The spirits of the forebears, going back several generations, have been seen to play a continuing role in the welfare of the family. Until recently, children were widely believed to be re-incarnated ancestors and were given the names of grandparents and great-grandparents. After the death of a father, the Yoruba of Nigeria used to compete to conceive children because with the first new son the departed parent would return to the world of the living. Moreover, the birth of children has always been crucial to the ancestral shades, for their immortality in the spirit world depends on the performance of the proper rites by their descendants.

Children also offer a hope of economic security during the parents' old age. Even when Africans have migrated to the cities in search of employment, as they have in growing numbers, they seem to have carried over the countryman's belief that many children are economically advantageous. Although this is not accurate—the city dweller has no way of employing children as the peasant could—nonetheless Africans transplanted to the cities have an indirect justification for their desire for many children. In the absence of provisions for old age security, the African parent can say: "If I have many children, there is at least a chance that one of them may prove to be both prosperous and dutiful." The position is: children are a hedge against the terrifying prospects of an impoverished old age.

Africa, it is apparent, is in the grip of a downward cycle of degradation. An exploding population of young adults means, at the least, that the available land be worked more intensively and with greater disregard for prudent agricultural practice. Family holdings must be subdivided; periods of fallow are shortened and often eliminated altogether. And marginal lands, lands of minimal fertility, are precisely the lands that must be exposed to systematic overexploitation. The drought and famine that struck Africa in the mid-1970s are, in part, attributable to the pressure of overpopulation on fragile lands.

Children are seen as a hedge against the destitution of old age in large part because those social security provisions that may have once existed have been swept away by the IMF's demands for austerity. Africa is saddled with a heavy burden of debt. In such circumstances the International Monetary Fund prescribes some bitter financial medicine as the price of new loans. Among the services that the IMF characteristically proscribes are old age security payments.

When Africa received independence, circa 1960, from its European masters, European colonies were transformed into political autonomies based on the model of the European nation. The model, however, has never shown a high degree of congruity with the African cultural reality. As was seen in the traditional African's religious view of the importance of children, so does the African entertain a religious view of ethnicity and kinship. The bonds that unite and reciprocally obligate members of an extended kinship group—brothers, sisters, cousins, parents, children, uncles, aunts—are infinitely more influential than are the claims of a common "nationhood." The idea of a "nation" is a foreign European idea. The claims of kinship on personal loyalties are, in large part, responsible for the nepotism and corruption that are endemic in African states.

The idea of African nationhood is a precarious one when considered from an economic point of view. Many thoughtful Africans have concluded that the nation state is not economically sustainable in the sense that the nations of the continent, as currently constituted, do not provide sufficient economic latitude to let indigenous manufacturing enterprises survive. What some thinkers envisage is that African nations will one day be replaced by a small number of regional confederations.

DESERTIFICATION AND FAMINE

* 4.5 *

Dahlberg, Kenneth A. *Beyond the Green Revolution: The Ecology and Politics of Global Agricultural Development.* New York and London: Plenum Press, 1979. LC 78-11271. ISBN 0-306-40120-7.

"[W]hen agriculture is analyzed from a global perspective that takes evolution seriously, one sees that the ecological risks as well as the energy and social costs of modern industrial agriculture make it largely inappropriate for developing countries. Beyond that, one can see a great need within industrialized countries to develop less costly, less risky, and more sustainable agricultural alternatives." Modern industrial agriculture, sometimes known as the "green revolution," is a combination of high-yielding varieties of grain, fertilizers, pesticides, and modern irrigation techniques.

Perhaps the most damning criticism of modern industrial man that can be made is that the prospects of survival of the human species within the global ecosphere are problematical.

To avert irreversible ecological decline, the species must adopt new measures to safeguard the earth's irreplaceable resources. Of these resources, water is obviously crucial to human survival. Moreover, water in the global cycle exists in an essentially fixed amount.

Currently there exists a grave threat to the delicate balance of the earth's hydrologic cycle—the cycle that links climate with soil, air, water, and humankind's use of all three resources. Expressed in the simplest possible terms, the cycle counterpoises the processes of evaporation, precipitation, and run-off over and from land with those of evaporation, condensation, and precipitation over the sea. When the earth's water cycle is allowed to function in its natural state, without human interference, 100 cubic kilometers of run-off from land into the oceans equals, on a daily basis, 100 cubic kilometers of precipitation that reaches land from the sea. When the hydrologic interchange between land and sea is disrupted through some form of human degradation such as deforestation and extensive irrigation, then water tables will fall and ocean levels will rise. Deforestation alters the hydrologic cycle by increasing the run-off from soil that has lost its absorbency. This augmented run-off not only causes soil erosion but also depletes critical reserves of groundwater.

An accelerated use of irrigation in arid and semi-arid lands, particularly in those lands that show evidence of erosion, further depletes critical groundwater reserves. Moreover, in times of severe drought, water for irrigation may simply be unavailable. "The amount of water required per acre in the Sahara for conventional irrigation is 5-10 times as much as that required in Morocco and 30-50 times as much as that required in southern Italy." Dahlberg quotes Bergstrom, with approval, "In harsh hydrological terms this can almost be formulated to mean that groundwater reserves never should be used for regular crop production but held in abeyance for drought relief in critical times."

Irrigation and deforestation are also implicated in the alteration of climates, both regionally and globally, although the exact mechanisms of action require a great deal of further investigation. It is thought that deforestation and irrigation effect changes in the apportionment of heat release from the earth's surface as between sensible heat and latent heat of vaporization. Sensible heat is available immediately to drive atmospheric motions; latent heat is released when vapor condenses and precipitates and it does so at different altitudes and longitudes.

* 4.6 *

Grainger, Alan. *Desertification: How People Make Deserts, How People Can Stop and Why They Don't*, edited by Jon Tinker. An Earthscan Paperback. London: International Institute for Environment and Development, c.1982, 1984. ISBN 0-905347-37-4.

Deserts expand primarily because human beings err in subjecting arid and semi-arid lands to: 1) over-cultivation, 2) overgrazing, 3) deforestation, and 4) poor irrigation practice. The first three errors strip vegetation from the soil, then deplete it of organic and nutrient content, and finally leave it vulnerable to the eroding forces of sun and wind. Having become extremely dry, the topsoil dissipates in the wind. The remaining subsoil then tends to become so hard and impervious that it can no longer absorb rain. Flowing water carries off the remaining soil and scars the surface with deep gullies that become increasingly deeper with each passing year.

The four primary causes of desertification are compounded by other influences, such as climatic change, population growth, and social and economic changes. Sheer increase in the numbers of people leads to a demand for more food. Very important as social and economic changes are development plans that call for intensive cultivation of cash crops for export in order to earn foreign exchange. Usually such cultivation entails an increase in the acreage, an expansion of the irrigated acreage, and a shortening of the periods of fallow on fragile lands.

As a consequence of the expansion of the acreage of cash crops, nomadic pastoralists have been forced to withdraw from the higher rainfall regions where they previously had grazed their cattle onto the most fragile and marginal lands. The density of their herds has increased sharply. Excessively large herds grazing on marginal lands cause soil compaction and sealing from the trampling by stock near waterholes. Another destructive result of overgrazing is "damage to vegetation on crests of formerly stable dunes, so that the sand becomes bare and starts to move."

If, because of a poor design, the water distributed by an irrigation system is not allowed to drain from the soil, the soil itself will become saturated, or waterlogged, and salts will not be leached away. With saturation, the water level, or water table, rises. Then the high temperatures associated with arid and semi-arid zones cause a continual evaporation from the surface of the soil. Evaporation sets in motion a form of "pumping" action that brings salts up from the subsoil and deposits them in the topsoil. This process, known as salinization, severely impairs the soil's fertility. Saline soils, nonetheless, retain a good structure and are therefore potentially reclaimable. However, the same processes of inadequate drainage, saturation, high water tables, and evaporation also bring alkalis to the surface. Because alkaline soils tend to be highly compacted, the roots of trees and shrubs cannot penetrate them.

Deforestation of watersheds in arid and semi-arid zones leads to increased stream flow, a lowered water table, and an increased concentration of salts dissolved out of the soil. The unprotected soil will then further erode and become increasingly saline.

Although the technical means of combatting desertification are known, the social, economic, and political means have not been found. Among the reasons that have thus far prevented effective action are the indifference of governments of affected nations, the apathy of donor nations and international development agencies, the apathy of the general public, and the sheer magnitude of the task.

* 4.7 *

The Green Revolution Revisited: Critique and Alternatives, ed. by Bernhard Glaeser. London and Boston: Allen & Unwin, 1987. LC 86-17302. ISBN 0-04-630014-7.

Pierre Spitz, one of the nine contributors to this volume, explains the origin of the slogan "green revolution." William S. Gaud, U.S. AID administrator, used it for the first time in a speech before the Society for International Development in March of 1968. Gaud explicitly opposed "green" to "red" and, by this color symbolism, signalled, as with a flag, that social reform in the Third World was not necessary since technical advances in agriculture alone would end hunger and thus obviate a "red" revolution.

In India, the main thrust of agricultural research under the auspices of the "green revolution" has been the development of the "superior cereals" and particularly irrigated wheat. To achieve the year-round cultivation the traditional Indian farmer had, it is necessary to revert to relay-cropping and intercropping. The intercropped fields of the traditional Indian farmer had a low productivity but they guarded against the disaster of a failing monocrop. Complex agricultural systems should combine scientific and vernacular knowledge. "This implies that the quest should not be for solutions in terms of large regional units, but for local solutions in each ecosystem and that climate especially should be treated more as a resource than a constraint, in order to fully utilize the human and natural resources of each microsystem."

The Indian government has made a major effort to build extensive irrigation works that have been seen as a solution to erratic droughts and floods. Unfortunately, it has not made a corresponding investment in water drainage systems. Irrigation systems, a key component in the "green revolution," subject the land to new ecological threats when they do not function properly: waterlogging and salinization. These of course only compound soil deterioration initially caused by deforestation. Deforestation, followed by inadequately designed irrigation systems, followed by monocropping supplemented by pesticides and fertilizers, is a prescription for the water and soil crisis that afflicts India today.

These agricultural practices "were designed for temperate climates, with mild and well-distributed precipitation, low insolation [exposure to sunlight] and a naturally-imposed fallow. The persuasiveness of Western (and therefore superior) science and technology is such that they have been readily adopted with little consideration of their relevance to the Indian context. This 'intellectual colonialism' (now neocolonialism) persuades Indian scientists to swear by a *modus operandi* which is incongruent with the objective reality of their country."

Attempts to introduce energy-intensive industrial agriculture in Nigeria and the forest zone of West Africa have failed. The failure gives strong support to the conclusion that, while traditional agriculture should be improved, emphatically it should not be replaced with an alien system. The undoubted ecological knowledge of the traditional farmer should be relied on to restore an ecologically sound alternative strategy. The elements that have composed traditional farming in West Africa include, among others, mixed cropping, substitute cropping, vertical stratification, and areal patterns; these vary according to the unit of organization, such as compound garden, farm, village. "In the context of energy-use management, the patterns at the village level are most significant." Frequently, there are three zones. Zone 1, the nearest to the village, includes the compound gardens. Energy is saved because some of the most bulky crops, which require great energy expenditure in transportation, are often grown here. Zone 2 is a mosaic of intensively managed land and fallow land. Zone 3 is the surrounding forest.

Although alternatives to the "green revolution" are urgently needed throughout the Third World, there can be no return to an unscientific past. Alternatives must take the form of an interfusion of traditional ecological knowledge with modern Western agricultural science.

* 4.8 *

Independent Commission on International Humanitarian Issues. *Famine: A Man-Made Disaster?: A Report.* 1st Vintage ed. New York: Vintage Books, 1985. LC 85-10533. ISBN 0-394-74252-1. Originally published in Great Britain by Pan Books, Ltd., London.

The recurrent famines that besiege sub-Saharan Africa are anthropogenic in their basic causation. The precondition for famine in Africa as elsewhere is a level of population in excess of the region's carrying capacity. Overpopulation engenders constant economic pressure on agriculturalists to expand their agricultural base by making deeper and deeper inroads on the still remaining forests. The lands that become available for exploitation by marginal farmers are scrub, woodlands, and barely green savannah, such soils being fragile and low in nutrients. Erosion follows in the wake of deforestation, thus further degrading them. The damage is compounded by over-cultivation and overgrazing. Intensive cultivation depletes the soil and grazing cattle compact it. The total conditions are then ripe in sub-Saharan Africa for further expansion of the desert.

Although some meteorologists believe that total precipitation in sub-Saharan Africa has declined over the last fifteen years, evidence for the claim is by no means conclusive. There has been less rainfall in recent years, but it is not clear whether this "marks the low point of a normal cycle" or a break with all past weather patterns. However this climatological dispute is resolved, there is one certainty:

> [E]nvironmental deterioration, once set in motion, can become self-reinforcing although the reasons for this are only partly understood. The loss of vegetation cover adversely affects the amount of rainfall, and as the former depends on rain its own decline is also then speeded up.

The authors of the report do not advocate new irrigation schemes to arrest the growth of the desert. Instead they argue for a partnership that is "modest in its financial dimensions, but far-reaching in its implications."

"The natural environment is never a neutral and passive force. People and nature interact." One manifestation of interaction is the reinforcement of weather failure by agricultural methods. Conversely better, more appropriate, methods that are more closely attuned to local conditions can cope with weather failure and act to reverse desertification. Tools, trees, and better seeds are the weapons needed, not mega-dams. Agricultural researchers must take seriously the peasant's farming experience and ecological knowledge. Often that experience is a sounder guide than the "scientific" knowledge of the learned. The advice that sub-Saharan farmers should plant high-yielding varieties of maize because they are more efficient can be fatally bad advice. HYVs of any crop require as a rule pesticides, fertilizers, and sufficient water. When any one of these factors is absent, the HYV may either yield less than a traditional variety or fail altogether.

Other components in the report's recommended program are

1) growing crops between rows of fast-growing trees, which both protect the soil from wind and water erosion, and provide fodder for animals;
2) small-scale water collecting schemes;
3) sowing crops without initially tilling the soil, and
4) mixed cropping.

For these and other reasons, the report answers its title question in the affirmative: famine is a man-made disaster.

* 4.9 *

Lappé, Frances Moore, Rachel Schurman, and Kevin Danaher.
Betraying the National Interest. A Food First book. New York: Grove
Press, 1987. LC 87-12067. ISBN 0-8021-0012-0.

Since the end of World War II, the framers of the foreign policy of
the United States have taken a markedly Manichaean attitude toward
world enmities. They have conceived the world conflict as a heroic battle
between the Children of Light and the Children of Darkness. Foreign
policy has been designed pre-eminently as a means of buttressing,
supporting, and augmenting the alliance of nations ranged against the
Soviet Union and its allies. To this end, the United States has earmarked
a large percentage of its total foreign monies to "economic support
funds" (ESF). Such funds are never used to feed the poor of Third
World countries, but rather to shore up the governments of countries
considered essential to the security of the United States. The point is well
illustrated by the government's long-term support for Ferdinand Marcos
of the Philippines:

> Despite Ferdinand Marcos' long record as a cruel dictator,
> U.S. aid not only continued but increased. Between its
> declaration of martial law in 1972 and 1985, the Marcos
> government received over a billion dollars in ESF and
> military aid. And in 1983, President Reagan pledged almost
> $1 billion more aid over the next five years. In the eyes of
> American officials, only continued support for Marcos
> assured U.S. access to Clark Air Base and Subic Naval
> Base, both deemed essential to U.S. national security.

It has invariably been the case that while U. S. development
assistance funds do promote growth and increase disposable income of
the relatively affluent, at the same time they deepen the poverty of the
poor majority who live in the recipient nation. In fact, the following is
a typical chain of partial successes and bitter disappointments: U.S.
development funds are allocated to the construction of an irrigation
system in a semi-arid land. In order to secure good local cooperation, aid
officials enter into commitments to the richest landowner in a district.
The system is built, and technically it works well, but the economic and
social infrastructure has been deliberately left unmodified. The result is
that the irrigation system becomes the exclusive property of the rich
landowner who proceeds to raise the cost of water as a first step toward
the consolidation of his land holdings.

Development must be redefined as a social process, and not simply
as a technological and economic process. To be effective, development
plans must entail changes in the relationships of people because such
relationships determine access to resources. An adequate development

proposal is one "in which people join together to build economic and political institutions serving the interests of the majority."

The authors observe that nothing could be more "Scroogelike" than to criticize food aid, and yet the grounds for doing so are compelling. They note that ninety percent of U.S. food aid does not go to emergency famine relief. "The bulk [of it] is sold by foreign governments to those among their peoples *who can afford it*" (emphasis theirs). A cogent economic reason for rejecting food aid is the following:

> Food can be even more problematic for the poor than economic aid if it undercuts prices that poor farmers need to stay in business. And long-term food security can be harder to achieve if food aid contributes to changing tastes toward foods which are difficult to produce locally.

U.S. foreign aid has failed to achieve any of its announced goals. Wealth has not become more evenly distributed in Third World countries. The quality of life has not improved appreciably. The countries themselves do not enjoy any greater degree of political stability than they ever did. In these failures, the framers of U.S. foreign aid policies have betrayed the national interest because the national interest requires that these goals be achieved.

* 4.10 *

Revel, Alain, and Christophe Riboud. *American Green Power.* A translation of *Les Etats-Unis et la Stratégie Alimentaire Mondial*, by Edward W. Tanner. Baltimore: Johns Hopkins University Press, 1986. LC 86-2709. ISBN 0-8018-2436-2 (pbk.)

An idiomatic translation of the French title might be: "The United States and Its World Food Strategy," a phrase that far more aptly delimits the subject of the book than does the official translated title. In their laudatory account of the American agricultural model, Revel and Riboud contend that the United States government has in fact attained its goal of becoming "number one around the world." Its strategy for the achievement of world agricultural supremacy has been the fullest possible development of those technologies known collectively as "green revolution."

Green power by definition intensifies a system's dependence on petroleum. By examining the productivity data for American agriculture during two time periods, 1959 to 1972 and 1972 to 1979, one can clearly see the effects of the 1972 oil crisis. The period of 1959 to 1972 showed a significant advance in most of the eleven measures of productivity. The period of 1972 to 1979, however, showed an overall decline, or negative growth, on two productivity measures. These are 1) productivity of fertilizers and pesticides; and 2) machine productivity. The first had an average annual rate of growth of -6.0 percent; the second had a -1.6 percent. These percentages being output-input ratios, negative values denote an annual decrease by the indicated amount. Despite these significant decreases, farm output and global productivity both showed average annual growth rates for 1972 to 1979 of +2.3 and +1.2 respectively.

Revel and Riboud attribute much of the continued growth in American agriculture to the success of two new varieties of winter wheat, called hard red and soft red. Statistics amply confirm their position. In 1959 to 1961, the average annual production of winter wheat was 28.0 million tons. In 1975 to 1984, production reached 53.4 million tons.

> Even more significant is the development during the 1970s of "soft" wheats, such as the Soft Red Winter, in the Corn Belt and in the Southeast. The share of this wheat in total production increased from 13 percent in 1970 to 26 percent in 1981, and its share of exports increased from 3.5 to 24 percent. But its share in the 1986 production decreased to 15 percent because of adverse economic and climatic conditions.

On the question of the sustainability of American agricultural growth, the authors express an almost unqualified optimism. Although they acknowledge that there is reason to be concerned with soil erosion, they are confident that "the vast majority of American farmers are aware of this problem." In our opinion, the optimism of the authors is not in accord with the data presented by other authorities. See in particular Gever et alia in *Beyond Oil: The Threat to Food and Fuel in the Coming Decades*.

The success of the American model is shown in the statistics of productivity before and after the energy crisis of 1973.

* 4.11 *

Understanding Green Revolutions: Agrarian Change & Development Planning in South Asia; Essays in Honour of B. H. Farmer, edited by Tim Bayliss-Smith and Sudhir Wanmali. Cambridge: Cambridge University Press, 1984. LC 83-14434. ISBN 0-521-24942-2.

The Green Revolution has given rise to passionate assertion and counter-assertion. In its early days, proponents of the new agricultural technologies saw in them enormous potential for increased production.

> They [the proponents] were fired with enthusiasm and faith, excited at the way in which the new dwarf wheats and rices shifted yield potentials to new high levels. Attention was concentrated on geographical areas which were well en-

dowed with irrigation water and infrastructure, most notably the Punjab and Haryana in India where the new seed-fertilizer-water technology was exploited very quickly. The spectacular trebling of wheat production in the Indian Punjab during the decade of the 1960s encouraged optimism. As the Green Revolution spread to other crops, some saw the prospect of banishing hunger from the world.

The pessimists, primarily social scientists concerned with political economy, were preoccupied with who gained, and who lost, from the new technologies.

Many studies showed that the new technologies were captured by and benefitted rural elites and those in the more favoured regions. Social scientists' attention was drawn especially to the new high-yielding varieties of foodgrains, which they found being planted, fertilized, and protected by pesticides, most where there was irrigation, and most on the fields of the larger and more prosperous farmers. Biplab Dasgupta concluded from his study of the Green Revolution in India that some of the major social and economic consequences of the new technology included "proletarianization of the peasantry and a consequent increase in the number and proportion of landless households." In their negative assessments, some social scientists saw the Green Revolution sharpening social tensions, and some spoke of it turning red.

The primary lesson that social scientists have learned from their studies of the social effects of technological change is that caution is necessary in assessing that change.

Unless interpretations are empirically based, tested for selective perception, and open to qualification, they are liable to serious error. More broadly, the history of ideas about rural poverty and rural development in the 1960s and 1970s is sobering. So many insights have become available so late; so many professions and professionals have been so wrong so much of the time, and yet so sure they are right.

Past failures indicate that what is needed is a new sort of analysis for which three guiding principles and requirements are appropriate.

1) The first requirement is that changes be those in which the poor can gain while those who are less poor do not lose and may even gain. Year-round irrigation systems, which give the poor more work and

which may generate labor shortages and thus raise daily wages, illustrate the first requirement of beneficial change.

2) The second requirement is that attention be concentrated on common property resources of land, water, grassland, forests, and fisheries. The poor should gain control of and benefit from increases in the productivity of such resources.

3) The third requirement is that existing disciplines, professions, and departments be studied to ascertain what potentials in rural development they systematically overlook. Such an inquiry may reveal that there are unrealized programs of great potential for the benefit of the poor.

* 4.12 *

Wolf, Edward C. *Beyond the Green Revolution: New Approaches for Third World Agriculture.* Worldwatch Paper, no. 73. Washington, DC: Worldwatch Institute, 1986. LC 86-51251. ISBN 0-916468-74-7.

Although the green revolution led to some spectacular increases in yield for Third World farmers who had access to irrigation systems and markets for their crops, it did not benefit subsistence farmers who raise food for their own families on marginal, rainfed land. Their agriculture remains not only unproductive but highly vulnerable to crop failure due to drought and other forms of natural catastrophe. Third World subsistence farmers remain the poorest in their societies.

Because the green revolution has failed most of the Third World, it has become necessary for modern agricultural experts to disabuse themselves of what amounts to contempt for the traditional methods, tools, and seeds of the indigenous farmer. When they do this, they make a remarkable discovery: they discover that the traditional ways of farming actually possess some undoubted ecological strengths. Among these strengths, it is important to specify the following:

1) They use few external inputs;
2) They accumulate and cycle nutrients effectively;
3) They protect soils and soil fertility;
4) They rely on, and hence preserve and perpetuate, genetic diversity; and
5) They make efficient, and readily affordable, use of available water.

These ecologically sound principles are illustrated in the agroforestry practices found in the Sahelian (sub-Saharan) region of Africa. Sahelian farmers have traditionally interspersed their sorghum and millet crops with trees of the *Acacia albida* species. *Acacia albida* returns organic matter to the topsoil, draws nutrients to the surface, fixes nitrogen, and changes soil texture so that rain will infiltrate the topsoil more readily. "Fields that include acacia trees produce more grain, support more livestock, and require shorter fallow periods between crops than fields sown to grain only." Moreover, farmers do not need to purchase fertilizers year after year.

Wolf quotes Gerald Marten of the East-West Center in Hawaii on the relationship that should exist between modern Western agriculture and indigenous traditional agriculture. "Neither," he says, "in their present forms, are exactly what will be needed by most small-scale farmers. The challenge for agricultural research is to improve agriculture in ways that retain the strengths of traditional agriculture while meeting the needs of changing times."

PESTICIDES AND THE THIRD WORLD

* 4.13 *

Bull, David. *A Growing Problem: Pesticides and the Third World Poor*. Oxford: OXFAM, 1982. LC 83-120823. ISBN 0-85598-064-8.

In agro-ecosystems that maintain themselves within natural biological controls, there is a complex interaction between pest and predator, crops, farm animals and humans. This is true of agro-ecosystems in all climates, temperate as well as tropical; however, tropical agro-ecosystems are distinguished from those in temperate zones by the fact that there exists in the tropics a much higher level of genetic diversity. This heightened genetic diversity becomes a key factor in any new agro-eco-system that results when agriculturalists insert chemical killing agents into the system. The addition of pesticides disrupts the previously existent balance between pest and predator. In the tropics, such chemically mediated disturbances of a natural balance can, do, and will continue to have devastating consequences. It is of the utmost importance to understand why it is that the same pesticides that have been highly beneficial to temperate agriculture should be either ineffective or even, at times, counter-productive in the tropics where most of the Third World peoples live.

The introduction of pesticides into a tropical agro-ecosystem will kill many of the natural enemies of the target pest; furthermore these natural enemies may take longer to recover from the application of pesticides than do the target pests themselves. "Thus freed from some of the natural controls which previously acted upon it, the population of the original pest may explode to unprecedented numbers." Even more divergent from the intended effect is the fact that a pesticide often kills large numbers of the natural enemies of a species *other than the target pest*, a species which was unnoticed and innocuous earlier but which can, in its new condition of immunity from predation, reproduce unhindered, very much to the detriment of the Third World farmer and his crops. This is known as a secondary pest outbreak, a phenomenon that occurs with great frequency in the tropics as a consequence of their enormous diversity of species. There have been field experiments that demonstrate "that by carefully timed and measured applications of pesticides it is quite possible to increase the pest population by as much as 1,250 times."

The most intractable difficulty that arises from the use of pesticides in the tropics is the extraordinary resistance that insect species have shown to insecticides. With their rapid breeding cycles and genetic diversity, insects have demonstrated a capacity to evolve new strains that resist the killing powers of previously effective pesticides. In the Rio Grande Valley of Mexico, the once prosperous cotton industry was devastated when the tobacco budworm, a cotton pest, became resistant to a wide range of pesticides. Before the introduction of pesticides, this pest had been kept under control by natural biological control. Bull quotes the University of California entomologist, Robert van den Bosch, to this effect:

> In ignoring the ecological nature of pest control and in attempting to dominate insects with a simplistic chemical control strategy, we played directly into the strength of those formidable adversaries. As a result, today, only a third of a century after the discovery of DDT's insect-killing powers and despite the subsequent development of scores of potent poisons, the bugs are doing better than ever, and much of insect control is in shambles. (In *The Pesticide Conspiracy*, Prism Press, 1980.)

A resurgence in the incidence of malaria, one of the dread mosquito-borne diseases that seemed almost at the point of extinction some years ago, is also attributable to the phenomenon of resistance. The chain of entomological cause and effect probably follows this course: "The pesticides used in agriculture often kill some of these mosquitos, as well as the agricultural pests. The surviving mosquitos breed in ditches, ponds and rivers where their offspring may in their turn be exposed to pesticides at the susceptible larval stage. The more susceptible larvae are killed, while the more resistant ones survive. *The adults which finally emerge from this environment may by then have developed some resistance to the pesticides used in malaria control programmes.*"

The fact of resurgence is easily documented. In India, the incidence of malaria had declined to just 49,000 cases by 1961. By 1976, it had risen to 6.5 million cases. The "bugs" had indeed made a comeback. It is the Third World poor who pay the cost of this tragic resurgence of diseases once naively thought to have been virtually eradicated. Malaria is a disease that afflicts primarily the rural poor in the tropics. It reaches its peak during the rainy season "when rural people have the most work to do." The poor of the Third World have become trapped in a vicious cycle of poverty, disease, and death. The trap exists in part because of the First World's conviction that it could dominate the Earth's insects through a simplistic strategy of chemical control.

Those who spray, or otherwise distribute, insecticides on crops to be protected from insects must be literate and informed if they are to carry out their task effectively and safely. It is unfortunately the case that many, perhaps most, of the Third World poor are neither literate nor informed. Manufacturers and exporters often do not properly label or describe their products or prescribe adequate safety precautions even when Third World poor users can read. And even when they can read safety recommendations, often there is no way they can in their own villages purchase the recommended pieces of safety equipment (e.g., goggles or rubber boots). Then even if such equipment can be purchased in their own villages, the poor lack the means by which to make the indicated purchases.

The poor of the Third World are the victims of the greed and irresponsibility of manufacturers, exporters, importers, and distributors of pesticides; of the greed and callousness of Third World officialdom at all levels; and finally of the scientific myopia of all who believe that humankind's most formidable enemies, the insects, can be dominated by a chemical strategy.

* 4.14 *

Weir, David. *The Bhopal Syndrome: Pesticides, Environment, and Health*. San Francisco: Sierra Club Books, 1987. LC 86-45430. ISBN 0-87156-797-0. The International Organization of Consumers Unions in Penang, Malaysia, published an Asian edition of this book.

A syndrome is a set of signs and symptoms collectively pointing to the presence of a pathological condition. Pesticide manufacturing plants that huge national and multi-national chemical corporations own and operate in Third World countries constitute such a pathology. The leading symptoms of the Bhopal syndrome are: 1) a double standard of safety codes and controls wherein standards so lax that they would not be tolerated in Europe, Japan, or the United States are tolerated in Third World countries; 2) workers in Third World chemical plants who have not been adequately trained; 3) a deficiency of waste disposal plants in the countries concerned; 4) an insufficient understanding among Third World workers of how dangerous pesticide plants are; 5) a lack of skilled regulatory personnel.

The syndrome takes its name from the massive aerosol cloud of methyl isocyanate (MIC) that escaped from a storage tank at Union Carbide's plant in Bhopal, India, early in the morning of 3 December 1984. Prior to the disaster, in fact, more than two years before it occurred, Union Carbide's headquarters staff in the United States were aware of the gravity of the situation in their Bhopal installation. A May 1982 internal report to Union Carbide's management spoke of a "serious potential for sizeable releases of toxic materials, either due to equipment failure, operating problems, or maintenance problems." Because this solemn and unambiguous warning was ignored, the residents of Bhopal were destined to suffer a night of death and horror. Two-hundred thousand people were exposed to the chemical contamination; at least 2,500 died and 17,000 more were permanently disabled.

Defects found in the safety equipment in the Bhopal plant included temperature and pressure gauges that "were so notoriously unreliable that workers ignored early signs of trouble." Other safety components had been turned off for maintenance, or for replacement parts, or for reasons unspecified. Similar failures of safety equipment and flaws in managerial judgment are characteristic of the operation of pesticide plants throughout the Third World. It is for this reason that the name of a city in India has become a synecdoche for an epidemic disease of potentially catastrophic proportions.

Given the probability that the symptoms of the Bhopal syndrome cannot be eliminated or even appreciably modified, then it is obvious that pesticide plants, like other components of the "green revolution," are inappropriate for Third World countries. However, it is highly unlikely that the governments of these countries will consent either to forgo new plants or to dismantle those that now exist. The only realistic remedy is to create a body of law that mandates greater social responsibility on the part of both governments and large chemical corporations.

On 3 December 1984, some people living near the Union Carbide plant in Bhopal ran toward the fire thinking that they would help put it out; in doing so, they collided with the company work force running desperately away from the crippled plant. Local Bhopal residents, it is clear, understood nothing of the hazards with which they lived day by day. No one, not officials of Union Carbide and not the government of India, had seen fit to inform them either of their routine hazards or of the catastrophic dangers they would face as a result of an accident. The Bhopal syndrome could be mitigated if the legal principles of the right to know and freedom of information were to be widely adopted and implemented. Armed with adequate information about impending technological installations in their communities, local residents could participate intelligently in those economic decisions that affect their welfare, their health, even at times, their lives. Further, they would be in a position to demand compliance with reasonable precautions such as the construction of safety zones around plants making dangerous chemicals.

The need for full dissemination of information becomes even more imperative in the light of clear evidence that chemical companies are gradually turning away from the manufacture of traditional pesticides. Public outcries against pesticide residues in food has only reinforced a tendency to abandon chemical killing agents in favor of the forms of patented life of the "biorevolution." Biotechnology only magnifies the dangers to an ill-informed public. Weir summarizes his final argument as follows:

> For too long, the narrow boundaries of corporate self-interest, enlightened or otherwise, have confined the discussion of how each of us gets our food on the table. It is time now for that discussion to be brought out into the open, with free access to information and a strong commitment to the public's right to know.

Weir adds that vast numbers of us have left the land to live in the cities in recent centuries, thus relinquishing our traditional knowledge of how food is grown. In doing so, "we have entered into dependence on technologies that neither we nor the best human science fully understands."

* 4.15 *

Weir, David, and Mark Schapiro. *Circle of Poison: Pesticides & People in a Hungry World.* San Francisco: Institute for Food & Development Policy, 1981. LC 81-13384. ISBN 0-935028-09-9 (pbk.)

U.S., European, and multinational chemical corporations make a routine practice of dumping pesticides that the EPA has banned for domestic use onto the overseas market. This practice, chemical company executives insist, is merely "good business." They have even engaged in extensive advertising campaigns abroad to stimulate sales of agricultural chemicals that may not be legally sold in the United States. It has been estimated that thirty percent of all pesticides produced in the United States are exported. To further augment their sales, manufacturers encourage farmers to use pesticides according to pre-set schedules, not as the need for particular pesticides has been determined locally. In Central America, the use of pesticides is probably forty percent higher than necessary to achieve optimum results. This commercial tactic of deliberately misleading users on optimum quantities has contributed to a radical overuse of pesticides in the Third World.

It is also important to note that most of the pesticides imported into Third World countries are applied to fields of luxury crops destined for export. "The poor and hungry may labor in the fields, exposed daily to pesticide poisoning, but they do not get to eat many of the crops protected by pesticides." Poor agricultural field workers are often treated in an incredibly cavelier fashion by plantation owners. When aircraft fly overhead to spray fields with dangerous chemicals, the workers may or may not leave, as they see fit, but their employers rarely afford them even rudimentary means of self-protection. The inevitable result is that exposure rates are intolerable and the people thus exposed run aggravated risks of incurring cancer, birth defects, sterility, and nerve damage.

Chemical company executives claim they sell pesticides to Third World countries in order to meet a demand—a demand for chemical products to feed a hungry world. This claim—that they only satisfy an existing market—cannot withstand criticism. It is apparent that chemical companies have employed advanced marketing techniques to create a demand for products that may not legally be sold in the countries of their manufacture. Companies such as the well-known Dow, Shell, Chevron, Monsanto, Dupont, Imperial Chemicals, and American Cyanamid, have taken advantage of venal government officials to insert huge quantities of destructive chemicals into countries that lack necessary protective environmental laws.

The "circle" of poison refers to the fact that chemicals banned in the United States are exported to Third World countries where these same U.S.-banned poisons may contaminate crops later imported into the United States.

PETROCHEMICALS AND FOOD PRODUCTION

* 4.16 *

Gever, John, Robert Kaufmann, David Skole, and Charles Vörösmarty. *Beyond Oil: The Threat to Food and Fuel in the Coming Decades.* A Project of Carrying Capacity, Inc. Cambridge, MA: Ballinger, 1986. LC 85-20007. ISBN 0-88730-074-X.

In 1982, the authors, all associated with Carrying Capacity, Inc., asked the Complex Systems Research Center at the University of New Hampshire to model the energy future of the United States and then to project the effects of that future on the U.S. agricultural system. The CSRC's two primary conclusions were: 1) Future energy supplies will not be as plentiful as is currently believed; and 2) A long-term downturn in U.S. gross national product is likely soon, probably starting in the 1990s.

Our economy is maturing and our resource base is aging. When a new petroleum deposit is first exploited, the supply seems bountiful and the costs of extraction are low. As the supply diminishes, two things happen; first, extractible petroleum is of a lower quality and the costs of extraction rise markedly. To the argument of "Why not just build better, more efficient extraction equipment," the answer is available in the production statistics from 1973 to 1985. "Despite quadrupled prices for oil and gas products and a 280 percent increase in drilling, the United States is producing less oil today [1985] than it did in 1973." Accepting the finality of diminished supplies, there are only limited options open to us. We can develop alternative fuels; we can increase the efficiency of our fuel use; we can radically reduce the amount of energy used; or we arrive at a compromise solution. Neither the supply of alternative fuels nor the nation's energy efficiency can be increased quickly enough to completely offset the effect of declining supplies of oil and gas, which now account for almost seventy percent of U.S. fuel use. Therefore we must take cognizance of the implication of our oil dependence.

Being as heavily oil-dependent as it is, U.S. agriculture is exceedingly vulnerable to diminishing petroleum supplies. That its resource base is declining is reflected in the fact that the amount of food produced per unit of energy has been declining. It is necessary that farmers adopt less fuel-intensive methods of producing food and that they do so without undue delay. Carrying Capacity recommends sustainable, organic, and regenerative farming, combined with integrated pest management. Such approaches not only greatly reduce the amounts of energy used but also energy costs. They also result in less degradation of the land, less erosion, and higher soil fertility.

Important examples of sustainable and regenerative agriculture are perennial grains. Clearly much traction energy can be saved by using grains that grow again from their roots each year. Another example is tree crops, such as pod and nut-bearing trees. Tree crops not only sharply reduce both required traction energy and soil loss, "but in many cases produce an annual soil gain."

Although the development of alternative fuels is a secondary remedy, it is still an important one. Carrying Capacity indicates that photovoltaic energy holds the greatest promise for the future. "These no-moving parts devices are the only method of producing electricity whose price is falling, but more importantly they are the only method of producing electricity with a rising energy profit level." The significance of the energy profit ratio is illustrated. The 1972 energy profit ratio of 1.0 meant that it took as much energy to make a photovoltaic cell as the cell could produce. Today conservative estimates place the ratio as high as 10.0.

Other recommendations of Carrying Capacity are: a) raise fuel taxes and/or impose import duties; b) develop cogeneration capacity; c) conserve through efficiency; d) encourage the federal government to set an example.

* 4.17 *

Green, Maurice B. *Eating Oil: Energy Use in Food Production*. Boulder, CO: Westview Press, 1978. LC 77-21577. ISBN 0-89158-244-4.

The phrase "eating oil" acknowledges the fact that vast amounts of fossil fuel energy are injected into each successive stage of the production, processing, distribution, and preparation of food. Energy inputs may be direct as in the fuels needed to drive tractors and harvester combines or indirect as in fuels used to make fertilizers and pesticides, or to transport, preserve, and cook food. The "oil-eating" food systems found in the developed countries are successful in providing adequate nutrition for most of the citizens of those countries. Where starvation and malnutrition exist in the developed countries, they derive from a mal-distribution of purchasing power. In the Third World, sporadic or chronic malnutrition is the rule while periods of acute famine are frequent.

A common compassionate response to the specter of famine in the Third World is the proposal that U.S. agricultural technology be exported. Green says flatly that such an effort "is totally impracticable from the point of view of fossil fuel energy requirements." With respect to the imposition of the "green revolution" on Third World countries, Green is dismissive.

> The complete failure of the so-called green revolution is an outstanding example of the futility of attempting to tackle the problems of a complex system by trying to alter one aspect of that system without studying the effects of what is proposed on the system as a whole. Systems analysis is an absolutely essential technique to apply to any propositions aimed at assisting the Third World to feed its people.

Nonetheless the Third World needs to increase its food production urgently. Technical advisors from the West, aware that energy-dependent food systems cannot be duplicated in the Third World, must scrupulously seek out, identify, and develop programs that do not rely on the expenditure of fossil fuels. Conversion of animal or vegetable wastes into fuel gas by biological fermentation is one technology that holds "tremendous potential for the Third World." Assume that an Indian village of 500 people has in total 250 cattle. "If seventy-five percent of the dung produced could be collected and a yield of 0.19 m^3 of fuel gas obtained from each kg of dung (a low figure in the light of known technology in this field) the gas output would be 2.4 GJ [gigajoule] per day."

It is important to note that the output of 2.4 GJ from biological fermentation is much greater than the Indian government's expected output of only 0.4 GJ/day from its rural electrification project, a project that is dependent on fossil fuels.

There is, moreover, a valuable derivative benefit from biological fermentation. The fuel gas takes out only carbon and leaves residual nitrogen as a fertilizer. The paramount difficulty with a proposal of this kind lies in securing the skill and capital to set up the fermentation plants. The costs will be high, and ways of making this technology simpler and cheaper still need to be found.

Another possibility is to grow plants—not suitable for crops—on water, specifically for biological fermentation. "The water hyacinth is a ubiquitous weed which could, if not already present, be introduced to areas of water. One ha [hectare = 2 and one half acres] of water hyacinth harvested and used for biological fermentation would provide 1.5 GJ per day of energy as fuel gas plus 3 t [tonnes = 1.1 U.S. tons] per yr of nitrogen which, when used as fertilizer, could be expected to increase crop yields to give about an extra 600 MJ [megajoule] per day of metabolically utilizable food energy."

"It is technology of this type—and possibly others not yet discovered—which do not use fossil fuel, which the developed nations should concentrate on developing and installing with whatever money and resources they are willing to make available to help alleviate the world food shortage." Aid administrators should decide on suitable technologies solely on the basis of full analyses of costs and benefits in the widest sense. "Conservation of limited and irreplaceable world supplies of fossil fuel energy should weigh very heavily on the benefit side."

Technologies such as these will not be sufficient to contain food shortages in the Third World. To eliminate the specter of famine globally, the conclusion is irresistible:

> [I]f a developed country such as the United States really wants to help ameliorate the hunger of the Third World countries, it should divert to those countries a substantial amount of the fertilizers and pesticides which it produces instead of allowing them to be used in domestic agriculture, and should make available to those countries a substantial proportion of the fossil fuel which it at present uses itself in order to enable them to irrigate their land and cultivate it efficiently.

* 4.18 *
Steinhart, John S., and Carol E. Steinhart. "Energy Use in the U.S. Food System." *Science* 184 (19 April 1974): 307-17.

Energy used in the U.S. food system, in all three stages of use—on farm, the processing industry, and commercial and home—has increased from a total of 685.5 in 1940 to 2172.0 in 1970, both values being multiplied by 1012 kcal (caloric units of food content). Thus while the caloric value of the food produced has enormously expanded in thirty years, so has the amount of energy injected into the system. Some of the energy inputs in each stage are: on farm—fuel, fertilizer farm machinery, irrigation; processing industry—food processing machinery, glass containers, transport; commercial and home—commercial refrigeration and cooking, home refrigeration and cooking, and home and commercial refrigeration machinery. This last component has increased by a factor of six in thirty years.

The large expenditure of energy required to place food on the table has made it very expensive by world standards.

> In 1970 the average annual per capita expenditure for food was about $600.00. This amount is larger than the per capita gross domestic product of more than thirty nations of the world which contain the majority of the world's people and a vast majority of those who are underfed. Even if we consider the diet of a poor resident of India, the annual cost of his food *at U.S. prices* would be about $200.00—more than twice his annual income.

Because the U.S. food system is energy-intensive, the caloric unit cost of food is perhaps the highest in the world. It is also an integrated system in which the components at the three stages of food production require each other for the full benefit and effect. The system has worked well in this country, albeit with some disquieting indicators for the future, but the system cannot be exported to hungry nations segmentally. We cannot export a piece of the system, say, high-yield varieties of seeds, to the Third World threatened with malnutrition or even famine, because HYVs require fertilizers, pesticides, and usually elaborate irrigation systems. Poor nations that are also poor in energy resources cannot afford these components of the "green revolution." Even if money and energy could be found for fertilizers, pesticides, and irrigation works, it is apparent that the lack of transport facilities would fatally cripple an effort to impose the "green revolution" on any nation that lacked the technological and economic infrastructure needed to implement it.

We have no alternative, therefore, but to work for a reduction of the energy needed to maintain an agricultural system. Some proposals to accomplish such a reduction are

1) a greatly increased use of natural manures,
2) an augmented use of crop rotation and interplanting,
3) an expanded use of biological methods of pest control, to replace the present excessive reliance on chemical methods,

4) "Plant breeders might pay more attention to hardiness, disease and pest resistance, reduced moisture content—to end wasteful use of natural gas in drying crops—reduced water requirements, and increased protein content, even if it should mean some reduction in overall yield."

The Steinharts have at best only a guarded optimism for the world's future freedom from hunger. They conclude with these words:

Food is basically a net product of an ecosystem, however simplified. Food production starts with a natural material, however modified later. Injections of energy (and even brains) will carry us only so far. If the population cannot adjust its wants to the world in which it lives, there is little hope of solving the food problem for mankind. In that case the food shortage will solve our population problem.

Chapter V

Time's Arrow and the Human Prospect

> *History does not repeat itself,*
> *but sometimes*
> *it rhymes.*
> [Remark attributed to Mark Twain]

Just as the meaning we ascribe to a word is determined by the context in which it is uttered, so too the importance we assign to events is determined by the context in which we perceive them. Disputes over the interpretation of pattern and trend in history arise not only because people look at different sets of facts but more fundamentally because different people consider the same facts in widely contrasting contexts.

The subconscious narrative which each of us employs to endow events with meaning can at times clash markedly with other narratives that govern the subliminal trajectory of time's arrow in the minds of others. This is often why those who formulate public policy admit to being confused and fail to act decisively on the problems that face them. They are assailed with conflicting versions of what is happening and immobilized by competing visions of what steps to take next.

What, then, is the appropriate context in which to view our contemporary ecological predicament? From what vantage point can we hope to discern pattern, identify trend, and seek to formulate effective public policy? What is the shape of time's arrow for the human prospect?

There is no one answer to this question, even for a single individual. We all live simultaneously in several different contexts, and each provides its measure of meaning for our lives.

Nevertheless, not all narratives are a matter of individual taste, reflecting simply the scenarios we may personally prefer to perceive. Objective measures of human performance are discernible, and objective conditions generated by specific public policy choices will turn out to shape our lives whether or not we perceive them or wish to include them in the stories we tell about ourselves.

Scientific research has helped to clarify a variety of objective narratives of human activity that enable us to see the human story in a new context. In the nineteenth century it became customary to separate "natural history" from "human history," but we are now beginning to realize that this separation of disciplines involved a falsification of both.

The two approaches to history are now being reunited in a new and different kind of narrative about the human prospect.[1]

From the study of ecosystems science, we are learning that as individuals, groups, and as a species we have been imbedded in objective narratives or scenarios of natural process, whether we like it or not—or even, whether we know it or not. It is to these objective scenarios of natural process that those who formulate public policy should now direct their most serious attention.

What we are discovering from the natural science approach to human history is that as a species humankind acts—often unknowingly—as a powerful transforming agent in a complex ecosystem. We have been intruding upon natural ecosystemic process, unleashing cycles and generating scenarios of ecological change over the entire course of human history. Moreover, this intrusion has accelerated enormously since the advent of industrial civilization, just when many people have come to think humankind was "freed" from the constraints of nature.

The ecological "foot print" of industrial civilization is something which we have only begun to document in depth, and we only dimly perceive some of its most obvious dimensions. But, although much remains to be learned, this much we do know and can affirm. Our intrusion into the natural bio-geo-chemical processes has been so massive and our transformation of ecosystemic parameters so thorough that responsible public policy in all realms must now direct itself toward moderating the human impact on its environment or we will face ecosystemic collapse and massive human catastrophe on a vastly greater scale than has ever been recorded in human history.

The contemporary problem of biotic extinction makes this dramatically apparent. Geologists, paleontologists, and evolutionary biologists are now reporting evidence in their professional journals that we are currently in the midst of a global "extinction event" which equals or exceeds in scale those catastrophic episodes in the geological record that marked the extinction of the dinosaurs and numerous other species. Biologists reassure us that the invertebrates and microbial species are likely to survive our current epoch relatively unscathed. Yet, for mammals like ourselves, this message provides small comfort when one begins to realize that the larger point is that *life as we know it* is undergoing massive extinction.[2]

At least two important differences exist between this extinction episode and those previously documented in the geological record. First, in previous events of similar magnitude the question of agency and the sequence of species extinctions have remained largely a mystery. In the current extinction event, however, we now know with a high degree of certainty what the effective agent of systemwide collapse is, and we have a fairly good notion of the specific dynamics and sequence of species extinctions.

Secondly, previous events of this nature seem to have involved extraterrestrial phenomena, like episodic meteor collisions. Alternatively, the long-term fluctuation of incoming solar radiation that results from the harmonic convergence of the earth's asymmetrical path around the sun and the "wobble" on its axis also drives systemwide changes generating periodic advances and retreats of continental ice sheets in high latitudes. These too cause systemwide transformations and have precipitated extinction events in the past.

In contrast to the celestial phenomena that served as the forcing functions behind previous mass extinctions, the current extinction event results from an internally generated dynamic. The relatively stable exchanges between varied biological communities have shifted in a short period of time into an unstable phase of runaway, exponential growth for a small sub-set of the species mix—namely, human beings, their biological symbionts, and their associates.

The seemingly unrestrained growth of these populations has unleashed a pattern of accentuated parasitism and predation of these growing populations upon a selected number of proximate species that were deemed by them to be useful. This accentuated parasitism led to the creation of anthropogenic biological environments which, in turn, drove hundreds of other species directly into extinction—sometimes within periods of only a few centuries or decades. More significantly, however, this pattern of unrestrained growth and subsequent collapse has repeated itself again and again, engendering in each instance a syndrome of generalized habitat destruction and over time precipitating the cumulative extinction of thousands of species.

For a variety of reasons humans remain fundamentally ignorant of or collectively indifferent to the fate of other species, insisting instead that measurements of human welfare should be the only criteria for governing human behavior. Yet it is upon the enduring presence of other life-forms and the integrity of systemwide functions they perform that human survival depends. Because of this ignorance and indifference anthropogenic biological systems periodically thrust themselves into episodes of radical instability driven by the agency of the dominant species engaged in paroxysms of self-aggrandizing self-destruction.

Thus, we live in the midst of an unresolved but rapidly escalating ecological paradox. In evolutionary and historical terms we are too successful for our own good. We refashion the natural world to suit our perceived needs and wants, yet—to date—these anthropogenic microcosms have proved to be ecologically unsustainable and in the long run collectively suicidal for human welfare.

At times it seems as if industrial culture feels itself to be at war with the natural world. The good news *and* the bad news is that we are winning. The human tragedy is that by winning such a war, we defeat ourselves. Those who persist in characterizing the problem as one of human life, human jobs, or human comforts *versus* the environment have misunderstood some basic facts about biological process. The continuity of human life itself requires the preservation of countless other life-forms that we are only now beginning to discover, catalogue, and understand. Those who formulate public policy would do well to remember that if humans pit themselves *against* natural processes, in the long run we cannot help but lose. In short, without some strong and governing principle of limit built into public policy, humans are bound to accelerate their own demise as a species. What is true for all other life-forms in the ecosystem will ultimately prove true for our own species: unfettered growth and unrestrained expansion in a finite system is a formula for extinction.

From an ecosystem perspective the problem can be stated quite starkly. Given its pervasiveness, its pugnacious propensity to alter its environments, and its increasingly powerful technologies, the human species can reasonably be characterized as the latest large scale "natural disaster" which the other life communities on earth have had to endure. In this sense, the evolutionary uniqueness of humans as a species resides not so much in its cognitive capacities or its predilection for symbolic manipulation or its much flaunted intelligence but rather in the fact that it is the first species in evolutionary history capable of inventing and engineering the means of its own extinction.

In assessing our contemporary circumstance, then, it is essential for policy makers to keep the long-term historical and archaeological record in mind, for public policy necessarily deals with large-scale and potentially long-term problems. While numeric precision in forecasting may not be possible, several clear patterns emerge from this long-range perspective. In the first place, while we do not know how far current populations are from reaching the earth's carrying capacity, it seems clear that two trends are unfolding: 1) the carrying capacity of at least some local environments is declining measurably; and 2) the population (and hence resource-use) load is simultaneously increasing. (See graphic presentation in figure 1.)

Beyond this, it is not clear what will happen if both of these trends continue on their current trajectory (see figure 2). Nor is it clear what time frame is remaining in which we must as a society and a world community find solutions to these problems.

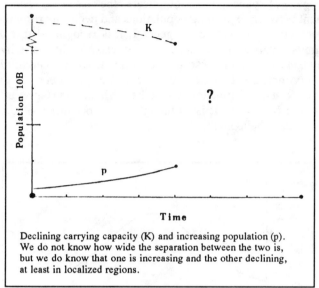

Declining carrying capacity (K) and increasing population (p).
We do not know how wide the separation between the two is,
but we do know that one is increasing and the other declining,
at least in localized regions.

Figure 1: Current Circumstances

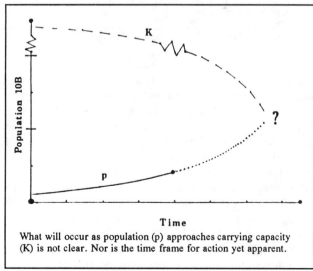

What will occur as population (p) approaches carrying capacity
(K) is not clear. Nor is the time frame for action yet apparent.

Figure 2: Continuation of Current Trends

Two general phenomena complicate the issue of achieving an adjustment between expanding populations and declining resources. First is the problem of perception. In general, it is recognized that there are upper limits involved in the amount of information that an individual or a society can successfully absorb and act upon. After a certain threshold as the environment becomes more complex, a society's ability to recognize or use information about its own circumstance effectively declines (see figure 3).[3] It is as though things become too complicated to know what is happening.

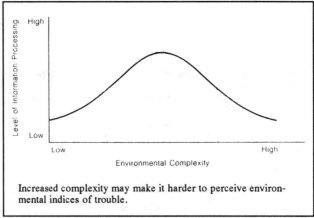

Increased complexity may make it harder to perceive environmental indices of trouble.

Figure 3: The Problem of Perception

This sad circumstance may already reflect our current position with reference to the Third World. Delegates from southern nations at the 1992 Rio summit reached this conclusion after witnessing the apparent lack of urgency on the part of the richer northern nations to reverse the patterns of environmental deterioration in the Third World. In reality ecological problems are now global in scope, and we will need to develop a matching degree of perception. Tropical deforestation affects both local weather and worldwide climate patterns. Food from Iowa feeds both Boston and Burundi. Currently, it is in the Third World that global ecological crises become most pronounced, but it would be a major mistake of perception for Western leaders to assume that the problems in the Third World are merely the Third World's problem.

A second threshold problem seems to be reflected in the general pattern of cooperation observable in societies faced with ecological stress (see figure 4). Initially, as ecological stress mounts, so does cooperation. Society members express a common determination to overcome difficulty. After a certain threshold of stress, however, this cooperation degenerates, and open conflict can result, leading to political fragmentation. Current famines in Africa are often said to result as much from patterns of ethnic or civil strife as they do from natural phenomena of deficient rainfall or locust plagues. Moreover, as the current disaster in Somalia demonstrates, the shortage of food itself becomes a powerful motivation for warfare. This self-reinforcing syndrome of ecological and social decline is violent and devastating to both human populations and natural ecosystems on an ever-expanding scale in Africa.

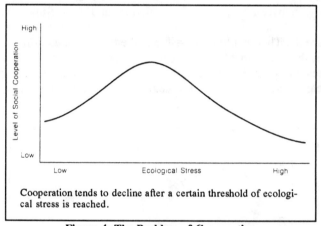

Cooperation tends to decline after a certain threshold of ecological stress is reached.

Figure 4: The Problem of Cooperation

Africa is not the only locus of these kinds of eco-social syndromes of fragmentation and collapse. The deterioration of ecological conditions in the former Soviet Union and throughout eastern Europe initially inspired the cooperative effort of many groups to overthrow the outmoded political structures. Nevertheless, as the resulting fragmented communities become anxious about the ecological hazards or waste generated by their neighbors, their willingness to cooperate has declined and their readiness to blame each other has increased.

One troubling aspect of these threshold phenomena is that it is often not clear where the upper levels of tolerance or the breaking points of irreversible deterioration are situated. It would seem that there is a considerable amount of inter-cultural and inter-societal variation in these matters. In addition, unpredictable disasters like the Chernobyl nuclear accident appear to alter both the level of what populations perceive as stressful in their environment as well as how willing they are to cooperate.

The vision of public leaders can no doubt play a key role in determining the thresholds of perception and cooperation in any given society.[4] For this reason it is vitally important for public policy makers to develop a clear understanding of the nature and scope of global problems even if they address themselves primarily to national, state, or local issues. As stresses increase in the global realm, only the broadest vision of public responsibility is likely to avert the self-consuming syndromes of ecosocial decline that have characterized both past civilizations and contemporary circumstances in the Third World.

Broadly speaking, two alternate patterns emerge from the evolving interaction between a growing population and a declining carrying capacity. First, it is possible that a stable adjustment can be achieved (see figure 5). This would be possible if the entire population concerned perceives the problem of adjustment as a real one, and simultaneously cooperates to achieve stabilization. Such a resolution implies that the society can exercise a remarkable degree of self-imposed restraint.

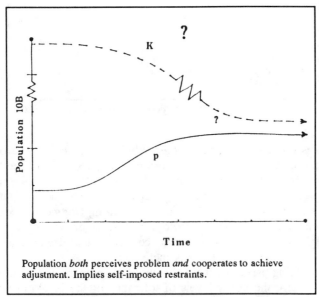

Population *both* perceives problem *and* cooperates to achieve
adjustment. Implies self-imposed restraints.

Figure 5: Possible Resolution #1: Stable Adjustment

An alternative resolution of current and future trends involves the phenomena of ecological "overshoot" and subsequent collapse (see figure 6). This would most likely occur either if the society did not perceive the problem at hand or if it did not succeed in achieving cooperation in a transition to a stable adjustment. The time lag involved between the overshoot and subsequent collapse is not at all clear. Nor is it clear just where we are located at the current moment in either of these two possible scenarios. Some scientists believe that we may already have exceeded the earth's capacity to sustain present populations on a permanent basis.[5] We are perhaps just beginning to witness the phenomena of collapse in indicative catastrophes ranging from repeated Bangladesh floods to chronic African famine.

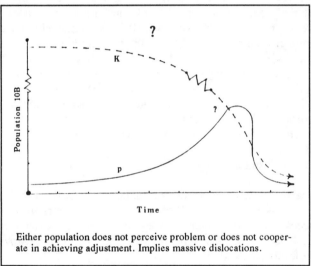

Either population does not perceive problem or does not cooperate in achieving adjustment. Implies massive dislocations.

Figure 6: Possible Resolution #2: Ecological "Overshoot" and Collapse

In considering our predicament in reference to these global trends three interlinked patterns in human affairs are troubling to historians of long-term process. First is the somewhat fitful but accelerating pattern of human population growth. Second is the concomitant pattern of global urbanization. Third is the increasing hyper-coherence of the world's food system, its increasing dependence upon fossil energy, and its potential vulnerability to perturbation.

We are so accustomed to notions of an expanding economy with annual interest rates that vary between 3% and 5% that it is difficult for us to understand that in ecosystems this kind of expansion for any given population is unstable, unsustainable, and most often tragic. It is even quite rare in the full course of human history. The industrial era in world history marks an unprecedented period in human evolution from this perspective. Never before have global human populations experienced such high rates of growth for such sustained duration, reaching a world-wide climax with an average annual population increase of 2% during the decade from 1965 to 1975. The demographic historian, Paul Demeny, has described this extraordinary period quite succinctly:[6]

> It took countless millennia to reach a global 1700 popula-
> tion of somewhat under 700 million. The next 150 years,
> a tiny fraction of humankind's total history, roughly
> matched this performance. By 1950 global human numbers
> doubled again to surpass 2.5 billion. The average annual
> rate of population growth was 0.34% in the eighteenth
> century; it climbed to 0.54% in the nineteenth century, and
> to 0.84% in the first half of the twentieth. In absolute
> terms, the first five decades following 1700 added 90
> million to global numbers. Between 1900 and 1950, not
> withstanding two world wars, and influenza pandemic, and
> a protracted global economic crisis, the net addition to
> population size amounted to nearly ten times that much.

As Dr. Demeny summarized the situation:

> Clearly, viewed in an evolutionary perspective, the 250
> years between 1700 and 1950 have witnessed extraordinary
> success of the human species in terms of expanding
> numbers, *a success that invokes the image of swarm-
> ing.*[emphasis added]

For demographic historians, then, it would seem that humans in the modern era are behaving much like a plague of locusts.

What is even more striking is that the pattern of distribution of this burgeoning population is one of rapid relocation into massive urban agglomerations. In 1700 less than 10% of the total world population of 700 million lived in cities. By 1950 a full 30% of the global population lived in cities. In North America the urban proportion of the population had reached 64% by that time while in Europe it was 56%.

In 1700 only 5 cities in the world had populations of 500,000 people. By the turn of this century that number had risen to 43 cities in the world with populations of 500,000 or more. Of those, only 16 cities had populations over 1,000,000. By now, however—that is to say in a span of under 100 years—there are nearly 400 cities that exceed 1,000,000, and there will soon be scores of cities with populations in excess of 10,000,000 people, particularly in the Pacific rim countries. Once again the insect image seems appropriate. It is as if collectively we are swarming, moving, and landing in concentrated hives of human activity.[7]

These two major patterns of recent human history are striking enough to raise the question as to whether either one or both can be sustained. So far these remarkable phenomena have been made possible only because of a matching increase in the output of agricultural production. Yet it is precisely with reference to the changing structure of the world food system that the third and perhaps most worrisome trend appears to be developing on a global scale.

Briefly put, industrial agriculture, and American agriculture in particular, has achieved enormous levels of output through a pattern of substituting human agricultural labor with fossil fuel-driven machines and chemicals. This is not an especially new or original insight. As long as twenty years ago, concerned analysts of American agriculture warned that, while there has been a substantial decrease in the human labor used on American farms during this century, there has been an overall *increase* in the energy subsidy required to obtain one calorie of consumable food in the American food system (see figures 7 and 8).[8]

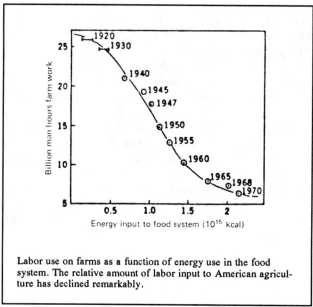

Labor use on farms as a function of energy use in the food system. The relative amount of labor input to American agriculture has declined remarkably.

Figure 7: Declining Labor Input

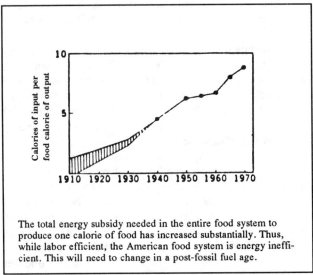

The total energy subsidy needed in the entire food system to produce one calorie of food has increased substantially. Thus, while labor efficient, the American food system is energy ineffi- cient. This will need to change in a post-fossil fuel age.

Figure 8: Increasing Energy Subsidy

Moreover, the vast majority of the energy subsidy provided to the food system in the United States is not reflected in the amount of food energy actually consumed (see figure 9). That is to say, more and more of the energy absorbed in the food production system as a whole is going into the necessary but ancillary aspects of agricultural production—the transport systems, the food processing systems, the cold storage systems, and so on.

Finally, the long-range trend from the 1920s until the present suggests that increases in energy inputs into the system have been approaching a point of diminishing returns in terms of overall food production. In other words, if this trend persists, future increases in food output will require even higher rates of energy inputs (see figure 10) for correspondingly diminished returns. This is a disturbing circumstance, particularly in view of the total collapse of food self-sufficiency of large numbers of Third World countries.

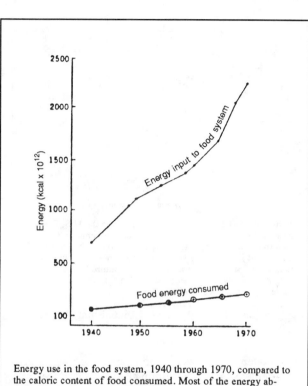

Energy use in the food system, 1940 through 1970, compared to the caloric content of food consumed. Most of the energy absorbed in the food system has not been reflected in a corresponding output of food.

Figure 9: Comparison of Energy Input and Food Energy Consumed

In an aggregate sense, of course, it may well be true that there is more food per capita in the present world than ever in history. This does not alter the fact that more people are dying of starvation now than at any point in human history. It could be argued that this is just a "distribution problem," having to do with politics more than agriculture or long-term ecological viability of the global food system, but such an argument misses the main point about the inter-connected nature of social and ecological issues.

The fact that these structural vulnerabilities in the world food system have been well known by experts and warned about for decades is not encouraging, for virtually nothing has been done by way of crafting public policy to reverse these circumstances in the intervening years. On the contrary, since the 1950s more and more people have come to

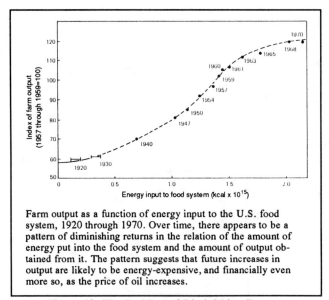

Farm output as a function of energy input to the U.S. food system, 1920 through 1970. Over time, there appears to be a pattern of diminishing returns in the relation of the amount of energy put into the food system and the amount of output obtained from it. The pattern suggests that future increases in output are likely to be energy-expensive, and financially even more so, as the price of oil increases.

Figure 10: The Problem of Diminishing Returns

depend upon fewer and fewer crop species grown more and more intensively on depleted soils and diminished land surfaces in regions that are farther and farther away from the points of consumption. The entire food system requires an already enormous and steadily increasing subsidy of fossil fuels to maintain itself. It will require even more to expand in relation to growing human populations.

These trends cannot persist for very long into the future without exhibiting increased vulnerability to variable weather patterns, oil price stability, pest and predator outbreaks, and various forms of economic and political instability. The current famine and total collapse of civil order in Somalia demonstrates with brutal ferocity the consequences for millions of people when a region becomes exclusively dependent upon external sources for food. Yet the same syndromes of underdevelopment and growing food dependency manifest so dramatically in that case are now in various stages of evolution in scores of Third World countries.

In order to survive in the coming decades those who formulate public policy will need to transform global agro-ecosystems away from petro-based toward bio-sustainable forms of agricultural technology. We cannot predicate our agriculture on fossil fuels and expect that agriculture to outlast the supply of this resource.

Unless public policy decisions are made in the near future to reverse the rapid increase in global dependence upon petroleum-based agriculture, we can expect wide-scale dislocations including famine, ensuing disease and open armed conflict to emerge on an expanding scale as supplies of that non-renewable resource decline and competition to control its use intensifies. We live in a highly industrialized, urban society, but it is important to remember that although we think we possess a "post-industrial" culture, there is no such thing as a "post-agricultural" society. Policy decisions concerning agriculture, our environment and the future construction of our economic infrastructure —water projects, transport systems, land-use patterns, and so on—all need to reflect this fundamental truth. Cultures that failed to understand this in the past have proved to be short-lived. We will be no exception to this repeated pattern in human history.

In effect, these three global trends of population growth, urbanization, and petro-intensification in agriculture form a powerful interacting syndrome of self-reinforcing and accelerated environmental decline. Each component in the syndrome works to aggravate the others. Population growth, particularly in impoverished rural regions, forces people off the land and into the cities. Growing urban populations are politically unstable unless cheap food supplies can be assured. The demand for cheap food in cities drives the expansion of the global trend toward petro-intensification in agricultural production as well as the concomitant growth of long-distance trade in foodstuffs.

The petro-intensification of agriculture works to benefit agricultural firms with sufficient capital to purchase the mechanical and chemical inputs, but it frequently reduces income and welfare of competing peasant households.[9] The response of the peasant household is to increase its output by increasing its labor input—that is, by having more children to provide the vital manpower. Thus, it is in the poorest of rural regions that one often finds the largest surge of population growth.

The lands in rural regions become increasingly impoverished for two broad reasons. Either the expanding petro-intensive technologies work to change the soil structure, accelerate soil erosion, contaminate ground or surface water supplies, and so on.[10] Or peasant agriculturalists, in the face of declining real prices for foodstuffs and cash crops, resort to over-cropping and over-grazing already marginal lands and frequently fight to retain or restore land rights to more fertile areas.[11]

The net effect on the overall interacting system is similar. Peasants are either displaced from their lands by the growing mechanization of agriculture or they migrate off the remaining marginal lands as their declining fertility no longer affords a sufficient return for their expanded families. In either case these landless peasants find their way to the cities, reinforcing the global pattern of urbanization and subsequent demand for continuous cheap food. The vicious circle or syndrome of accelerating environmental decline is complete.

It is important to recognize that there is no self-limiting or self-corrective counter tendency in the interaction of these three major components that can assure sustainability. In ecosystemic terms, there is no natural negative feedback loop to assure systemwide stability. On the contrary, these three global trends form interlocked components in a massive and powerful positive feedback loop driving a global syndrome of runaway environmental decline.

Only the careful elaboration of deliberate public policy can hope to slow and eventually reverse this global syndrome of decline and lead to stable ecosystemic adjustment. Those who argue, on the contrary, for the reduction of governmental attention to these matters—suggesting instead that some "invisible hand" will bring about the requisite adjustments—are abandoning global urban civilization to suffer the historical fate of all positive feedback syndromes: inevitable overshoot and collapse.

While the archaeological and historical record is filled with tragic reoccurrences of this syndrome, previous tragedies have been largely local or regional phenomena. Now, however, we face the prospect of wide-scale and potentially global disruptions. Markets in oil and food are global. Increasing urbanization is universal and aggregate population growth is occurring at a rate of nearly 1.8% per annum. Disruptions in any one of these interacting trends will intrude upon each of the others on a scale never before witnessed in human history.

To reduce the scale of such tragedy, those who make public policy must come to realize that it is unwise to shape our environment and continue to construct the urban and agricultural infrastructure in a manner that commits global agricultural production irretrievably to a non-renewable resource in a time of continuous population expansion. Such a strategy may well succeed in generating decade-long or even generation-long spurts of production to provision the cash wealthy and politically influential populations in expanding urban centers. Nevertheless, in the long run this course of action will prove to be a public policy blunder. In ecological terms, the short term success would be a recipe for long-term disaster. The world cannot continue to support current rates and patterns of global urbanization, and the cities themselves cannot sustain the growing disparity of income and welfare between the wealthy few and the impoverished masses, particularly in the Third World.

The time remaining to engineer a global transition toward a post-petroleum agriculture, sustainable urban forms, and a stabilized population is not long when measured in the span of decades and centuries that are normally necessary for successful social adaptation to technological innovation. If Somalia-like catastrophes are to be averted throughout the Third World and elsewhere in the years and decades ahead, those responsible for formulating public policy must begin now to arrest and reverse the syndromes of environmental decline that have led in the past and will lead in the future to the tragic pattern of overshoot and collapse in urban civilizations.

There are encouraging signs that at least some political leaders are beginning to see the scope of the problem at hand. Moreover, concerted research is now underway to analyze the favorable combination of changed circumstances and personal leadership abilities that enable courageous public figures to forge new and imaginative public policy when it is most needed. The results of this research on innovative policy formulation are likely to go a long way to help us understand the kind of leadership our global urban civilization will need to survive in the twenty-first century.[12]

For its part, however, the public must now learn both to demand and to reward public figures who are courageous enough to demonstrate environmental leadership on a global scale. It will no longer be sufficient to elect to local or national office those figures who simply succeed in putting together temporary coalitions of 50 percent plus one of the active electorate. A larger vision of community is essential.

Just as more imaginative leadership is called for, so to a larger understanding of citizenry will be required to reverse both local and global patterns of environmental decline. And this, in turn, will require a massive public education effort conducted through both the mechanisms of formal education and the broader public media. As catastrophic events like earthquakes and hurricanes demonstrate, public-minded citizens respond spontaneously and generously when they are informed of disasters in such a way that they feel themselves to be connected to the victims of tragedy. In reality, we are all connected to the victims of accelerated environmental decline throughout the world, and we must develop the means of communicating this in such a way as to engender and inspire a growing sense of global citizenry in the complex and interdependent ecosystem we have come to inhabit.

During 1992, the Carnegie Endowment for International Peace in Washington convened a *National Commission on America and the New World* to examine the crisis of leadership provoked by the decline of Soviet power and the shift of international focus in the post-Cold War world toward problems of environmental change and sustainable development. This blue ribbon commission included distinguished elected officials, civic leaders, academic experts, and business people, and in August 1992 it published a summary report of its findings and recommendations. As part of its assessment of the American's new international responsibilities the report draws to a close with this sober observation:[13]

We conclude where we began—foreign policy begins at home. We must make real for our own people the values we champion on the international scene even as we must manage our national resources in responsible fashion.

Changing our domestic ways also compels reexamination of our structures of government and our education for international affairs. For we are a country ill-equipped for new priorities. Our institutions creak with anachronisms. Many leaders proclaim change but act as if nothing has changed. And we are not preparing the next generation of Americans to understand, much less lead, in a transformed world.

The commission goes on to emphasize that: "It will be the character and quality of people, not the adequacy of machinery, that will determine success."[14] The report ends by underscoring the fact that far more than the change of particular policies is at stake:[15]

...this Commission has concluded that simply altering our policies will not suffice.

"The release of atom power," Albert Einstein once noted, "changed everything except our way of thinking."

What troubled Einstein troubles us. We have to change our "way of thinking."

The Carnegie Commission has articulated in new and compelling terms what ecosystem scientists have been urging us to consider for years. Our leadership as well as the public at large must come to understand that our way of thinking requires substantial change. The clarity of our thought about global ecological circumstance—the larger context within which we consider all human activity—will determine whether or not we will be able to devise effective public policy for secure survival. Only if we succeed in generating a new kind of leadership supported by an informed and motivated citizenry will the shape of time's arrow promise significant hope for the human prospect in the twenty-first century.

* * *

NOTES

1. The effort to re-unite natural history and human history is apparent in several recent attempts by scientists to write narratives that highlight the impact of natural process on human societies. Climate history has provided the archetype of this approach. See, for example, Reid Bryson and Thomas J. Murray, *Climates of Hunger: Mankind and the World's Changing Weather* (Madison: Univ. of Wisconsin Press, 1977); H.H. Lamb, *Climate History and the Modern World*, (London: Methuen, 1982); the collection of papers edited by Richard L. Wyman, *Global Climate Change and Life on Earth* (London: Routledge, 1991); and Stephen H. Schneider and Randi Londer, *The Co-Evolution of Climate and Life* (San Francisco: Sierra Club Books, 1984).

In addition, scientists have examined biological and human agency as an aspect of natural history. Geography, historical geology, environmental archaeology, and historical epidemiology as well as the history of plant and animal invasions or migrations have provided much of the case material for these kinds of narratives. See: Peter Westbroek, *Life as a Geological Force: Dynamics of the Earth* (New York: W. W. Norton, 1991); Neil Roberts, *The Holocene: An Environmental History* (Oxford: Basil Blackwell, 1989); I.G. Simmons, *Changing the Face of the Earth: Culture, Environment, History* (Oxford: Basil Blackwell, 1989); R.H. Groves and J.J. Burdon, eds., *Ecology of Biological Invasions* (Cambridge: Cambridge University Press, 1986); and Ann F. Ramenofsky, *Vectors of Death: The Archaeology of European Contact* (Albuquerque: Univ. of New Mexico Press, 1987).

Moreover, traditional historians of human endeavor have sought to reexamine the natural setting and the ecological transformations engendered by deliberate or inadvertent human activity. Studies have emphasized the interaction or co-evolution of human and natural environments. In addition to the works discussed in Chapter II above, see, for example, Redcliffe N. Salaman, *The History and Social Influence of the Potato* [First printed in 1949; revised impression edited by J.G. Hawkes] (Cambridge: Cambridge Univ. Press, 1987); William H. McNeill, *Plagues and Peoples* (New York: Doubleday/Anchor, 1976); Emmanuel Le Roy Ladurie, *Times of Feast, Times of Famine: A History of Climate Since the Year 1000* (Garden City, NY: Doubleday, 1971); and Meredeth Turshen, *The Political Ecology of Disease in Tanzania* (New Brunswick, NJ: Rutgers Univ. Press, 1984).

Finally, we are beginning to see the development of large-scale historical narratives that try to synthesize what is known about human historical ecology. See, for example, Daniel J. Hillel, *Out of the Earth: Civilization and the Life of the Soil* (New York: The Free Press, 1991); Paul Colinvaux, *The Fates of Nations: A Biological Theory of History* (New York: Simon and Schuster, 1980); Stephen Boyden, *Western Civilization in Biological Perspective* (New York: Oxford Univ. Press, 1987); and Clive Ponting, *A Green History of the World: The Environment and the Collapse of Great Civilizations* (New York: St. Martin's Press, 1991).

2. The issue of contemporary extinctions is often discussed under the general category of declining "biological diversity." See: E. O. Wilson, ed., *Biodiversity* (Washington, DC: National Academy Press, 1988); and John Terborgh, *Where Have All the Birds Gone?* (Princeton: Princeton University Press, 1989).

Recent popular accounts of the present extinction spasm include: Niles Eldredge, *The Miner's Canary: Unraveling the Mysteries of Extinction* (New York: Prentice Hall Press,

1991); and R.J. Hoage, *Animal Extinctions: What Everyone Should Know* (Washington, DC: Smithsonian Institution Press, 1985).

A particularly important type of extinction that has concerned scientists in recent decades is the loss of plant genetic diversity in food crop species. See: Cary Fowler and Pat Mooney, *Shattering: Food, Politics, and the Loss of Genetic Diversity* (Tucson: Univ. of Arizona Press, 1990); Robert and Christine Prescott-Allen, *Genes from the Wild: Using Wild Genetic Resources for Food and Raw Materials* (London: International Institute of Environment and Development, 1983); and Vandana Shiva, et al., *Biodiversity: Social and Ecological Perspectives* (Penang, Malaysia: World Rainforest Movement, 1991). The "genetic erosion" of plant cultivars has proceeded along with the simultaneous extension of petro-intensive forms of agriculture in many areas of the Third World. This phenomenon forms one of the themes of the critique concerning the trends in evolution of the global food system. See discussion and sources cited below.

3. The concepts represented in this and the following graphic are adapted from the analysis presented in Charles D. Laughlin, Jr. and Ivan A. Brady, "Introduction: Diaphasis and Change in Human Populations," in *Extinction and Survival in Human Populations*, edited by Charles D. Laughlin, Jr. and Ivan A. Brady (New York: Columbia University Press, 1978).

4. The perception and stress models here are adapted from those presented by Charles D. Laughlin, Jr. and Ivan A. Brady, "Introduction: Diaphasis and Change in Human Populations," in *Extinction and Survival in Human Populations* (New York: Columbia University Press, 1978), pp. 1-48.

5. In this connection see the views of several eminent members of the National Academy of Sciences as reported from a conference of biologists at Stanford: "'Population Bomb' Still Ticking," *UPI News*, 3 Sept. 1988, 11:57 am.

6. Paul Demeny, "Population," in B. L. Turner, et al., eds., *The Earth as Transformed by Human Action: Global and Regional Changes in the Biosphere over the Past 300 Years* (Cambridge: Cambridge University Press, 1990), p. 43.

7. For a detailed discussion of these and other figures on global urbanization trends, see: Brian J. L. Berry, "Urbanization," in B. L. Turner, et al., eds., *The Earth as Transformed...*, p. 103-119.

8. The graphs in figures 7-10 are adapted from: John S. Steinhart and Carol E. Steinhart, "Energy Use in the U.S. Food System," *Science* 184 (19 April 1974), pp. 307.

For an analysis of the trends in energy use in American and global agriculture, see: John Steinhart and Carol E. Steinhart, *Energy: Sources, Use, and Role in Human Affairs* (Duxbury, MA: Wadsworth/Duxbury Press, 1974); David Pimentel and Marcia Pimentel, *Food, Energy and Society* (New York: John Wiley, 1979); Maurice B. Green, *Eating Oil: Energy Use in Food Production* (Boulder, CO: Westview Press, 1978); and John Gever, et al., *Beyond Oil: The Threat to Food and Fuel in the Coming Decades* (Niwot, CO: University Press of Colorado, 1991).

9. See the annotations above on pages 161-182. In addition, for further social and economic critiques of the petro-intensive "green revolution," see: Andrew Pearse, *Seeds of Plenty, Seeds of Want: Social and Economic Implications of the Green Revolution*

(Oxford: Clarendon Press, 1980); and Vandana Shiva, *The Violence of the Green Revolution: Third World Agriculture, Ecology and Politics* (London: Zed Books, 1991). Because of the mixed outcome and inherent instabilities of the green revolution technologies, the promise of abundance from the "gene revolution" afforded by new types of biotechnology is often regarded with suspicion by analysts of the world food system. See: Henk Hobbelink, *Biotechnology and the Future of World Agriculture* (London: Zed Books, 1991); Lawrence Busch, William B. Lacy, Jeffrey Burkhardt, and Laura R. Lacy, *Plants, Power, and Profit: Social, Economic and Ethical Consequences of New Biotechnologies* (Oxford: Basil Blackwell, 1991); and Jack R. Kloppenburg, Jr., *The First Seed: The Political Economy of Plant Biotechnology, 1492 - 2000* (Cambridge: Cambridge University Press, 1988).

10. The petro-intensive nature of modern agriculture has degraded the environment and human health in many Third World areas. See the works annotated on pages 161-182 above, particularly, David Weir and Mark Schapiro, *Circle of Poison: Pesticides and People in a Hungry World* (San Francisco: Food First, 1981); David Bull, *A Growing Problem: Pesticides and the Third World Poor* (Oxford: Oxfam, 1982); and David Weir, *The Bhopal Syndrome: Pesticide Manufacturing in the Third World* (Penang, Malaysia: IOCU, 1986).

11. See particularly, Tom Barry, *Roots of Rebellion: Land and Hunger in Central America* (Boston: South End Press, 1987); and Robert G. Williams, *Export Agriculture and the Crisis in Central America* (Chapel Hill: Univ. of North Carolina Press, 1986).

12. A multi-year research project led by Professor John Montgomery of the John F. Kennedy School of Government at Harvard University is focusing the necessary characteristics and minimal components of what he calls "mega-policies," or genuinely new innovations in public policy, to face unprecedented circumstances.

13. Carnegie Endowment National Commission on America and the New World, *Changing Our Ways* (Washington, DC, Carnegie Endowment for International Peace, 1992), p. 85.

14. Carnegie Endowment, p. 86.

15. Carnegie Endowment, p. 87.

BIBLIOGRAPHY FOR CHAPTER V

CHANGING GLOBAL ENVIRONMENT

* 5.1 *

Global Warming: The Greenpeace Report, edited by Jeremy Leggett.
Oxford and New York: Oxford University Press, 1990. LC 90-40115.
ISBN 0-19-286119-0 (pbk.)

In 1988, the UN General Assembly established the Intergovernmental
Panel on Climate Change (IPCC) to advise world leaders on the gravity
of the threat of global warming. The scientists assigned to the panel did
in fact issue a warning of unrelenting sternness, but the IPCC itself
would not support its own scientists. The situation as it exists at present
is clearly stated in this quotation from the Greenpeace Report:

> ...the United Nations Intergovernmental Panel on Climate
> Change—its scientists excepted—has failed in its responsibil-
> ities in what has been the most important international
> consultation process in history. The policy-makers have
> consistently refused to listen to the dire and virtually unani-
> mous warnings from the world's climate scientists: they
> continue to recommend the distribution of a few bandages in
> the face of an effective plague warning...This is what makes
> the *Greenpeace Report* so important...it says what the IPCC
> should have said about how we must respond to the green-
> house threat.

The report opens with an explanation of the astrophysical mechanisms
that produce the greenhouse effect. Very briefly, they are these:

> Energy from incoming solar radiation reaches the Earth.
> Some is reflected. Most readily penetrates the atmosphere and
> warms the earth's surface. Invisible infra-red radiation is
> emitted by the Earth and cools it down. But some of this
> infra-red radiation is trapped by greenhouse gases in the
> atmosphere, which acts as a blanket, keeping the heat in.

Water vapor itself is a natural greenhouse gas, but when Greenpeace
speaks of the greenhouse gases, it is to be understood that they mean the
anthropogenic gases. The common, largely anthropogenic greenhouse
gases are: 1) carbon dioxide; its principal sources are fossil fuel burning

and deforestation; its contribution to global warming is fifty-five percent; 2) chlorofluorocarbons (CFCs) and related gases (HFCs and HCFCs); their sources are various industrial uses such as refrigerants, foam blowing, and solvents; their contribution is fifteen percent; 3) methane; its sources are rice paddies, enteric fermentation, and gas leakage; its contribution is fifteen percent; and 4) nitrous oxide; its sources are biomass burning, fertilizer use, and fossil fuel combustion; its contribution is six percent.

Although there are many threatening consequences of global warming, such as those that affect water resources and produce biotic impoverishment, one threat, the threat that rising sea levels pose to human settlements, is so menacing that it is perhaps legitimate to give special emphasis to it.

> World-wide, hundreds of millions of people would be displaced by the inundation of low-lying coastal plains, deltas, and islands in the next century if efforts to reduce greenhouse-gas accumulation in the atmosphere were unsuccessful. The IPCC Impacts Working Group merely touched on the problems of environmental refugees when it mentioned the "epidemics may sweep through refugee camps and settlements, spilling over into surrounding communities." These would be joined by countless millions displaced from the land as aridity and biotic impoverishment spread. If political and environmental refugees are a problem in 1990 in a world of 5.3 billion people, what will the problem be in 2000 or 2010 as the population soars above 6 billion?

Greenpeace is committed to the view that catastrophe can be averted, but only if governments throughout the world proceed to institute various policies designed to reduce the emission of greenhouse gases far below their current levels. The most compelling of such policies are summarized below.

Automobile Emissions

Chlorofluorocarbons and carbon dioxide are the two principal greenhouse gases that are attributable, in a very significant measure, to emissions from motor vehicles. Approximately one out of every eight pounds of CFCs manufactured in the United States "is used, and emitted, by motor vehicles." The contribution made by carbon dioxide to the total greenhouse effect is vastly greater. In the U.S. motor vehicle transport is responsible for almost thirty percent of the total CO_2 emissions. This staggering percentage requires that fuel-efficiency standards be made mandatory, not only in the U.S., but throughout the world.

Such mandatory standards must have these components:

1)   Stringent emission standards for CO, HC, and NO_x such that all new vehicles sold in the U.S. (and ultimately around the world) are equipped with state-of-the-art emissions controls.

2)   Carbon dioxide emission standards which will be sufficient to lower global-fleet emissions by twenty percent in the short term and fifty percent in the longer term. This likely means fuel-efficiency levels for future vehicles approaching forty mpg by the year 2000 and ninety mpg by 2030, unless growth in vehicle-miles travelled is constrained.

3)   Minimizing the potential for continued growth in the number of vehicles and their use. At very least, this should include the adoption of government policies which will provide attractive alternatives to the use of private cars.

Nuclear Power
    It is not possible to eliminate the threat of global warming by greatly augmenting our nuclear power capacity, first to supplement and ultimately to supplant fossil fuels as the prime source of electricity. Bill Keepin reaches this conclusion after a detailed feasibility analysis of the costs and consequences of an enormous expansion of the number of nuclear power plants throughout the world. "To displace coal alone would require the construction of a new nuclear plant every two or three days for nearly four decades."
    It is readily apparent that such a program of expansion rests on a body of economics that is, at the very least, infeasible. For the industrialized world, the economic strain would be extreme, if not disastrous. For the Third World, the strain would be disastrous. Aside from the economic infeasibility of massive expansion, the program presupposes the truth of three assumptions which are in fact manifestly false:

1)   Nuclear power is very inexpensive.

2)   Nuclear plants can be built relatively quickly.

3)   Nuclear power is perfectly *clean and safe*.

    An infinitely superior strategy for the industrialized nations of the world to pursue is fuel efficiency.

    ... in the United States, each dollar invested in efficiency
    displaces nearly seven times more carbon than a dollar

invested in nuclear power...even if the nuclear dream cost of 5 cents/kWh were realized, electric efficiency still displaces between two-and-a-half and ten times more carbon than nuclear power per dollar invested. And these numbers may be conservative...

Energy Efficiency
Amory Lovins declares that "it is generally cheaper today to save fuel than to burn it."

Avoiding pollution by not burning the fuel can, therefore, be achieved, not at a cost, but at a profit—so this result can and should be widely implemented in the market-place.

Lovins states the case for the "good news" as follows: 1) If we made full practical use of energy-saving technologies already on the market, we could save about three-quarters of the electricity currently being used; 2) If we made full practical use of the best demonstrated oil- and gas-saving technologies, we would save about the three-quarters of all oil now used. The bad news, however, is that governments of the world are less committed to market outcomes than they are to "corporate social-ism," or the bailing out of their favorite technologies despite the fact many of them are now dying of "an incurable attack of market forces."
Lovins has adduced all the evidence we need to state as a conclusion that energy need not limit traditional industrial expansion, but he adds that nonetheless goals other than indiscriminate growth are worthier. He asks: Why should Third World countries repeat the blunders of the developed world? An example of such a blunder is Los Angeles with its smog, pollution, traffic congestion, and water shortages. No sane country could wish to replicate Los Angeles. If rapid urbanization were in the offing, a developing country would surely seek ways to break up an incipient Los Angeles into small communities where people can both live and work and then to create a network of communities united by a good public transport system.

Agriculture
Agriculture makes a fourteen percent contribution to global warming, but as Anne Ehrlich reminds us:

Since the activities that generate the greenhouse emissions are central to the agricultural enterprise, complete elimination of greenhouse emissions from this sector clearly will not be possible.

Agricultural production being directly tied to global population size, production will inevitably be forced upward—and consequently the volume of greenhouse emissions—by population growth. The world's population now stands at 5.3 billion; it is projected to pass 6 billion by 1998 and 8 billion before 2020. In such circumstances agriculture's presently modest 15 percent share could double. If this happens, the expansion of agriculture might very well negate any advantage we might gain from increased energy efficiency.

Renewable Energy

Extracting renewable energy from its principal sources is technically possible, although economically the situation is more limited. It is not, however, as limited as most observers and analysts believe. The principal sources are: 1) photoconversion with solar technologies; 2) passive solar; 3) solar thermal; 4) photovoltaic; 5) photoconversion with biomass; 6) wind; 7) geothermal; 8) hydroelectric; and 9) ocean, consisting of wave, tidal, ocean thermal, and conversion.

Carlo LaPorta summarizes his position in these words: "Technically, renewable-energy systems can deliver energy reliably," and "Renewable-energy systems can be the preferred economic choice, even with today's seemingly expensive solar-energy technologies and historically low costs for conventional energy."

The report contains other important papers some of whose authors and titles are given below, such as, "Tropical Forests," by Norman Myers, "Third World Countries in the Policy Response to Global Climate Change," by Kilaparti Ramarkrishna, and "The Costs of Cutting—or Not Cutting—Greenhouse Gas Emissions," by Stephen H. Schneider.

* 5.2 *

Gore, Albert, Jr., *Earth in the Balance: Ecology and the Human Spirit.* Boston, New York, London: Houghton Mifflin, 1992. ISBN 0-395-57821-3.

In the first part of his book, Gore succinctly summarizes the evidence for environmental decline, covering such topics as ozone depletion, global warming and rising sea levels, air and water pollution, loss of species, and the relentless growth of human population. He notes, as have all observers of the environmental scene, that there are some, and some who hold the highest public offices, who refuse to accept the mounting evidence of global environmental decline as compelling. Relying on uncertainties concerning details in the anticipated course of degradation, these skeptics say action should be deferred pending further research. Gore dismisses this argumentative evasion.

But research in lieu of action is unconscionable. Those who argue that we should do nothing until we have completed a lot more research are trying to shift the burden of proof even as the crisis deepens. This point is crucial: *a choice to "do nothing" in response to the mounting evidence is actually a choice to continue and even accelerate the reckless environmental destruction that is creating the catastrophe at hand.* (Emphasis in the original).

Fundamentally, Gore urges us to cultivate in ourselves a form of religious-ethical consciousness that he calls "environmentalism of the spirit." This is his most original contribution to the environmental debate. Gore does not opt for any particular religious or ethical system, although he considers that every major religion has important environmental components, however cryptic and tenuous they may be in some cases.

As a first step in the necessary direction, Gore proposes that we re-examine the Cartesian dualism that sets rational man totally apart from a mechanical universe, a universe that we are empowered to manipulate to the fullest extent of our scientific capacity. According to this very respectable model, human manipulators of nature need have no feelings toward the natural systems they control or modify, any more than a watchmaker need have feelings toward the clock he works on. Gore proposes that we reject this Cartesian model, that we consider that nature is not a machine but an organism. And further, he advises us to consider that we as organisms are a part of a broad ecological system.

As a startling point of comparison with the Cartesian model, Gore directs our attention to the salutary spiritual environmentalism of Chief Seattle. When invited by President Pierce to sell his tribal lands to the U.S. government, Chief Seattle said:

This we know: the earth does not belong to man, man belongs to the earth. All things are connected like the blood that unites us all. Man did not weave the web of life, he is merely a strand in it. Whatever he does to the web, he does to himself.

One thing we know: Our God is also your God. The earth is precious to Him and to harm the earth is to heap contempt on its Creator.

These two propositions of Chief Seattle's: that man did not weave the web of life and that to harm the earth is to heap contempt on God are paradigmatic expressions of an environmentalism of the spirit.

Gore's views on the environmentalism of the spirit are a prelude to another important emphasis in his book. He calls for a new common purpose in our national life. From 1945 until 1990, the people and government of the United States, and to a lesser extent the peoples and governments of the Western alliance, had one common purpose, which was to contain and, if possible, to contract the domain of international communism. Most policies, both foreign and domestic, were adopted or rejected on the basis of the extent to which they served this one overarching goal. The containment of communism was the organizing principle of our national public life. Now, the threat of international communism having vanished, we are free to adopt a new common purpose, a new organizing principle. He proposes that we make the rescue of the environment our new central organizing principle and our new common purpose.

> Whether we realize it or not, we are engaged in an epic battle
> to right the balance of our earth, and the tide of this battle
> will turn only when a majority of the people of the world
> become sufficiently aroused by a shared sense of urgent
> danger to join an all-out effort.

An environmentalism of the spirit that is mediated through this new common environmental purpose creates the human conditions needed to right the balance of the earth. Free men and women who feel, and feel intensely, an individual responsibility for a particular part of the earth are absolutely essential to this effort. Only such people can serve as the earth's protectors, defenders, and stewards. Gore offers many apt illustrations of what a sense of individual responsibility working in tandem with an overarching purpose can mean. A woman in Maryland became aware that repair persons for General Electric refrigerators were venting CFCs from defective compressors through kitchen windows into the atmosphere. Lynda Draper, the woman in question, undertook a program of protests to everyone even remotely concerned with such routine environmental practices, whether in an official or unofficial capacity. Her perseverance ultimately prevailed. General Electric reversed itself and developed special equipment designed to salvage, not release, CFCs.

In order to right the balance of the earth, Gore proposes a "global Marshall plan." Recalling that the original Marshall plan was the Truman administration's response to the post-World War II devastation of the economies of Western Europe, Gore urges us to adopt a similar plan to contain and reverse the present devastation of the global ecology. The Marshall plan accomplished what its designers hoped it would. By enabling the European economies to recover, the plan also permitted

European peoples to resist an insidious slide into Soviet communism. By analogy, the task now is to resist a still more insidious slide into ecological devastation on a global scale. On page 297, Gore sets forth an outline of his plan.

> The scope and complexity of this plan will far exceed those of the original; what's required now is a plan that combines large-scale, long-term, carefully targeted financial aid to developing nations, massive efforts to design and then transfer to poor nations the new technologies needed for sustained economic progress, a worldwide program to stabilize world population, and binding commitments by the industrial nations to accelerate their own transition to an environmentally responsible pattern of life.

Gore's plan comprises five strategic goals, which are, in his own words and using his own emphasis:

> 1) *the stabilizing of world population*; 2) *the rapid creation and development of environmentally appropriate technologies*; 3) *a comprehensive and ubiquitous change in the economic "rules of the road" by which we measure the impact of our decisions on the environment*; 4) *the negotiation and approval of a new generation of international agreements*; and 5) *the establishment of a cooperative plan for educating the world's citizens about our global environment.*

Because the issue was virtually ignored at the June 1992 Earth summit in Rio de Janeiro, it is appropriate to fill in a few of the many details that Gore supplies under the heading of the stabilization of world population. Gore leaves little doubt of his sense of urgency about this issue. Before he states his own sub-goals for population stabilization, he adduces the evidence that establishes two demographic points of primary importance: first, that high literacy and education levels in a people lead to lower fertility rates; and second that low infant mortality rates likewise lead to lower fertility rates, because "the most powerful contraceptive is the confidence by parents that their children will survive." With these two points established, Gore then specifies three demographic sub-goals which are in his own words and reproducing his own emphasis:

> 1. *Allocate resources to fund carefully targeted functional literacy programs keyed to every society where the demographic transition has yet to come.*

2. *Develop effective programs to reduce infant mortality and ensure the survival and excellent health of children.*

3. *Ensure that birth control devices are made ubiquitously available along with culturally appropriate instruction.*

In unfolding his global Marshall plan, Gore's standard procedure is to close each major sub-section with a discussion of the U.S. role. He finds that the recent U.S. role in demographic matters under Reagan and Bush has been a tissue of ironies and equivocations where there should have been a strong assertion of leadership by the U.S. government.

* 5.3 *

Lyman, Francesca. *The Greenhouse Trap; What We Are Doing to the Atmosphere and How We Can Slow Global Warming*. Boston: Beacon Press, 1990. LC 89-43080. ISBN 0-8070-8503-0 (pbk.)

This book is one of the World Resources Institute's *Guides to the Environment*.

"During the last 100 years, human technology has proven it can alter the fundamental processes that govern the composition and 'behavior' of the atmosphere." One very important atmospheric alteration is the greenhouse effect, an effect that occurs when emissions from billions of tons of carbon dioxide and large amounts of other gases absorb the heat energy emanating from the surface of the earth. These gases trap "enough thermal radiation to warm the globe by several degrees." The consequences of such a warming of just 3.6 degrees Fahrenheit (2 degrees Celsius) for the human species will be the "hell" and "high water" of many direful forecasts. The hell will be drought and famine and high water will be rising sea levels worldwide, "enough to erode beaches and coasts, destroy wetlands, and bring severe flood damage to many low-lying countries."

The combustion of fossil fuels accounts for about eighty percent of all global emissions.

The gases responsible for this fundamental climatic alteration are the following:

1. *Carbon Dioxide (CO_2)*. The current contribution of the gas to global warming is 49 percent. Lifespan = 500 years.

Its primary source is fossil fuel combustion, but deforestation and soil destruction are also involved. Deforestation directly and indirectly causes the release of carbon dioxide into the atmosphere. It is a direct cause when felled trees are burned to clear land for cultivation. Indirectly it leads to a release of carbon dioxide because trees play an essential role in the recycling of the gas through photosynthesis.

2. *Methane (CH$_4$)*. The current contribution of the gas is 18 percent. Lifespan = 7-10 years.

Methane is produced when wood is burned inefficiently, when grasslands are set afire, and when fossil fuels are extracted and transported. Its principal sources are cattle, biomass, rice paddies, gas leaks, mining, and termites. Molecule for molecule, methane is "a much more potent greenhouse gas than carbon dioxide. Each molecule of methane has 20 to 30 times the heat-trapping effect of a molecule of carbon dioxide. Each year, about 50 more tons of methane enter the atmosphere than leave it."

3. *Nitrous Oxide (N$_2$O)*. The current contribution of the gas is 6 percent. Lifespan = 140-190 years.

Its primary sources are fossil fuels, soil cultivation, and deforestation. In addition to generation by coal burning and forest fires, nitrous oxide is a natural product of bacterial action of chemical fertilizers and the digestion of soil microbes.

4. *Chlorofluorocarbons (CFC$_{11}$ and $_{12}$)*. The current contribution of these gases is 15 percent. Lifespan = 65-110 years.

The primary sources of CFCs are refrigeration, air conditioning, aerosols, foam blowing, and solvents. "CFC's are far more effective than carbon dioxide in trapping Earth's thermal radiation. Indeed, one molecule of the most dangerous CFC has about 20,000 times the heat-trapping power of a molecule of carbon dioxide."

Chlorofluorocarbons pose a dual threat to the environment. Not only do they trap Earth's heat, but they also attack the ozone layer. Resisting chemical breakdown in the lower atmosphere, they drift skyward and collect in, and attack, "the stratospheric ozone layer starting some 15 miles above Earth's surface and extending upward." In the spring of 1985, British scientists discovered a 40 percent depletion in the ozone levels high above Antarctica. The consequences of the ozone hole for human beings range from skin cancers to immune diseases and eye cataracts. Excessive ultraviolet radiation, allowed to enter the atmosphere through the hole, may kill off vast numbers of sea-going plankton. The ozone in the ozone layer is often called the "good" ozone to distinguish it from the "bad"—the human-made ozone that is the principal ingredient in urban smog (see below).

5. *Ozone*. The current contribution of the gas is 12 percent. Lifespan = hours to days in upper troposphere; one hour in upper stratosphere.

Ozone is a blue, gaseous allotrope of oxygen, derived or formed from diatomic oxygen by electric discharge or exposure to ultraviolet radiation. It is the principal ingredient of urban smog.

Feedback Loops

Not only do these gases contribute directly to the greenhouse effect, they also interact in ways that are little understood. Such interactions, or feedback loops, may speed up the process of global warming beyond the point indicated by current predictive models. Possible mechanisms of interaction include the following:

1. As the temperature rises, methane from ocean sediments and tundra will be released faster.

2. Vegetation that can't adjust rapidly enough to climate warming will die off, decaying and giving off more carbon dioxide. But this increase should be offset in part because carbon dioxide stimulates the growth of plants that absorb carbon from the air.

3. The chemistry and circulation of the oceans could change as Earth warms, and oceans may no longer have as much capacity to absorb carbon dioxide.

4. Higher temperatures could lead to higher levels of ground-level ozone (smog)—a heat absorber that could, in turn, accelerate global warming.

To reduce or contain the extent of global warming, it is imperative that technically advanced societies reduce, by a substantial margin, their expenditure of energy obtained from fossil fuels. Two technological steps must be taken and one pre-condition must be met. The pre-condition for a concerted response to the threat of global warming is at the least a containment or, if possible, a reversal of the population explosion. If Earth's present population of 5.2 billion should double, then there will be no hope of arresting global warming. Even if population growth is brought under control, it will still be necessary to make much greater progress than we have in achieving fuel-efficient engines, and finally in replacing carbon-based fuels with cleaner-burning fuels, "including natural gas, alcohols, and hydrogen."

* 5.4 *

McKibben, Bill. *The End of Nature*. New York: Random House, 1989. LC 89-42791. ISBN 0-394-57600-2.

Our exposure to evolutionary thought has conditioned us to think that changes never happen quickly, that they unfold only over immense reaches of "geologic" time. This inference from the evolutionary record is both invalid and profoundly unfortunate when it is misapplied, as it all too frequently is, to anthropogenic change. It is unfortunate because it has diminished our capacity to grasp the imminence of the threat of global warming. Moreover, the idea that we as a species cannot effect irreversibly baneful changes, that all of our destructive, polluting acts of the past have been merely temporary in effect, that nature will somehow recover in spite of the worst we can do, has blinded us to the fact that we stand on the brink of committing global ecocide or, as McKibben puts it, of putting an end to nature. McKibben specifies the particulars of "the end of nature."

> The idea of nature will not survive the new global pollu-
> tion—the carbon dioxide and the CFC's and the like. This
> new rupture with nature is different not only in scope but also
> in kind from salmon tins in an English stream. We have
> changed the atmosphere, and thus we are changing the
> weather. By changing the weather, we make every spot on
> earth man-made and artificial. We have deprived nature of its
> independence, and that is fatal to its meaning. Nature's
> independence *is* its meaning; without it there is nothing but
> us.

Recognition that temperatures would rise globally as a consequence of sharply increased emission of carbon dioxide has been peripherally present as a possibility in the minds of some scientists for about one hundred years. The Swedish scientist and Nobel laureate, Svante Arrhenius (1859-1927), made the first systematic calculations of the effects of the carbon dioxide released into the atmosphere since the beginning of the industrial revolution in England. In making these calculations, he used measurements of infrared radiation from a full moon. He aptly called the process of burning fossil fuels "evaporating our coal mines into the air." The idea of global warming "floated in obscurity for a long time" until the 1930s when the British physicist, G.S. Callendar, speculated that rising carbon dioxide levels might account for "a warming of North America and northern Europe that meteorologists had begun to observe in the 1880s." In 1957 came the first systematic verification of the tentative warnings of Arrhenius and Callendar. In that year, Roger Revelle and Hans Suess published a paper in which they demonstrated that:

> [M]ost of the carbon dioxide being pumped into the air by
> millions of smokestacks, furnaces, and car exhausts would
> stay in the air, where presumably, it would gradually warm
> the planet.

In describing the anthropogenic damage being wrought, Revelle and Suess used a level of sarcasm rarely found in a scientific paper. "Human beings," they said, "are now carrying out a large-scale geophysical experiment of a kind that could not have happened in the past, nor be repeated in the future." To this, McKibben adds that with this experiment, human beings have begun to put an end to nature, in the special sense of this phrase analyzed above.

To say, as McKibben does, that nature has been rendered artificial does not mean that human beings have acquired control over it. One of the characteristics of the warming world will be the unpredictability of its violence. The old world was violent, but within limits we understood the cyclical patterns of its volatility. Despite its predictable violence, the world, or rather the biosphere, has, for the most part, been hospitable to the desire of our species to at least survive if not to thrive on our planet. With global warming, there can no longer be a question of thriving. Even survival is moot.

"The single most-talked-about consequence [of global warming] is probably the expected rise in global sea level as a result of polar melting." An effective way to realize the meaning of rising sea levels is to consider the effects of a one-foot rise on a single low-lying country. The Maldive Islands are an island nation in the Indian Ocean to the west of Sri Lanka. The Maldives rise only two meters above the ocean.

> If the sea level were to rise one meter, storm surges would become an enormous crippling danger; were it to rise two meters, a rise well within the range of possibilities predicted by many studies, the country would simply disappear.

In the words of its president, the Maldives are an "endangered nation." Other nations are also endangered, though to a lesser extent.

Bangladesh with a two-meter rise could lose twenty percent of land area. Most of the Nile Valley would be inundated. Nor would the Third World alone be victimized. The Netherlands could be utterly submerged under the North Sea. And many places up and down the Atlantic and Gulf coasts of the United States would be endangered.

* 5.5 *

Silver, Cheryl Simon, with Ruth S. DeFries, for the National Academy of Sciences. *One Earth, One Future: Our Changing Global Environment.* Washington, DC: National Academy Press, 1990. LC 90-5939. ISBN 0-309-04141-4.

By recovering the Vostok ice core from a drillhole in Antarctica, climate scientists have come into possession of "the record of 160,000 years of climate history, from the present warm period, or 'enterglacial', through the most recent 100,000-year-long ice age, through a previous warm period and back into an even earlier ice age." By analyzing the gas in bubbles trapped in the ice, it becomes demonstrable that greenhouse gases have undergone wide fluctuations over the glacial cycle. "Atmospheric greenhouse gases and climate generally shift in lockstep."

> As the earth moves into an interglacial period, for instance, temperatures rise, and so do concentrations of carbon dioxide. During the deepest part of the ice age, temperatures plummet, and so does carbon dioxide, to perhaps 60 percent of that during the inter-glacial periods.

As determined by air bubble analysis, concentrations of carbon dioxide have increased nearly twenty-five percent since industrialization began in the eighteenth century, the main cause for the increase being the combustion of fossil fuels. During combustion, carbon is oxidized to carbon dioxide and released into the atmosphere.

Prediction of the probable effects on future climate of rising levels of carbon dioxide is done by means of five different computer models. The five models are the NASA/Goddard Institute for Space Studies; the National Center for Atmospheric Research; the NOAA Geophysical Fluid Dynamics Laboratory; the Oregon State University; and the United Kingdom Meteorological Office.

> These are general circulation models (GCMs) that predict the ways in which temperature, humidity, wind speed and direction, soil moisture, sea ice, and other climate variables evolve through three dimensions and over time. They use mathematical equations to express the basic physical, chemical, and biological processes that govern the climate system.

The models do not agree on all specifics; the climate system is far too complex to permit agreement. Although uncertainties persist, the predictions of the five models are sufficiently close to justify the claim that we know enough to act. As human beings attempt to satisfy the demands of a growing population, there will be many ominous direct and indirect consequences of global warming. Among these are declining rates of food production, rising seas, depletion of the ozone layer, vanishing forests and vanishing species, and acid deposition.

The simulation of the potential effects of global warming on agriculture rests on general circulation climate models (GCMs). The models project these effects for agriculture:

In particular they find that warming will be greatest in the high latitudes, that soils will tend to be drier in mid-continental regions in summer, and that globally the hydrologic cycle will intensify—more rain, more evaporation—as the earth's surface warms. The models show that with an effective doubling of pre-industrial carbon dioxide concentrations (that is, with a combination of all trace greenhouse gases that equals the heat-trapping effect of a doubling of the concentration of carbon dioxide), evaporation on a global basis will increase by 7 to 12 percent. The atmosphere cannot store large amounts of water vapor, and so precipitation will increase. The increases will not be uniformly distributed, however; nor will the proportions of rain, snow, or dew necessarily remain the same.

In summary, the most disruptive effects of global warming on agriculture will be changes in seasonality and in amounts of precipitation and evapotranspiration.

There are two reason for climate scientists' prediction that the global sea level will rise.

First, as greenhouse gases accumulate in the atmosphere and eventually raise the earth's surface temperature, glaciers and land ice around the world will melt more rapidly, releasing water that will raise average sea level. Second, as the ocean absorbs additional heat from the air above it, the water will expand.

A rise in global sea level will be catastrophic for river deltas, "the wetlands that form when a river carries more sediment into a body of water than can be carried away by currents and waves." The sediment thus built up to form the delta functions as a barrier between land and sea. Under normal conditions, deltas continuously accrete and subside. Human interventions, however, to dam, divert, or channel rivers throw off this equilibrium with the result that accretion no longer offsets subsidence. For reasons of anthropogenic degradation alone, it is probable that "most of Louisiana's wetlands will be destroyed in the next century." Sea level rise will greatly compound the threat to the deltas caused by hydrological engineering. Hardest hit will be the Nile River Valley in Egypt, the deltas of Bangladesh, and the Mississippi River delta in the United States. It is estimated that sea level rise threatens the lives and livelihoods of 46 million people in Egypt and Bangladesh alone.

There is also a distinct possibility that global warming will intensify the severity and frequency of tropical storms.

> Currently, an average of one and one-half severe cyclones hit Bangladesh each year, and the storm surges advance up the rivers as far as 200 kilometers inland. If the storms increase in frequency and sea level rises, the storm surges will reach even further toward the main centers of population.

In 1974 it was hypothesized that chlorofluorocarbons (CFCs) were responsible for the depletion of the ozone layer. CFCs are synthetic compounds that are very stable in the lower atmosphere; they "rise unchanged through the lowest atmospheric layer, the troposphere."

> Even though CFCs are produced mostly in the industrialized countries of Europe and North America—where they are used in a variety of applications such as for solvents and refrigerants—they mix throughout the lower atmosphere, so that there are as many CFC molecules over Antarctica as over Colorado or Washington, DC. The researchers surmised that upon reaching the stratosphere, the CFCs encounter high-energy ultraviolet light, which breaks them down, releasing their chlorine atoms. The chlorine atoms can then engage with ozone in a catalytic reaction in which each chlorine fragment can destroy up to 100,000 ozone molecules before other chemical processes remove the chlorine from the atmosphere.

Because the ozone layer shields living creatures from damaging ultraviolet radiation, the health implications of ozone depletion are manifest. For example, "the EPA estimate in 1986 that the incidence of skin cancers would rise 2 percent for each 1 percent depletion of stratospheric ozone."

The tropics are extremely rich in the number of plant and animal species they enclose. Although the moist forests of the tropics cover only seven percent of the earth's land surface, they hold one-half of the estimated species. Moreover most of the species thought to be in the tropics have not yet been scientifically described and classified. The deforestation of the tropics is therefore extinguishing species before they are even known or their capabilities for human therapeutic benefit assessed.

The combustion of fossil fuels, particularly coal, releases, as gases, sulfur dioxide and nitrogen oxides which are then transformed into sulfuric and nitric acids through a series of chemical reactions in the atmosphere. These acids then fall back to the earth's surface dissolved in rain, snow, or fog, or as gases or dry particles. Acid deposition has engendered a great deal of transnational tension because often it will originate in one country but severely afflict another.

In an effort to ascertain the effects of acid deposition on lakes, acids have been deliberately introduced into an experimental lake. The effects of acidification on fish species are as follows:

> Scientists believe that the number of species in a lake declines continuously with increasing acidity below pH values of 6.5 to 7.0 and that species that are foraged by fish higher in the food chain are lost at pH values near 6.0. This disruption in the food chain means that large predatory fish can starve long before the direct toxic effects of acidification are evident.

The materials and analyses in this volume were presented to the Forum on Global Change and Our Common Future which was held on 2-3 May 1989 under the auspices of the National Academy of Sciences.

Author Index

Title Index